The Doctrines of the Mennonites

GERRIT ROOSEN, 1612-1711
Author of the Catechism, *Christian Conversation on Saving Faith*

The Doctrines of the Mennonites

By JOHN CHRISTIAN WENGER
Professor of Theology and Philosophy
Goshen College Biblical Seminary

A brief interpretation of the theology of the Anabaptists, correlated with the Schleitheim Confession of 1527, the Dordrecht Confession of 1632, the Christian Fundamentals of 1921, the Shorter Catechism of 1690, the Waldeck Catechism of 1778, and Roosen's Catechism of 1702 Prepared at the request of the Mennonite Commission for Christian Education and Young People's Work.

WIPF & STOCK · Eugene, Oregon

Wipf and Stock Publishers
199 W 8th Ave, Suite 3
Eugene, OR 97401

The Doctrines of the Mennonites
By Wenger, John C.
Softcover ISBN-13: 978-1-6667-4562-7
Hardcover ISBN-13: 978-1-6667-4563-4
eBook ISBN-13: 978-1-6667-4564-1
Publication date 4/15/2022
Previously published by Mennonite Publishing House, 1952

This edition is a scanned facsimile of
the original edition published in 1952.

TO OUR FOUR CHILDREN
GRACIOUS ENTRUSTMENTS OF GOD

DANIEL MARTIN
JOHN PAUL
MARY LOIS
ELIZABETH ANNE

IN THE HOPE THAT GOD MAY EVER
ILLUMINATE THEIR HEARTS WITH HIS TRUTH

I dedicate this book

Preface

Early this year Nelson E. Kauffman, secretary of the Mennonite Commission for Christian Education and Young People's Work, approached me as to the possibility of taking Chapter XIII of *Glimpses of Mennonite History and Doctrine,* breaking it up into chapters for study, and adding to it several Anabaptist and Mennonite confessions of faith. This I consented to attempt. As the work proceeded, my vision of what the appendix should contain expanded until it included three confessions and three catechisms. It may come as a distinct surprise to some modern Mennonites that confessions and catechisms played a large role in the Christian education materials of their spiritual forbears.

When the American Mennonite Church abandoned the German language in the nineteenth century and adopted the English, there was a tendency to discard the tried and proved literary materials of the brotherhood. Mennonite publishers, such as John F. Funk, provided English translations of some of the Anabaptist classics, and printed them in numerous editions. Nevertheless, it appeared for some decades as though the Anabaptist-Mennonite heritage was doomed to serious decline. The group appeared to have lost much of its original spiritual vigor, and had partially succumbed to formalism, Pietism, and other aberrations. In the latter part of the century a young German Mennonite scholar named John Horsch stepped to the side of Funk and began producing a stream of popular articles and scholarly monographs on Anabaptism which continued with some interruptions for half a century. Horsch was joined by younger scholars who were equally eager to recapture what Harold S. Bender has aptly termed "The Anabaptist Vision." The bibliography at the close of the present volume will furnish some insight into the literary activity of recent American Mennonite scholars. I hope that my modest effort in this book may also be of value in the Christian indoctrination of our youth.

A few words must be added about the form of the book. Following the discussions in each chapter there is a section giving selected Bible statements on the topic under consideration, then references to the confessions and catechisms, and finally a few study questions. In general I quoted from the King James Version of 1611. Whenever I used the American Standard Version of 1901, the letters "ASV" are found at the end of the passage. Occasionally I made my own translation in which case the word "Greek" follows the passage. All pronouns referring to the Deity are capitalized, and connectives such as *wherefore, and,* or *now,* are frequently omitted when they begin the verses cited. I also abolished the traditional form which makes each verse a paragraph. No attempt was

PREFACE

made to quote every section of each confession or every question of the three catechisms; nor did I hesitate to quote the same section or question more than once.

I also owe it to the reader to make clear that I do not desire to make the Mennonite brotherhood a creedal church. This book is offered to our families, congregations, and schools only with the deep conviction that our spiritual heritage is truly Scriptural, and with the hope that these studies may enhance our acquaintance with our historic faith and deepen our appreciation of its truth. I shall be delighted if God can use my labor of love to inspire our young people with a consciousness of the Biblical character of our faith, and to challenge them to a higher level of Christian life and devotion.

Goshen College Biblical Seminary J. C. WENGER
Goshen, Indiana
August 18, 1949

Introduction

The teaching mission of the church is continuous. Christ and the apostles were constantly occupied with this great task of bringing the facts of the Gospel to the adult mind. Men were challenged with the truth of divine revelation. To reason intelligently and convincingly with unconverted men, these Christian witnesses needed a knowledge of the facts, the fundamentals, the basic doctrines of the Christian faith. In this age also the Christian must be informed if he is to maintain his faith and propagate it to others.

In the past several decades the emphasis of the teaching program of the Protestants has been on the child level. The Mennonite Church has been influenced by this emphasis and has prepared superior curriculum materials for teaching children. However, there is a great need for a monograph that may be used to indoctrinate the adult membership of the church. It was for the purpose of meeting that need that the author was asked to prepare this volume.

We recognize the Scripture as the highest existing authority on all matters of doctrine. Doctrine, however, is invalid unless it is reflected and experienced in the lives of men and women. The books of the New Testament are not designed to give a systematic treatment of theology. They are experimental. When Christianity in the first century began to meet heresies, a definition of the Christian faith became necessary. Creeds came into being. The same condition existed in the sixteenth century in reformation times. As the Apostle Paul was not primarily a theologian but an evangelist and church builder, so the early Mennonites did not conceive their chief duty being to give a creed to the world, but to give to men a way of life after that of Jesus Christ, and made possible by His indwelling presence.

This Biblical faith was reduced to confessions by the exigencies of the times. They testify of the life and character of the early Anabaptists. A knowledge and understanding of these confessions give the Christian an application to the doctrine of the Word to the issues of the day. If we are to have virile, dynamic young Christians, able to meet the subtilty of today's world, our parents must be established in the faith and become champions of it. I have long felt the need of a compilation of the confessions of faith to which we are heir, that we might become familiar with them and have them easily accessible for use in a teaching program. I feel that this volume meets that need.

It gives me great pleasure to recommend this volume as a means of acquainting persons with the doctrines of the Mennonites. The Mennonite Commission for Christian Education and Young People's Work

INTRODUCTION

readily accepted my recommendation that as a part of the 1949 Major Emphasis of Adult Indoctrination, this volume should be prepared to be used by Sunday-school classes, midweek prayer meetings, Christian workers' training classes, winter Bible schools, ministers' meetings, and in other groups whose objective is to become acquainted with the basis of our Biblical and historic faith. There may be more material in some chapters than the class will have time to cover. The teacher should plan for what will be possible within the time limit.

The love of the author for the Word of God and the faith of the Anabaptists, together with knowledge of their sixteenth century life and thought, make him particularly qualified to write in this field. The Mennonite Church owes a great debt to the author and his colleagues at Goshen College Biblical Seminary for so ably presenting in the classroom and in writing the Biblical faith of our spiritual forebears.

I count the author's friendship one of the enriching gifts of God in my life. He has not ceased to challenge me to deeper devotions to God, to a better understanding of the Scriptures, and to a growing appreciation for the heritage of faith which has come to us.

It is my sincere prayer that this flame of holy love for the way of life taught by Christ and His disciples and lived by the Anabaptists may be kindled in the hearts of thousands of strong men in our congregations, and that they may earnestly contend for the faith once for all delivered to the saints, and accept the challenge to make it known around the world. To this end may God abundantly bless this volume.

NELSON E. KAUFFMAN, *Field Secretary* MENNONITE COMMISSION FOR CHRISTIAN EDUCATION AND YOUNG PEOPLE'S WORK
December 1, 1949
Hannibal, Missouri

Contents

Preface vii
Introduction ix
On the Use of This Book xii

Some Great Doctrines of the Christian Faith

1. The Doctrine of God 1
2. The Doctrine of Salvation 10
3. Present Grace and Future Glory 17

Some Unique Emphases in Anabaptist-Mennonite Doctrine

4. The Centrality of Evangelism 26
5. New Testament Church Ordinances 29
6. The Doctrine of Nonresistance 34
7. Biblical Simplicity of Life 40
8. The Finality of the New Testament 47
9. The Church as a Fellowship of Committed Disciples 52
10. The High Calling of the Church of Christ 56
11. The Heart of the Christian Life 61
12. Taking Up the Cross 64
    Appendixes 69
    1. The Schleitheim Confession 71
    2. The Dordrecht Confession 77
    3. Christian Fundamentals 88
    4. The Shorter Catechism 92
    5. The Waldeck Catechism 97
    6. Roosen's Catechism 113
    Bibliography 158

On the Use of This Book

As a church, we aim to base all our doctrine and practice upon the Scripture, the authoritative Word of God. How much help you derive from this study will depend largely upon you, the reader. If you merely skim over the material, your blessing will be small. But if you study earnestly, comparing the discussion with the standard helps in the back of the book, your benefit will be vastly greater. Above all, you should look up every Biblical passage cited and test every doctrinal statement by the Scriptures. The Word of God tells us, "Prove all things: hold fast that which is good" (I Thess. 5:21). "Thy word is truth" (John 17:17).

Summary Suggestions

1. Read each doctrinal discussion carefully and with an open mind.

2. Look up each portion of Scripture and seek to grasp its message in the light of the context and by comparison with other passages.

3. Read the pertinent material cited in the several confessions and catechisms in the Appendixes of this book.

4. Meditate on the questions for further study and on those which occur to you in your own thinking as you read.

5. Use this book merely as a signpost to some of the great themes of Scripture. Do not use it as a substitute for Bible reading.

6. For the most effective Bible study, you ought to make use of at least two translations, the King James Version of 1611, and the American Standard Version of 1901.

Chapter I
The Doctrine of God

Ideally the church of Christ is one. The truth of Scripture is not denominational truth. And no branch of the Christian church should consider itself the exclusive bride of Christ. Nevertheless with organized Christendom divided into differing groups, it is meaningless to announce that one has no doctrinal position, or to state that one simply "believes all the Bible." All groups of sincere Christians feel that way. And frequently when an individual announces that he cannot be loyal to the doctrinal standards of his denomination because they are man-made statements, he will be found to be an ardent adherent of a more recent Bible teacher or system of interpretation.

The position set forth in this book is known properly as the Anabaptist-Mennonite interpretation of Scripture. It is an attempt to reject the extra-Biblical doctrines and practices of the major branches of Christendom, the accretions of the last eighteen centuries. The Anabaptists were the religious radicals of the sixteenth century who insisted on abandoning the state church system, infant baptism, compulsion in matters of faith, participation in the magistracy and in warfare, and ecclesiasticism in general. It was their determined program to set up free congregations of committed disciples of Jesus, walking humbly and faithfully before the Lord, seeking to keep all His commandments blamelessly. Organized Christendom linked hands with the state to root the Anabaptists off the face of the earth, and the persecution unto death largely succeeded in its goal. Weak remnants survived in the Netherlands (the Mennonites), in Switzerland (the Swiss Brethren), and in Moravia (the Hutterian Brethren). The spiritual children of the Anabaptists in North America today, both of Dutch and Swiss backgrounds, are known as Mennonites.

A number of monographs on Anabaptism have been written and several books on Bible doctrine have been issued by Mennonite publishers, but the definitive Anabaptist-Mennonite theology is yet to appear. All that can be attempted here is a brief summary of the main outlines of the theology of the Anabaptists and Mennonites. One handicap to a historical survey is the paucity of theological treatises from the leaders of the brotherhood, for most of their writings treat of practical questions of Christian living, or matters of church discipline, or isolated doctrinal points. This is true even of Menno Simons' Works which will be quoted extensively in this discussion. This lack of theological treatises is not without its significance; it indicates the fundamental fact that Anabaptism and Mennonitism are more Biblical than theological.

One thing is certain: Anabaptism was essentially the logical outcome of the Protestant reformation. It was not an unbalanced, bizarre or fanatical movement. It was rather *a more earnest effort than the other Protestant groups made to break with religious and ecclesiastical tradition in order to render absolute obedience to the text of Scripture.* This point of view was regarded as revolutionary in the sixteenth century —as it is in modern Christendom. The Protestant reformers regarded Anabaptism as a dangerous acid that would eat away the very foundations of society. But the Brethren were determined to "live dangerously,"—if following the Scriptures is ever really dangerous. The Protestant "Revolution" itself involved definite hazards, but the rewards of facing those hazards far outweighed them. Since Anabaptism was simply a radical form of Protestantism, on the so-called fundamental doctrines the Anabaptists were in agreement with the Lutherans and the Reformed. This basic unity on the major doctrines of the Christian faith has often been overlooked by writers on the Anabaptists.

The following outline of the first three chapters will assist the reader in seeing more clearly some of the major doctrines on which the Anabaptists and present-day Mennonites enjoy a basic agreement with the larger bodies of Christendom:

SOME GREAT DOCTRINES OF THE CHRISTIAN FAITH

I. God (*Chapter I*)
  1. The Father
  2. Jesus Christ
  3. The Holy Spirit
II. Salvation (*Chapter II*)
  1. Sin
  2. Regeneration
  3. Holiness of Life
III. Present Grace and Future Glory (*Chapter III*)
  1. Divine Grace
  2. Eschatology
IV. The Inspiration of the Bible (*Chapter III*)

1. THE FATHER

The Brethren held to the same doctrine of God as did the Protestant reformers. They believed in His personality and goodness. In 1550 Menno Simons, 1496-1561, wrote his *Confession of the Triune, Eternal, and True God, Father, Son, and Holy Ghost.* This little treatise begins thus:

> We believe and confess with the Holy Scriptures, that there is an only, eternal and true God, who is a Spirit. One God, who created heaven and earth, the sea, and all that is therein Such a God whom heaven and the heaven of heavens cannot comprehend. Whose throne is heaven and earth His footstool; who measures "the waters in the hollow of His hand," who spanneth the heavens; who comprehendeth the dust of the earth in a measure, and weigheth the mountains in scales and the hills in a balance; who is as high as heaven, deeper than hell, lower than earth and broader than the sea; "Who only hath immortality, dwelling in the light which no man can approach unto; whom no man hath seen, nor can see"; who is an almighty, powerful and an over-ruling

King, in the heavens above and in the earth beneath, whose strength, hand and power none can withstand. A "God of Gods, and a Lord of Lords," there is none like unto Him, but He is a mighty, holy, terrible, praiseworthy, wonderful, and consuming fire, whose kingdom, power, dominion, majesty and glory is eternal, and shall endure forever, and besides this only, eternal, living, almighty over-ruling God and Lord, we know no other, and since He is a Spirit so great, terrible, and invisible, He is also inexpressible, incomprehensible and indescribable. . . . (*Works*, II, 183)

Pertinent Biblical Passages

1. On the Spirituality and Personality of God:
    John 4:24: "God is a Spirit."
    Cf. Luke 24:39. "A spirit hath not flesh and bones . . . ."
    Ex. 3:14: "And God said unto Moses, I AM THAT I AM."
    John 5:26: "The Father hath life in Himself."
    Read also the majestic passage in Isaiah 40.25-28.

2. On the Eternity of God:
    Ps. 90:2: "Even from everlasting to everlasting, Thou art God."
    Deut. 32:40: "I live for ever."
    Ps. 102:12: "Thou, O Lord, shalt endure for ever."

3. On the Omnipresence of God:
    I Kings 8:27: "Behold, the heaven and heaven of heavens cannot contain Thee."
    Ps. 139:8: "If I ascend up into heaven, Thou art there: if I make my bed in hell, behold, Thou art there."
    Acts 17:28: "In Him we live, and move, and have our being."

4. On the Omniscience of God:
    Ps. 147:4: "He telleth the number of the stars; He calleth them all by their names."
    Isa. 46:9, 10. "I am God, and there is none like Me, declaring the end from the beginning."
    Matt. 10:30: "The very hairs of your head are all numbered."
    Ps. 33:13, 14: "The Lord looketh from heaven; He beholdeth all the sons of men. From the place of His habitation He looketh upon all the inhabitants of the earth."

5. On the Omnipotence of God:
    Matt. 19.26. "With God all things are possible."
    Gen. 18:14: "Is anything too hard for the Lord?"
    Eph. 1:11: God "worketh all things after the counsel of His own will."
    Eph. 3:20: God "is able to do exceeding abundantly above all that we ask or think."

6. On the Truthfulness and Faithfulness of God:
    Num. 23:19: "God is not a man, that He should lie."
    Tit. 1:2: "God . . . cannot lie." Cf. Heb. 6:18.
    I Cor. 1:9: "God is faithful." Cf. I Thess. 5 24 and Phil. 1:6.

7. On the Holiness of God:
    I Pet. 1:16: "Be ye holy; for I am holy." Cf. Lev. 11:44f; 19:2 and 20:7.

Isa. 12:6: "Great is the Holy One of Israel in the midst of thee."
Ps. 5:5: "Thou hatest all workers of iniquity." See Hab. 1:13.

8. On the Justice of God:
Deut. 32:4: He is "a God of truth and without iniquity, just and right is He."
Rom. 2:5, 6: ". . . the righteous judgment of God; who will render to every man according to his deeds."
Ps. 7:9: "The righteous God trieth the minds and hearts." A.S.V.

9. On the Love of God:
John 3:16: "For God so loved the world, that He gave His only begotten Son, that whosoever believeth in Him should not perish, but have everlasting life."
Rom. 5:8: "God commendeth His love toward us, in that, while we were yet sinners, Christ died for us."
Rom. 8:32: "He that spared not His own Son, but delivered Him up for us all, how shall He not with Him freely give us all things?"
I John 4:10: "Herein is love, not that we loved God, but that He loved us, and sent His Son to be the propitiation for our sins."

Reading References in the Confessions and Catechisms
Dordrecht Confession, Article I.
Christian Fundamentals, Article II.
Shorter Catechism, Question 8.
Waldeck Catechism, Part First, Chapters I, II, IV.
Roosen's Catechism, Questions 6, 24-52.

Study Questions
1. Can man know anything about God apart from His Word? Give Scriptural proof.
2. What were some of the forms in which God appeared to the patriarchs and prophets?
3. In what way is Christ superior to the revelation of God made through the prophets?
4. Why is it legitimate to use human characteristics to describe God? What does the New Testament have to say about the divine image in man?
5. Does man naturally reach out for God? What passage in the Book of Romans speaks of this?

2. JESUS CHRIST

The Anabaptists also held to the Deity and the true humanity of Jesus Christ. They believed all that the Scriptures teach on His virgin birth, on His supernatural miracles, His vicarious and substitutionary death, His bodily resurrection, and His glorious second coming. Menno, in the same book on the Trinity, 1550, wrote as follows on Christ's Person:

And this same incomprehensible, inexpressible, spiritual, eternal, divine Being, which is begotten of the Father before every creature, divine and incomprehensible, we believe and confess to be Christ Jesus, the first and only begotten Son of God, "the first-born of every creature," the eternal Wisdom, the power of God, the everlasting Light, the eternal Truth, the everlasting Life, . , the Eternal Word. ... (*Works*, II, 183)

On the incarnation of the Son Menno stated:

. We believe and confess that this same eternal, wise, almighty, holy, true, living and incomprehensible Word, Christ Jesus, which in the beginning was with God and which was God, incomprehensible—born of the incomprehensible Father, before every creature, is in the fulness of time become, according to the unchangeable purpose and true promise of the Father, a true, visible, passive, hungry, thirsty and mortal man, in Mary the pure virgin, through the operation and overshadowing of the Holy Spirit, and is thus born of her Yea, that He was like unto us in all things except sin; that He grew up as other men; and at the appointed time was baptized and entered upon His ministerial office, the office of grace and love, which was enjoined upon Him from the Father, and which He obediently fulfilled .. (*Works*, II, 184)

On the Deity of Christ Menno wrote clearly:

... We believe and confess Christ Jesus, with His heavenly Father, to be truly God; and that because of the plain testimony of the holy prophets, evangelists and apostles, as we may learn from the following Scriptures, and also from other texts. Isaiah says, "Unto us a child is born, unto us a son is given; and the government shall be upon his shoulder; and his name shall be called Wonderful, Counsellor, The mighty God, The everlasting Father, The Prince of Peace " Again, "Say unto the cities of Judah, Behold your God! .." (*Works*, II, 185).

While it is true that the Obbenites and early Mennonites held to a strange view of Mary's relation to Jesus before His birth, the Swiss Brethren did not share this notion and the Mennonites themselves soon dropped it. Note the statement given in the third paragraph of Article IV of the 1632 Dutch Mennonite Confession of Faith: "But how or in what manner this worthy body was prepared, or how the Word became flesh, and He Himself man, we content ourselves with the declaration which the worthy evangelists have given ..."

Pertinent Biblical Passages

1. On His Eternal Existence:
    John 3:13: "He that came down from heaven, even the Son of Man."
    John 8:58: "Jesus said ... Before Abraham was, I am."
    John 17:5. "... the glory which I had with Thee before the world was."
    Col. 1:17. Christ "is before all things."
    Read also Phil. 2:5-11.

2. On the Incarnation and Virgin Birth:
    John 1:14: "The Word was made flesh, and dwelt among us."
    See Matt. 1:18-25 and Luke 1:26-38.
    Rom. 1:3: "Jesus Christ our Lord ... was made of the seed of David according to the flesh."

3. On His Supernatural Miracles:
    John 2:11: "This beginning of miracles did Jesus ... and manifested forth His glory; and His disciples believed on Him."
    Matt. 15:30f: "And great multitudes came unto Him, having with

them those that were lame, blind, dumb, maimed, and many others, and cast them down at Jesus' feet; and He healed them: insomuch that the multitude wondered, when they saw the dumb to speak, the maimed to be whole, the lame to walk, and the blind to see: and they glorified the God of Israel."

Acts 2:22: "Jesus of Nazareth [was] a man approved of God among you by miracles and wonders and signs."

4. On His Work as a Prophet:

John 7:16: "Jesus answered . . . , My doctrine is not mine, but His that sent me."
John 8:28: "As my Father hath taught me, I speak these things."
John 12:50: "Even as the Father said unto me, so I speak."
See also John 14:24 and 15:15.

5. On His Spiritual Kingship:

Luke 1:32f: "The Lord God shall give unto Him the throne of His father David: and He shall reign over the house of Jacob for ever; and of His kingdom there shall be no end."
Matt. 28:18: "And Jesus . . . spake unto them, saying, All authority hath been given unto me in heaven and on earth." A.S.V.
Eph. 1:20-22: God placed Christ "at His own right hand in the heavenly places, far above all principality, and power, and might, and dominion, and every name that is named, not only in this world, but also in that which is to come: and hath put all things under His feet."
Col. 1:13: God "hath delivered us from the power of darkness, and hath translated us into the kingdom of His dear Son."

6. On His Sinlessness:

Heb. 4:15: Christ "was in all points tempted like as we are, yet without sin."
II Cor. 5:21: Christ "knew no sin."
I Pet. 2:22: Christ "did no sin, neither was guile found in His mouth."

7. On His Deity:

John 1:1: "The Word was God."
Heb. 1:8: "Unto the Son He saith, Thy throne, O God, is for ever and ever."
Acts 20:28: "Feed the church of God, which He hath purchased with His own blood."

8. On His Vicarious Death:

I John 2:2: "And He is the propitiation for our sins: and . . . also for the sins of the whole world."
Eph. 1:7: "We have redemption through His blood, the forgiveness of sins."
Col. 1:20: Christ "made peace through the blood of His cross."
I Pet. 1:18, 19: "Ye know that ye were not redeemed with corruptible things, . . . but with the precious blood of Christ, as of a lamb without blemish and without spot."

9. On His Bodily Resurrection:
    Luke 24:39: "Behold My hands and My feet, that it is I Myself: handle Me, and see; for a spirit hath not flesh and bones, as ye see Me have."
    John 20:27f: "Then saith He to Thomas, Reach hither thy finger, and behold My hands; and reach hither thy hand, and thrust it into My side: and be not faithless but believing. And Thomas answered and said unto Him, My Lord and my God."
    I Cor. 15:4: "He was buried, and ... He rose again the third day."

Reading References in the Confessions and Catechisms

Dordrecht Confession, Article IV.
Christian Fundamentals, Article V.
Shorter Catechism, Question 9.
Waldeck Catechism, Part First, Chapter II, Questions 3-5; Part Third, Chapters I, II.
Roosen's Catechism, Questions 62-69.

Study Questions

1. Does the New Testament ever speak of Christ's ministry to God's people prior to His incarnation and birth?
2. What was the relation between the Old Testament sacrifices and Christ's death?
3. What New Testament passage compares Adam and Christ as race heads? Study it carefully.
4. In what sense is Christ now a spiritual King?
5. Which parable speaks most clearly of Christ as receiving a kingdom at His return?
6. Where does the New Testament refer to Christ's earthly body as not yet glorified (two references)?
7. How does Christ reveal the Father?
8. In what way are Christ and the Father one?
9. Why was Christ tempted?

THE HOLY SPIRIT

The Anabaptists also believed in the personality and Deity of the Holy Spirit, regarding Him as the One who convicts men of their sin and leads them to saving faith in Christ the Lord. Menno wrote:

... We believe and confess the Holy Ghost to be a true, real, or personal Holy Ghost; and that in a divine way—even as the Father is a true Father, and the Son a true Son; which Holy Ghost is a mystery to all mankind, incomprehensible, inexpressible and indescribable ... divine with His divine attributes, going forth from the Father through the Son, although He ever remains with God and in God, and is never separated from the being of the Father and the Son And the reason that we confess Him to be such a true and real Holy Spirit, is because we are impelled to this by the Scriptures, for He descended upon Christ at His baptism in the bodily shape of a dove, and appeared unto the apostles as cloven tongues like as of fire; because we are baptized in His name as well as in the name of the Father and of the Son, because the prophets through Him prophesied, performed miracles and works, had dreams and saw visions; for He is a Distributor of the gifts of God, and that according to His will (*Works*, II, 186f).

It is therefore evident that the Anabaptists believed in God as existing in three Persons, Father, Son and Holy Spirit. They engaged in no speculation concerning the philosophical aspects of the Trinity for they were Biblicists rather than theologians. Yet, Menno did write a brief treatise on the Trinity which contains the following:

> ... We believe and confess before God, before His angels, before all our brethren, and before all the world, that these three names, operations and powers, namely, the Father, Son and Holy Ghost (which the fathers called three persons, by which they meant the three, true, divine Beings) are one incomprehensible, indescribable, almighty, holy, only, eternal and sovereign God. ... And although they are three, yet in Godliness, will, power and operation they are one ... All the Father does and has wrought from the beginning, He works through His Son, in the power of His holy and eternal Spirit. ... If we deny the divinity of Christ, or the true existence of the Holy Ghost, then we counterfeit and depict unto ourselves a God who is without wisdom, power, light, life, truth, word, and without the Holy Spirit *(Works,* II, 187).

The interested reader should examine also "The Theology of Pilgram Marpeck," in *The Mennonite Quarterly Review,* XII, 205-256 (October, 1938), especially pages 214-217.

Pertinent Biblical Passages

1. On His Participation in the Creation:
   Gen. 1:2: "The Spirit of God moved upon the face of the waters."
   Job 26.13: "By His Spirit He hath garnished the heavens."
2. On His Striving with Sinners of Old:
   Gen. 6:3: "My Spirit shall not always strive with man."
   Isa. 63:10: "They rebelled, and vexed His Holy Spirit."
3. On His Blessings to Israelites:
   Ex. 31:3: "I have filled (Bezaleel) with the Spirit of God, in wisdom, and in understanding, and in knowledge, and in all manner of workmanship."
   Neh. 9:20: "Thou gavest also Thy good Spirit to instruct them."
   Ps. 51:11: "Cast me not away from Thy presence; and take not Thy Holy Spirit from me."
4. On His Convicting Power:
   John 16:8-11: "When He is come, He will reprove the world of sin, and of righteousness, and of judgment: of sin, because they believe not on Me; of righteousness, because I go to My Father ... ; of judgment, because the prince of this world is judged."
5. On His Work of Regeneration:
   John 3:5: "Except a man be born of water and of the Spirit, he cannot enter into the kingdom of God."
   John 3:8: "... So is every one that is born of the Spirit."
6. On His Sanctifying Work:
   Rom. 15:16: The believing Gentiles are "sanctified by the Holy Ghost."
   Gal. 5:16: "Walk by the Spirit, and ye shall not fulfil the lust of the flesh." A.S.V.

THE DOCTRINE OF GOD

7. **On His Ability to Lead:**
    Rom. 8:14: "As many as are led by the Spirit of God, they are the sons of God."
    Acts 15:28: "It seemed good to the Holy Ghost, and to us. . ."
8. **On His Enabling Christian Assurance:**
    Rom. 8:16: "The Spirit Himself beareth witness with our Spirit, that we are children of God." A.S.V.
    I John 3:24: "Hereby we know that He abideth in us, by the Spirit which He hath given us."
9. **On His Praying for Christians:**
    Rom. 8:26: "The Spirit Himself maketh intercession for us with groanings which cannot be uttered." A.S.V.
    Rom. 8:27: "He maketh intercession for the saints according to the will of God."
10. **On His Comforting Power.**
    Acts 9:31: "The churches . . . throughout all Judaea and Galilee and Samaria . . . were . . . walking . . . in the comfort of the Ghost."

Reading References in the Confessions and Catechisms

Christian Fundamentals, Article VII.
Shorter Catechism, Question 10.
Waldeck Catechism, Part First, Chapter II, Questions 6-8, Part Third, Chapter II, Questions 28-32.
Roosen's Catechism, Question 59.

Study Questions

1. Why is baptism to be "in the Name of the Father, and of the Son, and of the Holy Ghost"? Where is that reference found?
2. Find the location of this benediction: "The grace of the Lord Jesus Christ, and the love of God, and the communion of the Holy Ghost, be with you all. Amen."
3. To whom is prayer to be addressed? Give Scriptural support.
4. What is the meaning of praying in the name of Christ?
5. List some activities of the Holy Spirit which show that He is a person.
6. Find Scriptures which refer to the comforting power of the Spirit.
7. In what sense is there "one God," and in what sense are there three that are spoken of as God? Can the human mind comprehend this?

Chapter II

The Doctrine of Salvation

1. Sin

The Anabaptists believed in the sinfulness of human nature (original sin) and in man's total inability to deliver himself from sin. Menno commented thus on human depravity and sin:

> A carnal man cannot apprehend or comprehend divine things, for by nature he has not that discernment; but on the contrary his mind is depraved; God is not in his mind. A carnal man cannot understand spiritual things, for he is by nature a child of the devil, and is not spiritually minded, hence, he comprehends nothing spiritual; for by nature he is a stranger to God; has nothing of a divine nature dwelling in him, nor has communion with God. but is much rather at enmity with Him; he is unmerciful, unjust, unclean, not peaceable, impatient, disobedient, without understanding and unhappy. So are all men by nature according to their birth and origin after the flesh. This is the first or old Adam, and is comprised in the Scriptures in a single word, ungodly, that is, without God, a stranger and destitute of the divine nature (*Works*, I, 232; cf. II, 312f).

Pertinent Biblical Passages

1. On the Origin of Sin in the World:
    Read the Mosaic account in Gen. 3:1-19.
    Rom. 5:12: "By one man sin entered into the world, and death by sin; and so death passed upon all men, for that all have sinned. . . ."
    Rom. 5:19: "By one man's disobedience many were made sinners."
    I Cor. 15:22: "In Adam all die. . . ."

2. On the Meaning of Sin:
    I John 3:4: "Sin is lawlessness." A.S.V.
    I John 5:17: "All unrighteousness is sin."
    Rom. 14:23: "Whatsoever is not of faith is sin."
    James 4:17: "To him that knoweth to do good, and doeth it not, to him it is sin."

3. On the Universality of Sin:
    Gen. 6:5: "God saw that the wickedness of man was great in the earth, and that every imagination of the thoughts of his heart was only evil continually."
    Jer. 17:9: "The heart is deceitful above all things, and desperately wicked."
    Rom. 3:23: "For all have sinned, and fall short of the glory of God." A.S.V.
    Eph. 2:3: Prior to their conversion Christians "were by nature the children of wrath, even as others."

4. On the Consequences of Sin:
    Rom. 6:23: "The wages of sin is death."
    Rom. 8:6: "The mind of the flesh is death." A.S.V.

THE DOCTRINE OF SALVATION

Rom. 8.13: "If ye live after the flesh, ye must die." A.S.V.
John 3:36: "He that obeyeth not the Son shall not see life, but the wrath of God abideth on Him." A.S.V.
Rev. 20:15: "Whosoever was not found written in the book of life was cast into the lake of fire."

5. On the Blinding Effect of Sin:
   I Cor. 2:14: "The natural man receiveth not the things of the Spirit of God: for they are foolishness unto him: neither can he know them, because they are spiritually discerned."
   John 14:17: ". . . the Spirit of truth: whom the world cannot receive."
   I Cor. 1:18: "The preaching of the cross is to them that perish foolishness."

6. On Degrees of Guilt:
   Luke 12:48: "Unto whomsoever much is given, of him shall be much required."
   Matt. 10.15: "It shall be more tolerable for the land of Sodom and Gomorrha in the day of judgment, than for that city" [which rejects apostolic preaching]. Cf. John 19:11.

7. On the Lost Condition of All Those Not in Christ:
   Rom. 1:20: The creation speaks to all men of God's "eternal power and Godhead; so that they are without excuse."
   Rom. 2:12: "As many as have sinned without law shall also perish without law: and as many as have sinned in the law shall be judged by the law."
   James 2:10: "Whosoever shall keep the whole law, and yet offend in one point, he is guilty of all."

8. On Catalogs of Sins:
   Study Matt. 15:19f; Mark 7:21-23; Rev. 21:8; I Cor. 6:9f; Gal. 5:19-21.

Reading References in the Confessions and Catechisms
Dordrecht Confession, Article II.
Christian Fundamentals, Article IV.
Shorter Catechism, Question 16.
Waldeck Catechism, Part Second.
Roosen's Catechism, Questions 84-88.

Study Questions

1. Do any passages besides the ones cited refer to Adam's fall into sin?
2. Why do unsaved people not flee from God's wrath against sin?
3. Can a person sin unknowingly?
4. Are the children of the saints also born with original sin (depravity)?
5. Why are the heathen lost when they have never heard the Gospel?
6. How can sinners ever have any hope of eternal salvation?

2. REGENERATION

On the subject of the new birth Menno's friend and colleague, Dirck Philips, 1504-68, wrote:

Jesus testifies of this to Nicodemus and says: "Verily, verily, I say unto thee, Except a man be born again, he cannot see the kingdom of God Verily, verily, I say unto thee, Except a man be born of water and of the Spirit, he cannot enter into the kingdom of God."

Here the kingdom of God is absolutely denied to all who are not born again of God, and who are not created by Him anew after the inner man in His image . . .

This regeneration is not external, but in the mind, reason, and heart of man; in the reason or intelligence, and mind, in this that he learns to know the eternal, true and gracious God in Jesus Christ, who is the eternal image of the Father . . , and the brightness and express image of the Person of God. In the heart, in this that man loves this same almighty and living God, fears, honors and believes in Him, trusts in His promises, which cannot be without the power of the Holy Spirit, who must inoculate into the heart, as it were, with divine power, giving faith, fear, love, hope and all the divine virtues (*Enchiridion*, English Edition, 1910, 376f).

In his treatise on *The New Birth*, 1556, Menno wrote:

True repentance and the birth from above, must take place; we must believe Christ and His word, and we must abide by His Spirit, ordinance and example willingly, or eternal misery must be our portion This is incontrovertible *(Works,* I, 171).

Menno wrote further:

The new birth consists, verily, not in water nor in words, but it is the heavenly, living and quickening power of God in our hearts which comes from God, and which by the preaching of the divine Word, if we accept it by faith, quickens, renews, pierces, and converts our hearts, so that we are changed and converted from unbelief into faith, from unrighteousness into righteousness, from evil into good, from carnality into spirituality, from the earthly into the heavenly, [and] from the wicked nature of Adam into the good nature of Jesus Christ . . . *(Works,* II, 215).

Pertinent Biblical Passages

1. On the Agent of Regeneration:

    John 3:5: "Except a man be born of water and of the Spirit, he cannot enter into the kingdom of God."
    John 3:6: "That which is born of the Spirit is spirit."
    John 3:8· ". . . so is every one that is born of the Spirit."

2. On the Resulting Illumination:

    John 3:3: "Except a man be born again, he cannot see the kingdom of God."
    Eph. 1:18: "Having the eyes of your heart enlightened, that ye may know . . . ." A.S.V.
    II Cor. 4:6: God "hath shined in our hearts, to give the light of the knowledge of the glory of God in the face of Jesus Christ."

3. On the Spiritual Change Effected:

    Rom. 2:29: The true "Israelite" is the one whose "circumcision is that of the heart, in the spirit. . . ." Cf. Col. 2:11.
    II Cor. 5:17: "If any man be in Christ, he is a new creature: old things are passed away; behold, all things are become new."
    Gal. 6:15: "In Christ Jesus neither circumcision availeth any thing, nor uncircumcision, but a new creature."

4. On the Divine Cleansing in Regeneration:

    I Cor. 6:11: Ye Corinthian Christians used to be polluted sinners, "but ye are washed, but ye are sanctified, but ye are justified in the name of the Lord Jesus, and by the Spirit of our God."
    Titus 3:5: "Not by works of righteousness which we have done,

THE DOCTRINE OF SALVATION

but according to His mercy He saved us, by the washing of regeneration, and renewing of the Holy Ghost."

Heb. 10:22: In view of the adequate High Priest which we have in Christ, "Let us draw near with a true heart in full assurance of faith, having our hearts sprinkled from an evil conscience, and our bodies washed with pure water."

5. On the Spiritual Resurrection Involved:

Rom. 6:4: "We are buried with (Christ) by baptism into death: that like as Christ was raised up from the dead by the glory of the Father, even so we also should walk in newness of life."

Col. 2:11f: Christians have been cleansed from sin "by the circumcision of Christ: buried with Him in baptism, wherein also ye are risen with Him through the faith of the operation of God . . . ." Cf. Col. 2:13, 3:1.

6. On the Crucifixion of the Old Man·

Rom. 6.6: "Our old man was crucified with (Christ), that the body of sin might be rendered powerless." Greek. Study the context carefully.

Gal. 2:20: "I have been crucified with Christ; and it is no longer I that live, but Christ liveth in me: and that life which I now live in the flesh I live in faith, the faith which is in the Son of God, who loved me, and gave Himself up for me." A.S.V.

7. On the Conflict Which Remains in the Regenerated Person:

Rom 7:18: "I know that in me (that is, in my flesh,) dwelleth no good thing."

Rom. 8:23: Not only does the whole creation groan, "But ourselves also, which have the firstfruits of the Spirit, even we ourselves groan within ourselves, waiting for the adoption, to wit, the redemption of our body."

Gal. 5:16, 17: "This I say then, Walk in the Spirit, and ye shall not fulfil the lust of the flesh. For the flesh lusteth against the Spirit, and the Spirit against the flesh: and these are contrary the one to the other: so that ye cannot do the things that ye would."

8. On the Victory Which God Offers the Regenerated:

I Cor. 10:13: "There hath no temptation taken you but such as is common to man: but God is faithful, who will not suffer you to be tempted above that ye are able; but will with the temptation also make a way to escape, that ye may be able to bear it."

Rom. 8:37: "In all these things we are more than conquerors, through Him that loved us."

Reading References in the Confessions and Catechisms

Dordrecht Confession, Article VI.
Christian Fundamentals, Article VI.
Shorter Catechism, Questions 11, 13.
Waldeck Catechism, Part Third, Chapter III, Questions 6-11.
Roosen's Catechism, Question 100.

Study Questions

1. Does regeneration change the nature of the flesh? Are the passions of the body made different?
2. How does regeneration make itself evident?
3. Who are those who receive regeneration?
4. How may one know that he has been born again?
5. List the "fruit of the Spirit."
6. List the "works of the flesh."
7. How is victory over sin obtained?
8. When will our "vile body" be changed and made like unto Christ's?

3. HOLINESS OF LIFE

The Christian life is one of holiness, of following after Christ Jesus as Lord. Menno wrote:

> ... The chosen of God are the church of Christ, His saints and beloved, who washed their clothes in the blood of the Lamb, who are born of God, influenced by the Spirit of Christ; who are in Christ and He in them, who hear and believe His Word, who follow Him in their weakness, in His commandments, walk in His footsteps with all patience and humility, hate the evil, and love the good, earnestly desiring to apprehend Christ as they are apprehended of Him, for all who are in Christ are new creatures, flesh of His flesh, bone of His bone, and members of His body (*Works*, I, 161f).
>
> Behold, this is the word and will of the Lord, that all who hear and believe the word of God shall be baptized . . . , thereby to profess their faith, and declare that they will henceforth not live according to their own will but according to the will of God That for the testimony of Jesus they are prepared to forsake their homes, chattels, lands and lives, and to suffer hunger, affliction, oppression, persecution, the cross and death; yea, they desire to bury the flesh with its lusts, and arise with Christ to newness of life, even as Paul says, "Know ye not, that so many of us as were baptized into Jesus Christ were baptized into His death? Therefore we are buried with Him by baptism into death: that like as Christ was raised up from the dead by the glory of the Father, even so we also should walk in newness of life" (*Works*, I, 25f).

In 1582 John Wouters, a Mennonite of Dordrecht in Holland, was burned to death for his faith. While awaiting execution he wrote numerous letters to his friends. In a letter addressed to his only daughter, a child of about seven years, Wouters wrote:

> Thus, my dearest daughter, lay it to heart, despise it not, for it is of great importance to you; and diligently search (when you have received understanding from the Lord) the holy Scriptures, and you will find that we must follow Christ Jesus and obey Him unto the end, and you will also truly find the little flock who follow Christ. And this is the sign: they lead a penitent life; they avoid that which is evil, and delight in doing what is good; they hunger and thirst after righteousness: they are not conformed to the world; they crucify their sinful flesh more and more every day, to die unto sin which wars in their members; they strive and seek after that which is honest and of good report; they do evil to no one; they pray for their enemies; they do not resist their enemies; their words are yea that is yea, and nay that is nay; their word is their seal, they are sorry that they do not constantly live more holily, for which reason they often sigh and weep. Let not this, however, be the only sign by which you may know who follows Christ; but [they are] also these, namely, who bear the cross of Christ, for He says: "If any man will come after Me, let him deny himself, and take up his cross daily, and follow Me." ... For He has said: "If they have persecuted Me, they will also persecute you." . The apostle Paul declares to them and says that "all that will live godly in Christ Jesus shall suffer persecution" (*Martyrs' Mirror*, 1938, 915).

THE DOCTRINE OF SALVATION 15

Pertinent Biblical Passages

1. On Man's Total Lack of Holiness by Nature:
   Read Rom. 1:18—3:20.
   Rom. 3:23: "All have sinned, and fall short of the glory of God." A.S.V.
   Rom. 3:9f: "We have before proved both Jews and Gentiles, that they are all under sin; as it is written, There is none righteous, no, not one."

2. On the Promises of God to Those Who Seek Holiness:
   Matt. 5:6: "Blessed are they which do hunger and thirst after righteousness: for they shall be filled."
   John 7:37: "Jesus stood and cried, saying, If any man thirst, let him come unto Me, and drink."
   Rom. 8:13: "If ye through the Spirit do mortify the deeds of the body, ye shall live."

3. On the Absolute Demand of God for Holiness:
   Heb. 12:14-16: "Follow peace with all men, and holiness, without which no man shall see the Lord: looking diligently lest any man fail of the grace of God; lest any root of bitterness springing up trouble you, and thereby many be defiled; lest there be any fornicator, or profane person, as Esau . . . ."

4. On God's Desire for His Children to Be Holy:
   I Pet. 1:14-16: ". . . As obedient children, not fashioning yourselves according to the former lusts in your ignorance: but as He which hath called you is holy, so be ye holy in all manner of conversation [living]; because it is written, Be ye holy; for I am holy."
   Eph. 5:25-27: "Christ also loved the church, and gave Himself for it; that He might sanctify and cleanse it with the washing of water by the Word, that He might present it to Himself a glorious church, not having spot, or wrinkle, or any such thing; but that it should be holy and without blemish."

5. On the Significance of Holiness as a Means of Identification:
   Rom. 6:16: "Know ye not, that to whom ye yield yourselves servants to obey, his servants ye are to whom ye obey; whether of sin unto death, or of obedience unto righteousness?"

6. On the Lost Condition of Those Living in Sin:
   I Cor. 6:9: "Know ye not that the unrighteous shall not inherit the kingdom of God?" Read the list of sins excluding from the kingdom in verses 9 and 10.

7. On the Impossibility of a Saved Man Living in Sin:
   I John 3:9: "Everyone who is begotten of God does not practice sin; because His seed abides in him, and he is not able to be sinning, because he is begotten of God." Greek.

16   THE DOCTRINES OF THE MENNONITES

Reading References in the Confessions and Catechisms

Dordrecht Confession, Article VI.
Christian Fundamentals, Article X.
Shorter Catechism, Questions 11, 12.
Waldeck Catechism, Part Third, Chapter III, Questions 15-17
Roosen's Catechism, Questions 99, 100.

Study Questions

1. Why do men by nature lack holiness?
2. How may people become holy?
3. What do men indicate by their manner of life?
4. Can regenerated persons fall into sin?
5. Do saved people live in sin?
6. What is the relation of holiness to love?
7. Who is the best pattern of holiness?
8. Can Christians merit salvation by personal holiness?

Chapter III
Present Grace and Future Glory

1. Divine Grace

While the Anabaptists emphasized regeneration they also recognized that even those who have experienced the new birth continue to fall short of God's glory. But Christians enjoy the grace of God. Menno says expressly:

... For Christ's sake we are in grace, for His sake we are heard, and for His sake our failings and transgressions, which are committed involuntarily, are remitted. For it is He who stands between His Father and His imperfect children, with His perfect righteousness, and with His innocent blood and death, and intercedes for all those who believe on Him and who strive by faith in the divine word, to turn from evil, follow that which is good and who sincerely desire, with Paul, that they may attain the perfection which is in Christ . .

Mark, beloved reader, that we do not believe nor teach that we are to be saved by our merits and works, as the envious accuse us of without truth; but that we are to be saved solely by grace, through Christ Jesus ... (*Works,* II, 263).

To a troubled sister in the church Menno wrote:

... We must all acknowledge, whosoever we are, that we are sinners in thoughts, words and works .... In and by yourself you are a poor sinner . but in and through Christ you are justified and pleasing unto God, and accepted of Him in eternal grace as a daughter and child (*Works,* II, 402).

On the subject of God's grace Menno stated further:

... All the truly regenerated and spiritual conform in all things to the word and ordinances of the Lord; not because they think to merit the propitiation of their sins and eternal life; by no means; in this matter they depend upon nothing except the true promise of the merciful Father, graciously given to all believers through the blood and merits of Christ, which blood is and ever will be the only eternal medium of our reconciliation, and not works, baptism or Lord's supper ...

For if our reconciliation depended upon works and ceremonies, then it would not be grace, and the merits and fruits of the blood of Christ would be void. O no! it is grace, and will be grace to all eternity; all the merciful Father is doing or has done for us grievous sinners through His beloved Son and Holy Spirit is grace .. (I, 158).

... I have read in some books which they have written [undoubtedly he has in mind Luther, or perhaps Zwingli] that there is but *one* good work which saves us, namely, FAITH, and but *one* sin which will damn us, namely, UNBELIEF. Thus I will leave as it is, and not find fault with it, for where there is a sincere, true *faith,* there are also all manner of sincere, good fruits. On the other hand, where there is unbelief, there are also all manner of evil fruits, therefore, is salvation properly ascribed to *faith,* and damnation to *unbelief (Works,* I, 159).

Dirck Philips, Menno's fellow-elder (bishop), taught the same doctrine of grace. Indeed Menno himself stated unqualifiedly. "Dirck and we are of the same mind" (II, 96). Dirck wrote:

It must therefore be recognized that every Christian has sin and must confess himself a sinner, that he may humble himself under the mighty hand of God and pray the Lord for His mercy. Thus the Scripture remains true and unbroken which puts all men under condemnation and reproves them as sinners; but sin is not imputed to Christians, but has been forgiven them through the innocent death of Jesus Christ, and is covered with His everlasting love, by which He offered Himself up for us for an everlasting atonement for our sins, taking upon Himself our burden, and paying our debt with His bitter suffering, and making us a free gift of all that He has, so that He is one with us and we with Him, whereby we are made acceptable unto God, yea, accounted as saints of God. Therefore David says "Blessed is he whose transgression is forgiven, whose sin is covered. Blessed is the man unto whom the Lord imputeth not iniquity" (*Enchiridion,* English edition, 1910, 282).

Matthew Cervaes, c. 1536-1565, a Mennonite elder of the Lower Rhine who was beheaded June 30, 1565, at Cologne, wrote:

> ... We may not seek righteousness or salvation from our works, from what we do or do not do, for by the works of the law shall no flesh be justified before the Lord, as Paul says. Nor shall we be able to pay what we owe; but we hope to be justified and saved only through the grace of God, through the merits of our Lord Jesus Christ (*Martyrs' Mirror,* 1938 edition, 694).

In 1568 a Mennonite schoolteacher named Valerius was arrested as an Anabaptist in Zeeland in the Netherlands and after a long imprisonment was put to death as a heretic. During his imprisonment he wrote two books, one of which, *The Proof of Faith,* contains the following statement of salvation by grace:

> If then we are to be saved through God's mercy, we must repent, must be obedient children of God, born again of Him, and must follow Christ in the regeneration and the footsteps of faith, through the narrow way unto eternal life, nor are we then saved through the merit of good works, but by the grace which came through Christ ... For though we lived holy, blameless, and perfect in all righteousness (as the Scriptures require), and suffered for the truth a death more bitter than that of Christ, which with us men is impossible, yet we could not be saved through our own good works, but only by God's mercy, and the grace of our Lord Jesus Christ, who alone has wrought out our salvation. And if we sought or placed our salvation in our good works or our sufferings we should commit idolatry, and we were our own idol, if we trusted in ourselves. But now our salvation depends only on the mercy of God, and not on our running and following after ... though we should run and follow after ever so well (which is our bounden duty), so that we attained, and already had, the perfection (that for which we are apprehended of Christ), and had done all those things which are commanded us, and which it is our duty to do, we were yet only unprofitable servants ... How much more unprofitable then are we now, with our many defects, though we willingly strive after and should gladly perform that which is good, and are sorry that we are not perfect (Quoted in *Martyrs' Mirror,* 1938, 730f).

Pertinent Biblical Passages

1. On Man's Total Inability to Achieve Merit with God:
    Rom. 3:20: "By works of law shall no flesh be justified in His sight, for through law cometh a knowledge of sin." Greek.
    Acts 13:39: "By (Christ) all that believe are justified from all things, from which ye could not be justified by the law of Moses."
    Gal. 2:16: "A man is not justified by works of law but through faith in Christ Jesus, ...: for by works of law shall no flesh be justified." A.S.V. and Greek.
2. On the Grace of God in Repentance:
    Acts 16:14: "And a certain woman named Lydia ... heard us: whose heart the Lord opened to give heed unto the things which were spoken by Paul." A.S.V.
    John 6:43f: "Jesus therefore answered and said unto them ... No man can come to Me, except the Father which hath sent Me draw him." Cf. John 6:65.

Rom. 2:4: "The goodness of God leadeth thee to repentance." Cf. II Tim. 2:25.

3. On the Grace of God in the Plan of Salvation:
    Acts 15:11: "We believe that through the grace of the Lord Jesus Christ we [Jewish Christians] shall be saved, even as they [Gentile Christians]."
    Rom. 3:28: "We reckon therefore that a man is justified by faith, apart from works of law." Greek.
    Eph. 2:8f: "For by grace are ye saved through faith; and that not of yourselves: it is the gift of God: not of works, lest any man should boast."

4. On the Grace of God in Keeping Christians from Sin and Apostasy:
    John 10:27-29: "My sheep hear My voice, and I know them, and they follow Me; and I give to them life eternal, and not by any means shall they perish for ever, and no one shall snatch them out of My hand. My Father who has given them to Me is greater than all, and no one is able to snatch them out of the hand of the Father." Greek.
    I Cor. 1:7-9: Christians are "waiting for the coming of our Lord Jesus Christ: who shall also confirm you unto the end, that ye may be blameless in the day of our Lord Jesus Christ. God is faithful . . . ." Cf. Phil. 1:6.
    II Tim. 1:12: "I know Him whom I have believed, and I am persuaded that He is able to guard that which I have committed unto Him against that day." A.S.V.

5. On the Grace of God in Justifying Christians:
    Rom. 3:24: ". . . being justified freely by His grace through the redemption that is in Christ Jesus."
    Rom. 4:16: "Therefore it is of faith, that it might be by grace." Study the context.
    Rom. 11:5f: "Even so then at this present time also there is a remnant according to the election of grace. And if by grace, then it is no more of works: otherwise grace is no more grace. But if it be of works, then it is no more grace: otherwise work is no more work."

Reading References in the Confessions and Catechisms

Christian Fundamentals, Article VI.
Shorter Catechism, Questions 3-6.
Waldeck Catechism, Part Third, Chapter III, Questions 12-14.
Roosen's Catechism, Questions 70, 71.

Study Questions

1. How is it possible for imperfect people to be saved?
2. In what way does God show His love to sinful men outside of Christ?
3. Why are not all men saved who hear the Gospel?
4. Make a list of Scriptures which warn Christians against apostasy?
5. Is the grace of God adequate to keep believers from losing out as saints?

6. Are Christians saved by "being good" or by doing good deeds?
7. Why is salvation wholly of grace? (Cf. Eph. 2:9).
8. Can regenerated people afford to become cold and careless? Why not?
9. What effect will an awareness of God's grace have upon a Christian?
10. Does a true understanding of God's grace lead to carelessness or to love and devotion toward God?

2. Eschatology

The Swiss Brethren and the Mennonites also agreed with the Lutherans and the Reformed on eschatology. They looked for the personal return of the Lord Jesus to raise the dead, judge the world, and usher in the eternal state. The only "golden age" to which they looked forward was in heaven, not on this earth. Nicholas Blesdijk, c. 1500-1556, a Davidian, stated: "The followers of Obbe Philips, who are today called Mennonites, taught that no other condition of Christ's kingdom is to be expected than that which exists today, namely persecution by the world." The *Vindication* of Pilgram Marpeck, c. 1495-1556, contains fifty references to the Return of Christ. Menno Simons, after quoting from Luke 19, comments:

This Scripture clearly testifies that the Lord Christ must first come again before all His enemies are punished And how Christ will come again He Himself testifies, saying, "For the Son of man shall come in the glory of His Father, with His angels, and then He shall reward every man according to his works." Again, "For as the lightning cometh out of the east and shineth even unto the west; so shall also the coming of the Son of man be." "And then shall appear the sign of the Son of man in heaven: and then shall all the tribes of the earth mourn, and they shall see the Son of man coming in the clouds of heaven, with power and great glory " The two angels also testified how Christ would come again, saying, "Ye men of Galilee, why stand ye gazing up into heaven? This same Jesus, which is taken up from you into heaven, shall so come in like manner as ye have seen Him go into heaven."

Further, the evangelist says, that Christ will take account with His servants, which will not be until the day of judgment . . .

. . . "The Lord Jesus shall be revealed from heaven with His mighty angels, in flaming fire, taking vengeance on them that know not God, and that obey not the gospel of our Lord Jesus Christ" These angels will be the reapers who, at the end of the world, that is, in the day of judgment, will root up all the tares and cast them into the lake of fire. Until that time the tares will be left among the good seed; let none think that we should root up the tares now, or that we should now separate the goats from the sheep. "When the Son of man shall come in His glory, and all the holy angels with Him, then shall He sit upon the throne of His glory: and before Him shall be gathered all nations, and He shall separate them one from another, as a shepherd divideth His sheep from the goats; and He shall set the sheep on His right hand, but the goats on the left "

These words are as clear as the sun, yet some do not understand them . . (*Works*, II, 438f).

Pertinent Biblical Passages

1. On the Signs of the Second Coming of Christ:
    Matt. 24:14: "This gospel of the kingdom shall be preached in all the world for a witness unto all nations; and then shall the end come." (Worldwide missions.)
    Rom. 11:25: "Blindness in part is happened to Israel, until the fulness of the Gentiles be come in." (Many Gentiles will be saved before the end.)

PRESENT GRACE AND FUTURE GLORY

2. Rom. 11:32: "For God hath shut up all [the Jews] unto disobedience, that He might have mercy upon all." A.S.V. (Many Jews will be saved before the end.)
Great apostasy and tribulation. Matt. 24:9-12, Mark 13:9-13, II Thess. 2:3, 4; I Tim. 4:1-3; II Tim. 3:1-5.
The appearance of the man of sin, the antichrist. II Thess. 2:1-12; I John 2:18; 4:3; II John 7; Rev. 13.
Various signs and wonders: wars, famines, earthquakes, astronomical disturbances, abounding heresies. Matt. 24:7, 11, 29, 30; Mark 13:24, 25; Luke 21:25, 26.
A sensate and material culture and civilization. Luke 17:24-30.
A sense of security. I Thess. 5:3.
Matt. 24:36: "But of that day and hour knoweth no man, no, not the angels of heaven, but my Father only."

2. On the Nature of the Second Coming: Personal, Visible, Sudden, Glorious:

Matt. 24:44: "Therefore be ye also ready: for in such an hour as ye think not the Son of man cometh." Study the context; also parallels.
Acts 1:11: "This same Jesus, which is taken up from you into heaven, shall so come in like manner as ye have seen Him go into heaven."
Matt. 24:30: "And they shall see the Son of man coming in the clouds of heaven with power and great glory."
I Thess. 4:16—5:3: "The Lord Himself shall descend from heaven with a shout, with the voice of the archangel, and with the trump of God: and the dead in Christ shall rise first: then we which are alive and remain shall be caught up together with them in the clouds, to meet the Lord in the air: and so shall we ever be with the Lord. Wherefore comfort one another with these words. But of the times and seasons, brethren, ye have no need that I write unto you. For yourselves know perfectly that the day of the Lord so cometh as a thief in the night. For when they shall say, Peace and safety; then sudden destruction cometh upon them, as travail upon a woman with child; and they shall not escape."
II Pet. 3:3, 4, 10: "There shall come in the last days scoffers . . . saying, Where is the promise of His coming? . . . But the day of the Lord will come as a thief in the night; in the which the heavens shall pass away with a great noise, and the elements shall melt with fervent heat, the earth also and the works that are therein shall be burned up." Study the entire passage.

3. On the Purposes of the Second Coming of Jesus:

I Cor. 15:21-23: "For since by man came death, by man came also the resurrection of the dead. For as in Adam all die, even so in Christ shall all be made alive. But every man in his own order: Christ the firstfruits; afterward they that are Christ's at His coming."

Matt. 13:40-43: "... So shall it be in the end of this world. The Son of man shall send forth His angels, and they shall gather out of His kingdom all things that offend, and them which do iniquity; and shall cast them into a furnace of fire: in that place shall be wailing and gnashing of teeth. Then shall the righteous shine forth as the sun in the kingdom of their Father." (The Greek word *ekei* means "there;" "in that place.")

II Thess. 1:7-10: "... When the Lord Jesus shall be revealed from heaven with His mighty angels, in flaming fire taking vengeance on them that know not God, and that obey not the gospel of our Lord Jesus Christ ... When He shall come to be glorified in His saints ... in that day."

Rom. 8:18: "I reckon that the sufferings of this present time are not worthy to be compared with the glory which shall be revealed to us-ward." A.S.V.

Phil. 3:20f.: "For our citizenship is in heaven; whence also we wait for a Saviour, the Lord Jesus Christ: who shall fashion anew the body of our humiliation, that it may be conformed to the body of His glory...." A.S.V.

Rom. 8:21: "The creation itself also shall be delivered from the bondage of corruption into the liberty of the glory of the children of God." Study this passage in the American Standard Version, from which this verse is quoted.

II Pet. 3:13: "We, according to His promise, look for new heavens and a new earth, wherein dwelleth righteousness." Cf. Rev. 22:1.

Matt. 19:28: "And Jesus said unto them, Verily I say unto you, That ye which have followed Me, in the regeneration when the Son of man shall sit in the throne of His glory, ye also shall sit upon twelve thrones, judging the twelve tribes of Israel."

Reading References in the Confessions and Catechisms

Schleitheim Confession, third last paragraph of postscript.
Dordrecht Confession, Article XVIII.
Christian Fundamentals, Articles XIV-XVIII.
Shorter Catechism, Question 34.
Waldeck Catechism, Part Third, Chapter V.
Roosen's Catechism, Questions 139-148.

Study Questions

1. Why will the unsaved be unprepared for Christ's coming?
2. Will the righteous be caught unprepared at His coming?
3. Contrast His first and second advents.
4. What will happen to this sin-cursed earth at His coming?
5. Can we estimate the approximate time of His return?
6. Did Pentecost fulfill His promise to come again? Why not?
7. Why were the five foolish virgins not ready when the bridegroom came?
8. How can Christians best watch for the Lord's coming?

9. Does Scripture anywhere state the effect in the lives of those who entertain the hope of the Lord's return?
10. How many destinies will there be for the human family following the judgment?

3. INSPIRATION OF THE BIBLE

On the great doctrines of God, Christ, the Holy Spirit, the Trinity, depravity and sin, regeneration, holiness of life, grace, and eschatology, the Brethren held common views with the Protestant bodies. In some respects they agreed also on the doctrine of the church. And, in common with all branches of the Christian Church in the sixteenth century, the Brethren believed in the absolute authority of the Bible. Menno said it was "impossible" for the Word of God to prove untrue (II, 438). The Scriptures are "the true witness of the Holy Ghost and the plummet of our consciences" (I, 167).

... The whole Scriptures, both of the Old and New Testaments, were written for our instruction, admonition and correction, and .. they are the true scepter and rule by which the Lord's kingdom, house, church and congregation must be governed and adjusted ... Everything contrary to Scripture, whether it be in doctrines, faith, sacraments, worship or conduct, should be measured by this infallible rule, and demolished by this just and divine scepter, without any respect to persons, and brought to nothing (Menno's *Works*, I, 53f).

Brethren, I tell you the truth and lie not I am no Enoch, no Elias; I have no visions, am no prophet who can teach and prophesy differently from what it is written in the Word of God, (and whoever tries to teach something else will soon miss the right way and be deceived in his learning). I trust that the merciful Father will keep me in His Word so that I shall write or speak nothing but that which I can prove by Moses, the prophets, the evangelists or by other apostolic Scriptures and doctrines, explained in their true sense, spirit and intent of Christ. Judge ye that are spiritually minded. Again, I have no visions nor angelic inspirations, neither do I desire such lest I be thereby deceived. The Word of Christ alone is sufficient for me *(Works,* II, 248).

In view of the above discussion of the position of the Brethren on the major doctrines of the Christian faith—and on those doctrines the Swiss and Dutch Anabaptists largely agreed—it is not surprising to find Zwingli addressing the Brethren in these words: "If one looks into this matter closely it is seen that you contend only for unimportant outward things." At the Zofingen debates, 1532, the Swiss Reformed clergy stated: "We are of one mind in the leading articles of faith, and our controversy has to do only with external things which are not in accordance with the gospel ..." Again, Zwingli stated: "But that no one may suppose that the dissension is in regard to doctrines which concern the inner man, let it be said that they make us difficulty only because of questions such as these: whether infants or adults should be baptized and whether a Christian may be a magistrate."

In controversy however this basic agreement was quite overlooked and the Reformers spoke of the Anabaptists in most abusive terms. Zwingli stated that the Brethren "seek nothing but disturbance and confusion of affairs, both human and divine." Calvin referred to "the nefarious herd of Anabaptists." Luther spoke of the Anabaptists as "the devil's emissaries" and "the birds who devour the seed sown by the wayside." In the heat of their polemic the Reformers hurled charges against the Brethren which came wide of the truth. Indeed, most sixteenth century writers, no groups excepted, were lacking in grace and courtesy when they engaged in "religious" controversy.

Pertinent Biblical Passages

1. On the Inspiration of the Old Testament Scriptures:
    John 10:35: "The Scripture cannot be broken."
    II Pet. 1:20f: "No prophecy of the Scripture is of any private interpretation. For prophecy came not in old time by the will of man: but holy men of God spake as they were moved by the Holy Ghost."
    II Tim. 3:16: "All Scripture is given by inspiration of God, and is profitable for doctrine, for reproof, for correction, for instruction in righteousness."

2. On the Inspiration of the New Testament Scriptures:
    I Cor. 14:37: "If any man think himself to be a prophet, or spiritual, let him acknowledge that the things that I write unto you are the commandments of the Lord."
    II Thess. 3:12: "Now them that are such we command and exhort by our Lord Jesus Christ . . . ."
    Cf. II Pet. 3:16 where Paul's epistles are classed with "the other Scriptures."

3. On the Necessity of Recognizing the Word Only:
    Mark 7:13: Jesus condemned the Pharisees for "making the Word of God of none effect through your tradition . . . and many such like things ye do."
    Matt. 15:13: Jesus "answered and said, Every plant, which my heavenly Father hath not planted, shall be rooted up."

4. On the Divine Approval for Testing All Doctrine by the Word:
    Acts 17:11: The Christians at Berea were "more noble than those in Thessalonica, in that they received the Word with all readiness of mind, and searched the Scriptures daily, whether those things were so."

5. On Proclaiming a Message Which Is Grounded on Scripture:
    Acts 26:22f: Paul stated: "I continue unto this day, witnessing both to small and great, saying none other things than those which the prophets and Moses did say should come: that the Christ should suffer, and that He should be the first that should rise from the dead, and should show light unto the people [of Israel], and to the Gentiles."

6. On the Absolute Reliability of God's Word:
    Study the New Testament references to the fulfillment of Old Testament prophecy.
    Examine Paul's argument in Gal. 3:16.
    John 17:17: "Thy Word is truth."

Reading References in the Confessions and Catechisms

Dordrecht Confession, Article I, first paragraph; Article V.
Christian Fundamentals, Article I.
Waldeck Catechism, Part First, Chapter I, Questions 6-13.
Roosen's Catechism, Questions 7, 8, 14, 15.

Study Questions

1. Did God allow the several writers of Scripture to employ their individual styles of writing?
2. Did God allow the writers of Scripture to incorporate human error into His Word?
3. Is it necessary to understand all about inspiration before one can believe the testimony of the Bible as to its character?
4. Why did God allow certain lower ethical standards, such as divorce, in the Old Testament?
5. With what motive should one study the Word of God?
6. Why did God give mankind a written revelation of Himself?
7. In what sense is Christ the Word of God? How did He reveal God?
8. What is the function of the Scriptures in reference to Christ?

Chapter IV
The Centrality of Evangelism

The unique tenets and emphases of the Mennonites theologically can perhaps be subsumed under three heads, relating to the Bible, the church, and the Christian life. It is with these three great topics that the remainder of this book will deal. The following outline of this material will perhaps help clarify the discussion:

SOME UNIQUE EMPHASES IN ANABAPTIST-MENNONITE DOCTRINE

I. The Bible
    1. Evangelism, not Theology (*Chapter IV*)
    2. Biblicism
        a. Ordinances (*Chapter V*)
        b. Nonresistance (*Chapter VI*)
        c. Simplicity of Life (*Chapter VII*)
    3. Finality of the New Testament (*Chapter VIII*)

II. The Church
    1. Fellowship of Committed Disciples (*Chapter IX*)
    2. Kept Pure by Discipline (*Chapter IX*)
    3. High Calling of the Church (*Chapter X*)

III. The Christian Life
    1. Its Heart, Discipleship (*Chapter XI*)
    2. The Believer's Cross (*Chapter XII*)
    3. A Life of Penitence (*Chapter XII*)

1. EVANGELISM, NOT THEOLOGY

The Anabaptists were above all else men of the Word. They accepted the Bible, both the Old and New Testaments, as inspired of the Holy Spirit, as the very oracles of God. This was not unique with them for the Lutherans and the Reformed, as well as the Catholics, also believed in divine inspiration. But the Anabaptists made their attitude toward the Bible operate in daily life to a degree which seemed fanatical to many sixteenth century Christians. Furthermore, Luther in his reaction to ecclesiastical tradition and authority relaxed somewhat in his attitude toward the Biblical canon. Menno Simons took offense at Luther's derogatory remark concerning the Epistle of James (*Works*, I, 111). In brief, the Anabaptists used the Bible not so much to erect a human system of theology as to redeem men from sin. In this sense they had a "practical" attitude toward the Bible, making it function in the salvation and the sanctification of men, rather than placing much stress on systems of

THE CENTRALITY OF EVANGELISM

thought or entering into the speculative problems of theology. And there is something wholesome about this point of view. It is much easier to theorize about the order of the divine decrees than to win converts for the Lord Jesus. It is much easier to get an intellectual grasp of the doctrines of Scripture than to apply the Scriptures to the whole man, to all of life. A few quotations from Menno's works will help elucidate the redemptive and Bible-centered attitude of the Brethren:

> I have served you all with this small gift as I received it from my God I gladly would that I could serve you longer with great and abundant grace, to the praise of the Lord Therefore have I renounced praise, honor, ease, and forsaken all, and willingly submitted to the pressing cross of my Lord Jesus Christ, which ofttimes weighs very heavily on my weak flesh I seek neither gold nor silver (the Lord knows this), but am ready with faithful Moses to suffer affliction with the people of God rather than to enjoy the pleasures of sin for a season; and I esteem the reproach of Christ greater riches than the treasures in Egypt, for I know what the Scriptures have promised us. And this is my only joy and desire of my heart, that I may extend the borders of the kingdom of God, publish the truth, reprove sin, teach righteousness, feed the hungry with the word of the Lord, lead the stray sheep into the right path, and win many souls to the Lord through His Spirit, power and grace, and so act in my weakness, as He taught me who purchased me, a miserable sinner, with His crimson blood, and gave me this mind, by the gospel of His grace, namely Jesus Christ to Him be praise and glory and the eternal kingdom, Amen (*Works*, I, 75).
>
> ... The Word of God is eternal Neither princes, nor power, nor the commands of men with all their imperial edicts are to constitute faith, neither can a soul be saved by them. Only the heavenly counsel we must hear and follow, that which Jesus Christ, God's first and only begotten Son Himself brought from heaven and taught from the mouth of His Father and confirmed by signs and wonders, and finally sealed it with His crimson blood. This counsel stands and can never be changed or prevailed against by the gates of hell By this counsel we are, in common, taught that we must hear Christ, believe in Him, follow His footsteps, repent, be born from above, become as little children, not in understanding but in malice, be of the same mind with Christ, walk as He did, deny ourselves, take up His cross and follow Him. . (*Works*, I, 175).
>
> ... The surest and best fruits are to so preach the Word of God in power that many may be born of Him and be led to sincerely fear and love Him, to cordially serve their neighbors, to die unto flesh and blood, to believe on Jesus Christ with all the heart, and tremble at His Word, that they may do nothing contrary to it, may truly worship God and conform their whole life or walk according to His Spirit, Word and example... (*Works*, II, 24).

It was because of their wholehearted obedience to the Word of God, their determination to recognize only the Scriptures in matters of faith, that the Anabaptists defied all efforts of the state and of organized Christendom to coerce them in matters of faith. They were determined at all costs to follow God as He revealed His will in the Scriptures. They therefore demanded for themselves the right to have freedom of conscience. They resented and repulsed all efforts to settle matters of Christian faith by an appeal to church authority or to ecclesiastical tradition. In his *Exhortation to All in Authority* Menno wrote:

> O you high-renowned lords and princes, turn to the truth of God and receive reproof and wisdom, for through wisdom kings reign and princes decree justice. Observe how far your spirit, faith and lives differ from the Lord's Spirit, Word and life (*Works*, I, 77).
>
> Do not excuse yourselves, beloved sirs and judges, that you are the servants of the emperor; this will not acquit you in the day of vengeance . . (*Works*, I, 86).
>
> Do not interfere with the right and kingdom of Christ, for He alone is the Ruler of the conscience, and beside Him there is none other. . . (*Works*, I, 86).

28 THE DOCTRINES OF THE MENNONITES

Pertinent Biblical Passages

1. The Imperative of Evangelism and Missions:
    Matt. 28:18-20: "And Jesus came to them and spake unto them, saying, All authority hath been given unto Me in heaven and on earth. Go ye therefore, and make disciples of all the nations, baptizing them into the name of the Father and of the Son and of the Holy Spirit: teaching them to observe all things whatsoever I commanded you: and lo, I am with you always, even unto the end of the world." A.S.V.
    Mark 16.15f: "Go ye into all the world, and preach the gospel to every creature. He that believeth and is baptized shall be saved; but he that believeth not shall be damned."
    Luke 24:47f. ". . . And that repentance and remission of sins should be preached in His name among all nations, beginning at Jerusalem. And ye are witnesses of these things."
    John 20:21: "As my Father hath sent Me, even so send I you."
    Acts 1:8: "Ye shall be witnesses unto Me both in Jerusalem, and in all Judea, and in Samaria, and unto the uttermost part of the earth."
    II Cor. 5:19f: God "hath committed unto us the word of reconciliation. Now then we are ambassadors for Christ, as though God did beseech you by us: we pray you in Christ's stead, be ye reconciled to God."
    Rom. 10:14f: "How then shall they call on Him in whom they have not believed? and how shall they believe in Him of whom they have not heard? and how shall they hear without a preacher? and how shall they preach, except they be sent?"
2. On the Lost Condition of Those Not Evangelized:
    Rom. 1:20: The heathen, because of God's self-revelation in nature, "are without excuse."
    Rom. 2.12: "As many as have sinned without law shall also perish without law."

Reading References in the Confessions and Catechisms

Christian Fundamentals, Article IX.
Waldeck Catechism, Part Third, Chapter II, Questions 32-36; Chapter III, Questions 22-24.
Roosen's Catechism, Questions 89-92.

Study Questions

1. Why has much of the Christian church been inactive in missionary work?
2. What caused the early Anabaptists to lose their original active witnessing?
3. What is the central function of the Christian church?
4. How may a given member of the church support missions and evangelism?
5. Why do not more missionaries go to the unevangelized world?
6. How does God add converts to His church?
7. Ought compulsion ever be used in matters of faith? Give reasons.

Chapter V
New Testament Church Ordinances

BIBLICISM

The genius of Mennonitism has been to reject completely the traditional distinction between those New Testament commandments on the one hand which are binding both in form and spirit upon Christians for all time, and those on the other hand which are to be observed only in spirit. Most Christians hold that to the former class belong such items as baptism, communion and ordination, and that to the latter class belongs such commands as to greet one another with a holy kiss, to wash one another's feet, and to anoint the sick with oil. The Mennonites, however, in the course of time began to stress the parity of all New Testament commands; this is of course a parity in authority, not in significance. The Mennonite Church of today has numerous ordinances and restrictions.

ORDINANCES

Dirck Philips comments thus on (1) baptism (2) communion, and (3) feet washing:

... The penitent, believing and regenerated children of God must be baptized, and for them the Lord's Supper is ordained.... These two symbols Christ gave and left behind and subjoined to the gospel because of the unspeakable grace of God and His covenant, to remind us thereof with visible symbols, to put it before our eyes and to confirm it, in the first place by baptism, to remind us that He Himself baptizes within and in mercy accepts sinners, forgives them all their sins, cleanses them with His blood..., bestows upon them all His righteousness and the fulfilling of the law, and sanctifies them with the Spirit.... In the second place, by the Lord's Supper, which testifies to divine acceptance and redemption by Jesus Christ.., namely that all believing hearts who are sorry for their sins hasten to the throne of grace, Jesus Christ, believing and confessing that the Son of God died for them and has shed His blood for us.., obtain forgiveness of sin, deliverance from the law, everlasting justification and salvation, by grace through Jesus Christ....

These two symbols are left us by the Lord that they might admonish us to a godly walk.., to a crucifixion of the flesh, the burial of sin, a resurrection into newness of life, to thanksgiving for the great benefits which we have received of the Lord, to a remembrance of the bitter suffering and death of Christ, to the renewing and confirming of brotherly love, unity and fellowship... (*Enchiridion*, 1910, 386f).

[3] The third ordinance is the washing of feet of the saints which Jesus Christ commanded His disciples to observe [John 13 1-17], and this for two reasons. First, He would have us know that He Himself must cleanse us after the inner man, and that we must allow Him to wash away the sins which beset us. . (*Ibid*, 388).

The second reason why Jesus instituted the ordinance of foot washing is that we shall humble ourselves among one another ., and that we hold our fellow believers in the highest respect for the reason that they are saints of God and members of the body of Jesus Christ, and that the Holy Ghost dwells in them... (*Ibid*, 389).

(4) There seems to be no extended discussion of the holy kiss by the early Anabaptists. But Thomas of Imbroich, 1533-58, beheaded for Anabaptism at Cologne, wrote to his wife, "Greet all the saints with the

kiss of love, and all who love the Lord Jesus, and tell them to be kind . . . (*Martyrs' Mirror*, 1938, 581). The *Martyrs' Mirror* contains a number of cases of Brethren greeting one another with a kiss (471, 474, 591). In 1565 Matthew Cervaes several times encouraged his fellow believers to practice this "holy kiss of love" (M. M., 697, 700, 702). Menno Simons says that "the greeting or kiss of peace signifies the communion" [that is, Christian love in Christ's fellowship, the church]; he states that if an apostate should come "we should not greet him as a brother lest we have communion with him" (*Works*, II, 278). The Brethren were of course correct in regarding the "holy kiss" of the New Testament (Rom. 16:16; I Cor. 16:20; II Cor. 13:12, I Thess. 5.26; I Pet. 5:14) as a symbol of fervent Christian love. How often the Anabaptists practiced this greeting or on what occasions we do not know.

(5) There seems to be no mention in Anabaptist writings of anointing with oil. Modern Mennonites, when ill, sometimes send for the elders of the church and ask to be anointed with oil for the healing of the body (James 5:14, 15). How long this has been observed is not known. In 1527 Michael Sattler stated that the Roman Catholic sacrament of extreme unction is not identical with the oil mentioned in James 5. In the same year an Anabaptist martyr, a woman named Weynken was asked, "What do you hold concerning the holy oil?" With facetious "misunderstanding" she replied, "Oil is good for salad, or to oil your shoes with" (*Martyrs' Mirror*, 423; cf. 778). But the woman had in mind extreme unction, not the modern Mennonite practice of anointing with oil for God to heal the body.

(6) Because of Paul's teaching (I Corinthians 11:2-16) that women should be veiled when participating in the worship of God the baptized girls and women of a number of Mennonite conferences now wear, while worshiping, a special "covering" or veil on their heads to symbolize the headship of man. This point received no literary treatment by Mennonites in previous centuries, perhaps because in other Christian groups the women used to worship with their heads covered. Mennonite women have long worn a prayer veiling similar to that of the "Mennonite Church" of today. For example, in the beautiful painting by Rembrandt of "The Mennonite Minister Cornelis Claesz. Anslo," now in the National Gallery of Berlin, Germany, if not destroyed during the second World War, the woman is wearing a covering on her head much like that of the modern Mennonite church. (Claesz Anslo, 1592-1646, was a Waterlander Mennonite Minister, ordained in 1617. Rembrandt's painting was made in 1641, more than three centuries ago.)

Each of the above practices has a valuable symbolical significance; none has any value apart from faith and obedience. Baptism symbolizes the convert's faith in the power of Christ to cleanse from the guilt of sin. The Lord's Supper symbolizes faith in Christ as the One who has given His life for the redemption of the race. Feetwashing is a symbol of Christian brotherhood within the church. The holy kiss is a symbol of fervent

Christian love in the fellowship of the saints. Anointing with oil symbolizes the power of God to heal the body. The prayer veiling is a symbol of the pre-eminence of man in administration and function (not in importance or personal gifts).

(7) About the close of the nineteenth century certain ministers in the "Mennonite Church" began to teach that the Bible prescribes *seven* ordinances. In this sense an ordinance is a practice commanded in the Word of God, it is binding upon the Church; and it symbolizes a Christian virtue or truth. We have just listed six ordinances, but what is the seventh? The modern formulation is that it is marriage. Marriage is indeed a God-ordained relationship, and it therefore does seem appropriate for the wedding ceremony to be performed before the Christian congregation by a minister of the church. The *Martyrs' Mirror* indicates that some sixteenth-century Mennonite weddings did take place before the assembly (pages 515, 516, 675, 925, 927, 929, 936, 1004).

(8) One other rite has been committed to the church, namely the laying-on of hands in ordination (I Timothy 4.14; Titus 1:5; Hebrews 6:2; Acts 14:23). For four centuries the Mennonite Church has had three types of ordained men: (1) the elders or bishops, each of whom is the chief pastor of one or more congregations; (2) the ministers who serve as teachers of God's Word and as assistant pastors of the congregations; (3) the deacons who assist the elders in administering such ordinances as baptism and communion, and who have charge of administering the alms of the church.

As noted above Mennonites reject the traditional distinction between ordinances which are binding upon the church for all time and those which are to be kept only in spirit. They hold that all New Testament commandments are to be kept literally by all believers everywhere as long as the world stands. There is no exegetical consideration against the observance of feetwashing, for example, which would not also bear against the observance of baptism.

Pertinent Biblical Passages

1. On Baptism.
    I Pet. 3:21 Baptism is "the [covenant] of a good conscience toward God." The Greek word rendered covenant in the German version here seems to mean an avowal of consecration (Cf. Thayer's lexicon).
    Read Rom. 6.1-14 where baptism is shown to be a symbol of the Christian's death to sin and resurrection to newness of life.
2. On Communion:
    I Cor. 11:24-26. Jesus said, "Take, eat: this is My body, which is broken for you: this do in remembrance of Me . . . This cup is the new testament in My blood: this do ye, as oft as ye drink it, in remembrance of Me. For as often as ye eat this bread, and drink this cup, ye do show the Lord's death till He come."

Read the comparable passages in Matt., Mark, and Luke; also I Cor. 10:16f.

3. On Feetwashing:
    John 13:13-17: "Ye call Me Master and Lord: and ye say well; for so I am. If I then, your Lord and Master, have washed your feet; ye also ought to wash one another's feet. For I have given you an example, that ye should do as I have done to you ... If ye know these things, happy are ye if ye do them."

4. On the Holy Kiss:
    Rom. 16:16: "Salute one another with an holy kiss."
    Cf. I Cor. 16:20; II Cor. 13:12; I Thess. 5:26; I Pet. 5:14.

5. On Anointing with Oil:
    James 5:14f: "Is any sick among you? let him call for the elders of the church; and let them pray over him, anointing him with oil in the name of the Lord: and the prayer of faith shall save the sick, and the Lord shall raise him up. ..."

6. On the Worship Veil:
    I Cor. 11:5f: "Every woman praying or prophesying with her head unveiled dishonoreth her head; for it is one and the same thing as if she were shaven. For if a woman is not veiled, let her also be shorn: but if it is a shame to a woman to be shorn or shaven, let her be veiled." A.S.V.
    Read carefully the entire section (11:2-16) in the King James and American Standard Versions.

7. On Marriage:
    Eph. 5:31: "For this cause shall a man leave his father and mother, and shall be joined unto his wife, and they two shall be one flesh."
    I Tim. 5:14: "I will therefore that the younger women marry, bear children, guide the house, give none occasion to the adversary to speak reproachfully."
    Read Matt. 19:3-9, Mark 10:2-12; Luke 16:18; Rom. 7:2f; and I Cor. 7.

8. On the Laying on of Hands in Ordination:
    Acts 13 3f: On the sending out of Paul and Barnabas on the first missionary campaign, the Scripture reports: "And when they had fasted and prayed, and laid their hands on them, they sent them away ... being sent forth by the Holy Ghost."
    I Tim. 4:14: "Neglect not the gift that is in thee, which was given thee by prophecy, with the laying on of the hands of the presbytery."

Reading References in the Confessions and Catechisms

Schleitheim Confession, Articles I, III and V.
Dordrecht Confession, Articles VII, IX, X, XI, XII.

NEW TESTAMENT CHRISTIAN ORDINANCES

Christian Fundamentals, Article XII.
Shorter Catechism, Questions 13-27.
Waldeck Catechism, Part Third, Chapter III, Questions 21-34.
Roosen's Catechism, Questions 89-116.

Study Questions

1. Name by memory the seven ordinances which the New Testament enjoins upon the church.
2. Give one or more Scriptures which demand the observance of each ordinance.
3. What ordinances do most denominations observe literally?
4. Why do you believe that God has given ordinances to the church?
5. What truth does each ordinance symbolize?
6. What danger faces those who neglect many New Testament ordinances?
7. What temptations beset those who find satisfaction in a literal observance of all New Testament ordinances? Discuss fully.

Chapter VI
The Doctrine of Nonresistance

There are other portions of Scripture which are taken in an absolute sense by Mennonites but which are not so understood by most Protestant bodies. This accounts for some of the distinctive positions held by Mennonites in the field of Christian ethics.

Exposition

(1) A number of New Testament verses teach unqualified love for and nonresistance to evil men as the divine ethic for Christian believers. Among these passages are Matthew 5:38-48; Luke 6:27-36; John 18:36; Romans 12:17-21; I Thessalonians 5.15; II Timothy 2:24; Hebrews 12:14; I Peter 2:20-23; 3:8, 9, 13, 17. These verses require no "interpretation"; they are entirely clear. Consider the following, for example, from Romans 12:

> Dearly beloved, avenge not yourselves, but rather give place unto [God's] wrath: for it is written, Vengeance is mine, I will repay, saith the Lord. Therefore if thine enemy hunger, feed him, if he thirst, give him drink· for in so doing thou shalt heap coals of fire on his head Be not overcome of evil, but overcome evil with good.

In a simple acceptance of this as the Christian ethic Mennonites oppose the use of force in private life and also reject military service in every form. They hold this position humbly, aware of the fact that there are many believers who cannot understand them. They base their ethic of nonresistance on both the letter and spirit of the New Testament, believing that the Christian's calling is to "make disciples of all nations" (Matt. 28:19). The question is not so much "how far to take" the verses on nonresistance; it is rather this: If one seeks to obey these verses at all, can one participate in warfare? Can there be a more complete violation of the law of love than the waging of modern warfare?

It is because of these verses on nonresistance that Mennonites also refuse to do police service, or to be a magistrate. They frown even on jury service. *The calling of the Christian is evangelism, not the dispensing of justice in the state.* It does not follow, however, that Mennonites condemn the state. On the contrary the state is ordained of God to administer law and justice *in a society of evildoers.* In that sphere the state is absolutely necessary. Evil men must frequently be restrained by force. But that task is not assigned by God to the saints. Christians are obligated, however, to obey the government in all matters (Rom. 13:1-7; Titus 3:1; I Pet. 2:13, 14) save where the demands of a ruler may conflict with the law of God (Acts 4:19; 5:29). All taxes are to be paid (Matt. 22.15-21; Rom. 13:7). The Schleitheim Confession of Faith, 1527, asserts that the state is ordained of God *outside the perfection of Christ*. This is based on the belief that the Christian ethic is for Christians, not for the state. The only means which the church has to cope with transgressors is admonition, and finally excommunication in case of impenitence.

Critics of the nonresistant Anabaptists sometimes try to point out certain logical difficulties in connection with their position. But the critics have some difficult exegetical considerations to deal with themselves, as well as the problem of just how to divide a man into two persons: the Christian who seeks the welfare and salvation of all men, and the policeman or soldier who must take human life in the pursuit of his work.

History

From its very inception in 1525 the Mennonite Church has held the principle of nonresistance. Conrad Grebel, the founder of the Swiss Brethren Church, wrote in September 1524: "True, believing Christians are as sheep in the midst of wolves . . . . They use neither the worldly sword nor engage in war, since among them taking human life has ceased entirely, for we are no longer under the Old Covenant." Felix Manz, a colleague of Grebel, said, "No Christian smites with the sword nor resists evil." Pilgram Marpeck said of the Christians, "All bodily, worldly, carnal earthly fighting, conflicts and wars are annulled and abolished among them through such law." The Dutch Mennonites took the same stand as the Swiss Brethren. Dirck Philips testified that "The people of the Lord arm themselves not with carnal weapons . . . but with the armor of God, with the weapons of righteousness . . . and with Christian patience, with which to possess their souls and overcome all their enemies." Menno Simons wrote, "The regenerated do not go to war, nor engage in strife. They are the children of peace . . . and know of no war. They render unto Caesar the things that are Caesar's and unto God the things that are God's. Their sword is the sword of the Spirit which they wield with a good conscience through the Holy Ghost."

The Mennonites of Europe have largely given up the Anabaptist position on war. The first country in which the Mennonites weakened on the doctrine of nonresistance was Holland. After the Napoleonic period the Dutch Mennonites took a progressively weaker stand, and by the middle of the last century nonresistance among them was about dead. Mention has already been made of the determined group of Mennonites who emigrated from Balk, Holland, to New Paris, Indiana, in 1853, to maintain the doctrine of nonresistance. Very few Dutch Mennonites took a stand for the historic faith of the church during the first World War. However, the new "Gemeentedag" Movement has nonresistance as one of its emphases.

About the middle of the past century the Prussian Mennonites were also weakening in their stand for nonresistance. King Wilhelm I issued a cabinet order in 1868 which permitted the Mennonites to do noncombatant service, but in the Franco-Prussian war of 1870-71 many German

Mennonites voluntarily accepted combatant service. German militarism led many nonresistant Mennonites to emigrate to the western part of the United States, especially Kansas, in the nineteenth century. In World War I almost all the Mennonite soldiers of North Germany voluntarily bore arms. The doctrine itself was formally given up in 1934.

The story in South Germany is similar to that of Prussia,—a gradual giving up of the doctrine of nonresistance. A large emigration of nonresistant Mennonites took place to America between the years 1817 and 1860 because of a fear of military service. Today, however, there is an awakening interest in the historic doctrine of nonresistance on the part of many European Mennonites.

It was in France that compulsory military service began. Beginning in 1688 certain men were conscripted by lot. Since the time of Napoleon there has been no place in France for conscientious objectors to military duties. Everyone simply takes military training or faces the consequences, which means imprisonment at the least, or possible death in time of war. The French Mennonites of today are therefore not nonresistant. Many Alsatian Amish emigrated to America after 1815 to escape the rigid militarism of the French.

Switzerland is the only country where Mennonites suffered any hardships because of nonresistance prior to the time of Napoleon. Not only did the Swiss hire out their young men as mercenary soldiers to other countries, Berne also made a law making it obligatory for all her citizens to be armed. The Mennonites of course refused to carry any weapons and were constantly harassed on this account, even as late as the early part of the nineteenth century. They won the right to pay a fine in lieu of military service in 1815, but lost this right in 1874 when they were at last given the full privilege of citizenship. In 1937 when Bishop Johann Kipfer of Langnau, the oldest Mennonite congregation in existence, wrote a little confession of faith, he did not even mention nonresistance, though this was displeasing to some of his brethren. Most of the Swiss Mennonites today stop short of bearing arms, although all accept the military uniform. They are taking a stronger stand for nonresistance than any other European Mennonites.

When the Prussian Mennonites settled in South Russia in the last decades of the eighteenth century, they were promised military exemption forever. About 1870 it began to appear that the "forever" had already expired and the Russian Mennonites began to look for a new national home. A key man at this time of crisis was John F. Funk of Elkhart, Indiana. On June 11, 1895, Peter Jansen, 1852-1923, wrote to Funk as follows: "I would call your attention to the fact that the correspondence of Father with yourself was really the first step towards the Mennonite Immigration to the U.S. I recently found some of your letters written to Father in Russia in 1871 & 72." The father of Peter Jansen was Cornelius Jansen who led the Russian emigration of 1873 to North America.

THE DOCTRINE OF NONRESISTANCE

In the end, however, the Mennonites who remained in Russia were not required to bear arms. A system of nonmilitary forestry service was devised, a system which was fairly satisfactory to the church. The Russian Mennonites remained nonresistant until the crises of the first World War bore down upon them. When bands of ruthless bandits plundered in the Mennonite colonies of the Ukraine, some young men, unable to remain passive, disregarded the protests of the majority and took up arms, forming a self-defense corps. Even from a practical point of view, this was a mistake, for when the little Mennonite army was overpowered the abuse became more horrible than before. Since that time cold-blooded execution and Siberian exile have broken the organized church life of the Russian Mennonites. Nonresistance is probably one of their lesser worries, for even faith in Christ is probably dying in the younger generation.

Prior to 1940 nonresistance was not put to a test in the United States except in time of war. There is no guarantee in the constitution of the United States that pacifists shall enjoy military exemption. The Supreme Court of the United States in 1946 granted citizenship to a pacifist of some sort. The United States has, moreover, shown consideration to those whose conscience forbids participation in warfare. During the American Civil War, 1861-65, Mennonites secured military exemption by the payment of a fee of $300, or by hiring a substitute. Farm furloughs and release for relief work were provided for Mennonites, Friends, and Brethren during the first World War, 1914-18. The matter was handled quite admirably during the second World War, 1939-45, by creating Civilian Public Service camps and units. In "C.P.S.," as it was familiarly known to hosts of Mennonites, conscientious objectors to warfare did work of national importance, such as forestry service and soil conservation work, under civilian direction. Many objectors also served as attendants in mental hospitals where they rendered a splendid service. The cost of the C.P.S. program to the Mennonite Central Committee for the fiscal year ending November 30, 1945, was about $825,000. Congressional action prevented large numbers of inducted Mennonites from serving as relief workers in Europe and Asia during the war. Nevertheless the Mennonite Central Committee was able to launch a relief program, which by November 30, 1945, amounted to $285,000 per year. C.P.S. and relief for 1945 did not mean a retrenchment in missionary receipts. The Mennonite Board of Missions and Charities, which handles only a part of the contributions of one group, the "Mennonite Church," received over $390,000 for missions during the fiscal year which ended April 1, 1946.

Both Brazil and Argentina have compulsory military training. This creates a problem both for the Russian Mennonite colonists of Brazil and for the North American missionaries of the Mennonite Church who are working in Argentina.

Of the countries where Mennonites live only two guarantee them military exemption: Canada and Paraguay.

Nonresistance and believer's baptism were the two most distinguish-

ing tenets of the Swiss Brethren and the Dutch Mennonites. On the subject of nonresistance those interested may consult further Guy F. Hershberger's monograph, *War, Peace, and Nonresistance,* and John Horsch's treatise, *The Principle of Nonresistance as Held by the Mennonite Church;* also the writings of Conrad Grebel, Pilgram Marpeck, Menno Simons and Dirck Philips; and the several Mennonite confessions of faith.

Some of the writings of the early Dutch Mennonites seem to grant eternal salvation to good Christian rulers; note especially the last four paragraphs of page 87 of Part I of Menno's *Works,* and the last sentence of Article XIII of the Dordrecht Confession. It is extremely doubtful that these statements would have been acceptable to the Swiss Brethren. Modern Mennonites follow the Swiss in those points where they differed from the Brethren in the Netherlands.

Pertinent Biblical Passages

1. On Resisting Evil Men:
    Matt. 5:38f: "Ye have heard that it hath been said, An eye for an eye, and a tooth for a tooth: but I say unto you, That ye resist not him that is evil: but whosoever shall smite thee on thy right cheek, turn to him the other also" (Greek).
    Luke 6:29: "Unto him that smiteth thee on the one cheek offer also the other; and him that taketh away thy cloke forbid not to take thy coat also."

2. On Loving One's Enemies:
    Matt. 5:43-45: "Ye have heard that it hath been said, Thou shalt love thy neighbour, and hate thine enemy. But I say unto you, Love your enemies, bless them that curse you, do good to them that hate you, and pray for them which despitefully use you, and persecute you; that ye may be the children of your Father which is in heaven: for He maketh His sun to rise on the evil and on the good, and sendeth rain on the just and on the unjust."

3. On "Overcoming" One's Enemies:
    Rom. 12:17-21: "Recompense to no man evil for evil . . . If it be possible, as much as lieth in you, live peaceably with all men. Dearly beloved, avenge not yourselves, but rather give place unto [God's] wrath: for it is written, Vengeance is Mine; I will repay, saith the Lord. Therefore if thine enemy hunger, feed him; if he thirst, give him drink: for in so doing thou shalt heap coals of fire on his head. Be not overcome of evil, but overcome evil with good."

4. On Belonging to a Heavenly Kingdom:
    John 18:36: "Jesus answered, My kingdom is not of this world: if My kingdom were of this world, then would My servants fight, that I should not be delivered to the Jews: but now is My kingdom not from hence."

5. On the Christian's Weapons:
    II Cor. 10:3f: "For though we walk in the flesh, we do not war after the flesh: for the weapons of our warfare are not carnal, but mighty through God to the pulling down of strong holds . . . ."
6. On the Spirit of the Christian:
    II Tim. 2:24: "And the servant of the Lord must not strive; but be gentle unto all men, apt to teach, patient . . . ."
7. On Suffering and Abuse:
    I Pet. 3:8f: "Finally, be ye all of one mind, having compassion one of another, love as brethren, be pitiful, be courteous: not rendering evil for evil, or railing for railing: but contrariwise blessing; knowing that ye are thereunto called, that ye should inherit a blessing."
    I Thess. 5:15: "See that none render evil for evil unto any man: but ever follow that which is good, both among yourselves, and to all men."
8. On the Christian's Pattern:
    I Pet. 2:21-23: ". . . Christ also suffered for us, leaving us an example, that ye should follow His steps: who did no sin, neither was guile found in His mouth: who, when He was reviled, reviled not again; when He suffered, He threatened not; but committed Himself to Him that judgeth righteously . . . ."
    Matt. 5:48: "Be ye therefore perfect [in love], even as your Father which is in heaven is perfect."

Reading References in the Confessions and Catechisms

Schleitheim Confession, Article VI.
Dordrecht Confession, Article XIV.
Christian Fundamentals, Article XIII.
Shorter Catechism, Question 30.
Waldeck Catechism, Part Third, Chapter IV, Questions 1-6.
Roosen's Catechism, Questions 115-118.

Study Questions

1. Was the doctrine of nonresistance clearly revealed to Israel?
2. Does the Old Testament contain any teaching that warfare and force are sinful?
3. Do the writers of the New Testament ever base the doctrine of nonresistance on Old Testament passages?
4. Is it right for Christians to employ force under any circumstances, for example, with small children?
5. Is it more Christian to suffer wrong than to fight for justice? Support your answer with Scripture.
6. Does God ever allow a nonresistant Christian to suffer injury or death? If so, ought one then fight?
7. How can one convert an enemy into a friend?
8. What is the relation of nonresistance to regeneration? To the Christian's peace? To the function of the church?

Chapter VII
Biblical Simplicity of Life

The last chapter attempted to set forth the Biblical doctrine of love and nonresistance. The evangelical Anabaptists and their spiritual descendants, the Mennonites, understand the Bible to require the renunciation of all force in human relations, including warfare.

(2) The Bible also forbids Christians to sue at law. The New Testament advises that it is better for Christians to suffer injustice than to achieve their "rights" by resorting to litigation. This position is a particular application of the broad principle of love and nonresistance. The New Testament says expressly:

Dare any of you, having a matter against another, go to law before the unjust, and not before the saints? . . . Now therefore there is utterly a fault among you, because ye go to law one with another Why do ye not rather take wrong? Why do ye not rather suffer yourselves to be defrauded? Nay, ye do wrong, and defraud, and that your brethren (Cf I Cor. 6·1-7).

(3) Another point where Mennonites and other Protestant bodies differ is on the swearing of oaths. Jesus stated emphatically that although the Old Testament condemned only false oaths His followers should never swear at all. Rather they should let their every word be strictly truthful. The pertinent New Testament Scriptures are Matthew 5:33-37; 23:16-22; and James 5:12. Mennonites therefore merely make an affirmation when asked to take an oath.

Menno wrote in his *Clear Confession,* 1552:

We are aware that the magistracy claim and say, *We are allowed to swear when justice is on our side.* This we simply answer with the word of the Lord. To swear truly was allowed to the Jews under the law; but the gospel forbids this to Christians. . . *(Works,* II, 273).

In his *Epistle to Martin Micron,* Menno added:

The oath is required for no other purpose but that we shall truthfully testify. Can the truth not be told without being sworn? Do all testify to the truth, even, when under oath? To the first question you must answer in the affirmative, and to the last in the negative. . . *(Works,* II, 410).

. . Christ's foundation and doctrine is that Moses had commanded not to forswear thyself, but that under the New Testament one should not swear at all. James says that we should not swear "neither by heaven, neither by the earth, neither by any other oath. . . ." (Mark, he says neither by *any other oath*) and you gloze it . . . that it is not so but that we may swear to the truth. . . *(Works,* II, 410).

I will let you teach and counsel . . . to fight and retaliate as did Moses and the patriarchs. . . ; teach them to punish, scatter, imprison and destroy their enemies; to adjudge the criminals no matter whether they repent or not, as you write. Teach them also to swear and be sworn after the manner that Moses commanded the Israelites. But I shall and will by the grace of God faithfully teach and counsel all truly regenerated children of God and followers of Christ, both rulers and subjects, according to the sure word of the holy gospel, to use no other sword than the one Christ Jesus and His holy apostles used; to be merciful unto the penitent sinners as Christ is merciful unto us; mercifully to punish the impenitent and to admonish them in love as Christ admonished us; and scrupulously to stand by their yea and nay as the true Teacher and Executor of the New Testament, the ever blessed Christ Jesus Himself, has distinctly commanded and taught us with His guiltless mouth; no matter what the consequences to my person may be . . . *(Works,* II, 412).

(4) The awful oaths which bind the members of secret orders make it unthinkable for a non-swearing Christian to unite with such societies. But it is not only the oath which keeps Mennonites out of secret societies. The very principle of organized secrecy is unchristian. Jesus protested to the Jewish authorities that He had no secrets; His doctrine and teaching were open to all men (John 18:19, 20). It is the church which is to be *the* brotherhood of Christians. For a Christian to unite with a fraternal society, especially when some members are not even professing Christians, and share with this mixed body certain secret information which he may not divulge to his fellow believers in Christ's church, is utterly out of the question (II Corinthians 6:14—7:1). Furthermore, in the minds of many people secret societies are a substitute for church membership. Being a lodge "brother" is often regarded as practically equivalent to being a member of Christ's body, the church. All Mennonite conferences therefore oppose membership in secret societies.

(5) Mennonites also teach the permanence of marriage, permitting a second union only when a life companion dies, and allowing formal separation only for adultery. This position they base on the following Scriptures: Matthew 5:31, 32; 19:3-9; Mark 10·2-12; Luke 16:18; Romans 7:1-3; I Corinthians 7:1-16, 39. In his *Foundation* Menno wrote:

> We acknowledge, teach, and approve of no other matrimony than that one which Christ and His apostles publicly and plainly taught in the New Testament, namely one man and one woman [Matt. 19.4], and that they may not be divorced except in case of adultery [Matt. 5·32,] for the two are one flesh, but if the unbelieving depart, a sister or brother is not under bondage in that case [I Cor. 7 15]—*Works,* I, 83 (Cf. article "Ehe," in *Menn Lexikon)*

In speaking of Christ's kingdom Menno states:

> . . . Under this kingdom and under this King no other wedlock must be tolerated except between *one* man and *one* woman as God had in the beginning established in the union of Adam and Eve; and Christ has further said that these two are one flesh, and that they shall not separate, save for the cause of fornication [Matt. 5·32]— *Works,* I, 95f; cf. II, 277.

(6) Mennonites have for centuries placed much stress on simplicity of life. Considerable emphasis fell on the external appearance of the Christian; the wearing of jewelry, for example, is proscribed. Here are a number of quotations from the *Complete Works* of Menno Simons:

> And even as all things are pure to the pure, and are for the good of the pious, so also to the impure all things are impure, and to the evil all things are evil; because they are impure they use all the creatures of God impurely. They eat and drink to excess; they dress gorgeously; and engage in lewdness; they raise their children to idleness; they avariciously hoard gold, silver, houses and lands, and there is nothing they use purely according to the will of God, for they are impure, sensual, disobedient to the Word, and are earthly-minded, as the Scriptures say *(Works,* I, 71).
> Beloved reader, take notice that all the proud, haughty, avaricious, carnal and adulterous who call themselves Christians, but who are by no means such, testify by their disposition, heart, mind and walk that they hate and are inimical to Christ. . . .
> They say that they believe, and yet there are no limits nor bounds to their accursed

wantonness, foolish pomp, show of silks, velvet, costly clothes, gold rings, chains, silver belts, pins, buttons, curiously adorned shirts, handkerchiefs, collars, veils, aprons, velvet shoes, slippers and such like foolish finery; never regarding that the enlightened apostles, Peter and Paul [I Pet 3·3, 4, I Tim. 2 9, 10] have in plain and express words forbidden this to all Christian women If this is forbidden to woman how much more then should men abstain from it, who are the leaders and heads of their women, notwithstanding all this they still want to be called the Christian church *(Works,* I, 144).

This is not a kingdom in which a display is made of gold, silver, pearls, silk, velvet and costly finery, as is done by the proud, wicked world, and which also your leaders teach and give you liberty to do under this deception, viz, that it is harmless if you do not desire and serve them from your heart . . . *(Works,* I, 96).

(7) In recent years the Mennonite Church has had to resist the unnatural and unscriptural practice of women cutting their hair. Paul stated that it was "a shame for a woman to be shorn or shaven" (I Cor. 11:6). On the same point he asks, "Does not even nature itself teach you that if a man have long hair it is a shame unto him? But if a woman have long hair it is a glory to her . . . ." Then he adds these significant words, "for her hair is given her for a covering." The verb for *given* is in the Greek perfect tense which, as Professor G. G. Findlay states, "connotes a *permanent* boon." It was none other than God who gave woman long hair in the first place. It is God who intends that woman should wear her hair long. And it is God who regards woman's hair as a natural covering to accompany the prayer veiling. The prayer veiling in turn, as indicated above, symbolizes the authority of man.

(8) In recent decades Mennonites have also found it necessary to warn their young people against worldly recreation in general and the moving picture theater in particular. It is well known that the moving picture industry, with its sensuous stars divorcing and remarrying continually, caters to those human desires which are not spiritual. Commercial moving pictures, by gratifying the carnal mind deaden spiritual life and draw the human heart away from God and His Word. Moving pictures create in young people false standards of life in general. Particularly do they portray impossible economic standards and an utterly unchristian view of courtship and of home life. On the subject of the moving picture theater the warning of the Apostle John is apropos: "Love not the world, neither the things that are in the world. If any man love the world, the love of the Father is not in him. For all that is in the world, the lust of the flesh, and the lust of the eyes, and the pride of life, is not of the Father, but is of the world" (I John 2:15, 16), and Paul warns, "Therefore, brethren, we are debtors, not to the flesh, to live after the flesh. For if ye live after the flesh, ye shall die: but if ye through the Spirit do mortify the deeds of the body, ye shall live" (Romans 8:12, 13).

(9) From the very beginning of the church, Mennonites have emphasized the fact that the New Testament teaches church discipline. The Christian congregation, the entire brotherhood, is responsible to warn and restore those who may fall into sin (Gal. 6:1). In case the transgressor remains impenitent it becomes necessary to make known to the entire

brotherhood that he is no longer a member of the church. This is what Paul meant when he told the Corinthian Church to "put away from among yourselves that wicked person" (I Cor. 5:13). This is not a matter of a minister's self-will and selfish love of power or of lording it over the congregation, all of which is condemned in the New Testament (Matt. 20:25-27; Mark 10:42-45; Luke 22:25-27; I Pet. 5:3). It is rather a solemn act with a threefold purpose: (1) It makes known to the obdurate sinner his true state before God—for Scriptural excommunication is attended by divine sanction (Matt. 16.18; 18:18). (2) It indicates to the brotherhood the awfulness of unrenounced sin and warns believers against such social fellowship with the sinner as might lead them into sin (I Cor. 5:9-11; Rom. 16:17; II Thess. 3:14; Tit. 3:10, 11). (3) It protects the good name of the church, the members of whom are to glorify God by their life. Menno Simons sets forth his views on church discipline in his books, *Excommunication, Ban, Exclusion* . . . , Works, I, 239-268, revised by him in the latter years of his life; and *Scriptural Explanation of Excommunication,* II, 121-137.

(10) It is amazing to observe how severely the Anabaptists were maligned by the state churchmen four centuries ago for seeking to maintain Scriptural standards of life and faith in their congregations. It is because of the same desire to uphold Biblical standards in the congregations of today that the Mennonite Church continues to practice close communion. It is not intended to suggest that there are no children of God in other denominations; both Menno Simons and Pilgram Marpeck acknowledged that there were saved people in other religious groups. Nor is close communion an anathema published against all other Christians. Close communion is practiced because of a desire to maintain faithfully the Biblical ethic, for some professing believers are not Scripturally qualified to come to the Lord's table. Since it would be impossible and odd to try to exercise a Scriptural discipline over those who are not affiliated with one's particular group, the only position open to those who believe that the brotherhood is obligated to maintain Scriptural standards of faith and life is to offer the communion emblems only to those who share those standards and are faithful members of that Christian group.

In the liberalism of the present era this Mennonite "Biblicism" with its ordinances and restrictions may seem like a neo-legalism. It is not so intended. The obedience of love is never legalism; it is loveless conformity to a code which is legalism. A joyful awareness of the centrality and foundation of Christ's redemption and of God's grace will prevent this simple and earnest obedience to Christ's Word from degenerating into a formalistic legalism. Furthermore, the "danger" of taking the Bible too seriously is far less grave than the peril of secularism and worldliness.

Pertinent Biblical Passages

1. On Litigation:

    I Cor. 6:1, 6f: "Dare any of you, having a matter against another go to law before the unjust, and not before the saints? .... But brother goeth to law with brother, and that before the unbelievers. Now therefore there is utterly a fault among you, because ye go to law one with another. Why do ye not rather take wrong? Why do ye not rather suffer yourselves to be defrauded?"

2. On the Swearing of Oaths:

    Matt. 5:33-37: "Again, ye have heard that it hath been said by them of old time, Thou shalt not forswear thyself, but shalt perform unto the Lord thine oaths: but I say unto you, Swear not at all; neither by heaven; for it is God's throne: nor by the earth; for it is His footstool: neither by Jerusalem; for it is the city of the great King. Neither shalt thou swear by thy head, because thou canst not make one hair white or black. But let your communication be, Yea, yea; Nay, nay: for whatsoever is more than these is of the evil one." Cf. A.V. mg.

    Matt. 23 16, 19-22: "Woe unto you, ye blind guides, which say, Whosoever shall swear by the temple, it is nothing ... Ye fools and blind. for whether is greater, the gift, or the altar that sanctifieth the gift? Whoso therefore shall swear by the altar, sweareth by it, and by all things thereon. And whoso shall swear by the temple, sweareth by it, and by Him that dwelleth therein. And he that shall swear by heaven, sweareth by the throne of God, and by Him that sitteth thereon." Cf. Jas. 5 12

3. On Secret and Oath-bound Fraternities:

    James 5:12: "But above all things, my brethren, swear not, neither by heaven, neither by the earth, neither by any other oath: but let your yea be yea; and your nay, nay; lest ye fall into condemnation."

    John 18:20: "Jesus answered him, I spake openly to the world; I ever taught in the synagogue, and in the temple ... ; and in secret have I said nothing."

    II Cor. 6:14-18: "Be ye not unequally yoked together with unbelievers: for what fellowship hath righteousness with unrighteousness? and what communion hath light with darkness? and what concord hath Christ with Belial? or what part hath he that believeth with an infidel? and what agreement hath the temple of God with idols? For ye are the temple of the living God; as God hath said, I will dwell in them, and walk in them; and I will be their God, and they shall be My people. Wherefore come out from among them, and be ye separate, saith the Lord, and touch not the unclean thing; and I will receive you, and will be a Father unto you, and ye shall be My sons and daughters, saith the Lord Almighty."

4. On the Permanence of Marriage:

    Matt. 5 31f: "It hath been said, Whosoever shall put away his wife, let him give her a writing of divorcement: but I say unto you, that whosoever shall put away his wife, saving for the cause of fornication, causeth her to commit adultery: and whosoever shall marry her that is divorced committeth adultery." Cf. Matt. 19:3-9.

Mark 10:7-9: "For this cause shall a man leave his father and mother, and cleave to his wife; and they twain shall be one flesh: so then they are no more twain, but one flesh. What therefore God hath joined together, let not man put asunder."

Rom. 7:2f: "For the woman which hath an husband is bound by the law to her husband so long as he liveth, but if the husband be dead, she is loosed from the law of her husband. So then if, while her husband liveth, she be married to another man, she shall be called an adulteress: but if her husband be dead, she is free from that law; so that she is no adulteress, though she be married to another man."

5. On True Christian Adornment:

I Pet. 3:3f: "Whose adorning let it not be that outward adorning of plaiting the hair, and of wearing of gold, or of putting on of apparel; but let it be the hidden man of the heart, in that which is not corruptible, even the ornament of a meek and quiet spirit, which is in the sight of God of great price." Cf. I Tim. 2:9f.

6. On the Duty of Winning Again a Fallen Believer:

Gal. 6:1: "Brethren, even if a man be overtaken in any trespass, ye who are spiritual, restore such a one in a spirit of gentleness; looking to thyself, lest thou also be tempted." A.S.V.

7. On the Obligation to Expel Impenitent Sinners from the Church:

I Cor. 5:1, 13: "It is reported commonly that there is fornication among you. . . ." ". . . Therefore put away from among yourselves that wicked person."

8. On the Breaking of Fellowship with Excommunicated Persons:

Rom. 16:17: "Mark them which cause divisions and offences contrary to the doctrine which ye have learned; and avoid them."

II Thess. 3:14: "If any man obey not our word by this epistle, note that man, and have no company with him, that he may be ashamed."

Reading References in the Confessions and Catechisms

Schleitheim Confession, Articles II, IV, VII.
Dordrecht Confession, Articles XV, XVI, XVII.
Christian Fundamentals, Articles XI, XIII.
Shorter Catechism, Questions 29, 31-33.
Waldeck Catechism, Part Third, Chapter IV, 7-22.
Roosen's Catechism, Questions 119-138.

Study Questions

1. Since Christians may not sue at law, how should they settle their differences?

2. Why is it wrong to swear an oath? Why is it not wrong for God?
3. Why should Christians refuse to unite with secret orders?
4. Christians should not divorce life companions and remarry. Explain why.
5. Why did Moses permit divorce in the Old Testament law?
6. Are Christians free to marry whom they please?
7. How should the Christian seek to be beautiful?
8. Should Christians wear jewelry such as gold, pearls, and the like? Why?
9. Should Christian women cut their hair? Why not?
10. What does close communion signify and what is not implied? Why not throw open the service to every professing believer?
11. What is the Christian attitude toward fallen Christians? toward impenitent sinners?
12. What kind of "avoidance" is Biblical and what kind is not?

Chapter VIII
The Finality of the New Testament

All the ordinances and restrictions of the Mennonites, as shown above, are based on a literal obedience to the text of Scripture. Some of them, it should be noted, are also grounded on the distinction between the covenants of Moses and of Christ, a distinction which will here be examined briefly.

Mennonites regard the entire Bible as God's holy Word, "inspired and profitable." But they hold that Jesus Christ and His redemption stand at the center of time. All of God's dealings with man before Christ were in preparation for His redemption. The Old Covenant stood until the death of the One who instituted the New Covenant, until "the death of the Testator" (Heb. 9:16). The Old Covenant was not perfect in the sense that its blessings were inferior to those of the New (Heb. 8:6ff). The Old Testament prophets looked forward to the glory of the New Covenant with its deeper blessings, the New Covenant being less nationalistic and external and more personal and spiritual in character (Jer. 31:31-34; Heb. 8:7-13). Jesus Christ established this predicted New Covenant (Heb. 8:6; 9:13-17). The Old Testament *as a religious system* is therefore done away. It is displaced by the New Covenant with its better promises (Heb. 8:6), this New Covenant being in force since the death of Jesus (Heb. 9:15, 16). The New Covenant brought with it complete forgiveness for sin forever, with no need of further sacrifices for sin (Heb. 10:14-18).

Jesus Christ who established the New Covenant during His earthly life served as God's Prophet making known the will of God for man. All that Christ taught was by command of the Father. Christ's words were therefore the Word of God (John 12:49, 50). The four Gospels contain almost all that we know of the words of Jesus. In the fifth chapter of Matthew the Lord Jesus discussed His attitude toward the Old Testament, "the law and the prophets." He indicated first of all the durability and permanence of the Old Testament Scriptures; they will not fail (5:18). But they are fulfilled in Jesus and His teaching (5:17, 18). Then Jesus proceeded to give five illustrations of how He "fulfilled" the Old Testament. These relate to murder (5:21), adultery (5:27), divorce (5:31), oaths (5:33), and retaliation (5:38). In every case Jesus built upon the essential moral principles of the Old Testament and made those principles more penetrating and extensive than they had been in the law. Not only is killing wrong, but he who hates is equally guilty of a lack of love (cf. I John 3:15). Not only is adultery wrong, but the lustful gaze indicates the same corrupt heart (cf. Mark 7:21). Not only shall divorce be strictly legalized, it shall be restricted to but one ground, infidelity (cf. Matt. 19:9). Not only are all false oaths prohibited, but all oaths whatsoever are to be done away (cf. James 5:12). Not only is illegal retaliation wrong, but all retaliation shall be desisted from (cf. Romans 12:17-21). In every respect the disciple of the Lord shall take an attitude of perfect love toward his enemies and wrongdoers; he shall imitate the Father in heaven who is beneficent toward both the evil and the good, toward those who defy Him and those who obey Him. He shall be perfect in love, even as God is perfect (5:48).

With this general interpretation the leading reformers of the sixteenth century were in basic agreement. They too believed that there was a difference between the Old Covenant and the New; indeed John Calvin wrote an excellent discussion of the matter (*Institutes*, II, 11). The reformers also believed that Jesus had established the New Covenant. They believed further that Jesus gave His disciples an authoritative interpretation of God's moral law. But at that point the agreement ceases. The reformers ultimately limited that which Christ displaced to the Mosaic tabernacle, sacrificial system, priesthood, holy days and festivals, and ceremonially unclean foods. They refused to concede that what was permitted in the Old Testament could now be forbidden. They were of course not totally consistent in this point of view; for example, it was only in an awkward situation that Luther joined in permitting Philip of Hesse to have two wives. But the reformers did not believe in granting religious liberty to the "heretical" Anabaptists—and in the Old Testament they found abundant authorization to suppress deviation from the faith of the covenant people. Furthermore, since wars and oaths were freely engaged in by Israel of old, even with divine sanction, the reformers refused to believe that Christ and His apostles meant in an absolute sense what they said about being nonresistant and not swearing at all. In addition to this the Anabaptist stress fell on the *fulfillment* of the Old Covenant by the New, while the reformers emphasized the essential *unity* of the two covenants. Consequently it was natural for the reformers to think in terms of a national church with all children of the citizen-members being baptized as infants quite as Israelitish children were circumcised from Abraham to Jesus.

Little wonder then that the Anabaptists were regarded as heretics when *they stated that the Old Testament was done away and when they demanded New Testament backing for every church ordinance and for the entire ethic of the Christian.* Pilgram Marpeck compiled an entire volume consisting of contrasting citations from the two testaments on every conceivable point of doctrine. Dirck Philips wrote as follows on the unity in spirit of the two covenants:

> So then the gospel and the law are divided so far as the figures, shadows and the letter of the law are concerned, which are all done away by the gospel But it is essential that we take heed to the spirit of the law (for the law is spiritual, as Paul says . .) We will then find that the signification, purport and real meaning of the law accords and agrees in every way with the gospel, yea, that it is one and the same

truth. For as there is but one God so there is but one truth, for God Himself is the truth; but the letter (in which the truth is hidden) comes to an end. Thus the literal command of the Lord regarding circumcision of the flesh has come to an end, but the command regarding the spiritual circumcision of the heart remains [Rom. 2:25-29; Phil 3·3, Col. 2 11] Thus all symbols of the law (which are too numerous to speak of here) have come to an end so far as the letter is concerned, nevertheless the true and essential signification of these same figures remains and accords with the gospel. ... Thus the apostles and even the Lord Jesus Christ Himself many times proved and confirmed the truth of the gospel with sayings and testimonies of the law and the prophets, thereby showing us that the truth of the gospel is embodied in the law and the prophets *(Enchiridion, 260, 261)*.

But in the preface to his book, *Of Spiritual Restitution,* Dirck stated that he had written

... to the end that simple minds may be thereby instructed and that they may not be deceived by the false prophets who embellish and disguise their deceptive doctrine with the old leaven of the letter as shadows and figures, for whatever of the New Testament they cannot defend they try to prove with the Old Testament and with the letter of the prophecies. From this fallacy many sects have come, many false forms of worship have been established ... *(Enchiridion, 323).*

Menno Simons made numerous remarks regarding the necessity of having New Testament support for one's ethic and practice. Here are a few of them:

.. Even though an Elias himself were to come, he dare not teach anything against the foundation and doctrine of Christ and the apostles, but he must, if he would preach aright, teach and preach conformably to the same, for by the spirit, word, actions and example of Christ all must be judged and receive the last sentence; otherwise the whole Scriptures are false *(Works,* I, 97).

In the course of a discussion on baptism he wrote:

It is our determination in this matter as in all other matters of conscience ... that we will not be influenced by lords and princes, nor by doctors and teachers of schools, nor by the influence of the fathers, and long established customs, for in this matter neither emperors nor kings nor doctors nor licentiates nor councils nor proscriptions against the Word of God will avail. We dare not be bound to any person, power, wisdom or times, but we must be governed alone by the expressed and positive commands of Christ, and pure doctrines and practices of His holy apostles. . *(Works,* I, 31).

After condemning "infant baptism, masses, matins, vespers, caps (of cardinals, etc.), palms, crosses, chapels, altars, bells, etc.," Menno adds:

The true evangelical faith looks upon and has respect to the doctrine, ceremonies, commands, prohibitions and unblamable examples of Christ alone, and strives to conform thereto with all its powers .. *(Works,* I, 118).
... We acknowledge the ever blessed Jesus alone for our Redeemer, Mediator, Intercessor, spiritual King, Example, Shepherd, infallible Teacher and Master, ... we judge and prove all spirits, doctrines, councils, ordinances, statutes and ceremonies as far as regards spirit and faith with the spirit, doctrine, ordinances, commands and ceremonies of Christ, and thus esteem the commands and ceremonies of men which are contrary to the commands and ceremonies of God not only as vain and useless but also as accursed and idolatrous according to the Scriptures... *(Works,* I, 185).

The Anabaptists were above all else *men of the Word,* believers who insisted on striving to achieve absolute obedience to Christ and His New Testament.

Pertinent Biblical Passages

1. On the Divine Authority of the Old Testament Scriptures:
John 10:35: "The Scripture cannot be broken."

II Tim. 3.16: "All Scripture is given by inspiration of God, and is profitable for doctrine, for reproof, for correction, for instruction in righteousness...."

II Pet. 1:21: "The prophecy came not in old time by the will of man: but holy men of God spake as they were moved by the Holy Ghost."

2. On the Divine Authority of the New Testament Scriptures:

I Cor. 14:37: "If any man think himself to be a prophet, or spiritual, let him acknowledge that the things that I write unto you are the commandments of the Lord."

II Thess. 3:12: "Now them that are such we command and exhort by our Lord Jesus Christ...."

Cf. II Pet. 3.16: where Paul's epistles are classed with "the other Scriptures."

3. On the Fulfillment of the Old Testament by the New:

Matt. 5:17f: "Think not that I am come to destroy the law, or the prophets: I am not come to destroy, but to fulfil. For verily I say unto you, Till heaven and earth pass, one jot or one tittle shall in no wise pass from the law, till all be fulfilled."

4. On the Higher Demands of the New Testament:

Matt. 5:21-26: The Old forbade killing; the New requires a redemptive attitude toward every one.

Matt. 5.27-30: The Old forbade adultery; the New requires purity of heart and rigorous self-control.

Matt. 5:31f: The Old forbade informal separation of husband and wife; the New forbids all divorce except for unfaithfulness.

Matt. 5:33-37: The Old forbade false oaths; the New requires absolute truthfulness ever, without any oaths.

Matt. 5·38-42: The Old forbade illegal retaliation; the New requires absolute love and no retaliation at all.

Matt. 5.43-48: The Old forbade hating one's neighbor; the New requires loving all, even those who abuse and harm one.

5. On the Reliability of Old Testament Prophecy:

Matt. 1.22: "Now all this was done, that it might be fulfilled which was spoken of the Lord by the prophet...."

Matt. 21:4. "All this was done, that it might be fulfilled which was spoken by the prophet...."

Make a study of the phrase, "that it might be fulfilled," in a complete concordance such as James Strong's.

Study all the sayings of Jesus in Matt. 5 which begin thus: "But I say unto you." (In the Greek it is the word "I" which is emphatic, not the word "but.")

Reading References in the Confessions and Catechisms

Schleitheim Confession, Articles VI, VII.
Dordrecht Confession, Articles V, XIV, XV.
Shorter Catechism, Questions 29, 30.
Roosen's Catechism, Questions 72-74, 115-120.

THE FINALITY OF THE NEW TESTAMENT 51

Study Questions

1. How many kinds of law does the Old Testament Scripture contain?
2. What is binding upon the Christian from the Old Testament? what is not binding?
3. How can one explain the lower ethical standards of the Mosaic law?
4. Make a list of some of the higher standards of the New Testament in comparison with the Old.
5. What is the basic difference between Israel and the church? How did one become an Israelite? How does one become a Christian? Do these differences help explain the differing ethical standards?
6. Where does the New Testament speak of the *First Covenant* and of *the Second*?
7. Does the Jewish Sabbath belong to the Old Covenant or the New?

Chapter IX

The Church as a Fellowship of Committed Disciples

Luther and Zwingli both decided to continue with the state system, to have a *Staats-und Volks-Kirche*. In this arrangement the common people had no choice but to accept the official religion of their land or emigrate. But large numbers of them did not take the matter of religion very seriously, as the reformers themselves lamented. In the early years of Luther's reform work his colleague, Philip Melanchthon, 1497-1560, stated that "Many believe themselves very pious and holy when they upbraid priests and monks or eat meat on Friday." This agrees with Menno's severe charge against the Lutherans:

If anyone can simply say with them, Ah! what dishonest knaves and villains these desperate priests and monks are; . . . The ungodly pope with his shorn crew, say they, have deceived us long enough with purgatory, confession, and fasting; we now eat as we have hunger, fish or flesh, as we desire; for every creature of God is good, says Paul, and is not to be rejected. But what follows they do not want to understand or know; namely to [live as] the believing who know the truth and enjoy it with thanksgiving. They further say, How shamefully they have deceived us poor people; they have robbed us of the blood of the Lord and directed us to their mummery and to their enchanting works. God be praised, we now know that all our works avail nothing, for the blood and death of Christ alone must blot out and pay for our sins. They begin to sing a *psalm: Der Strick ist entzwei und wir sind frei*, etc., i e , *The cord [of restraint] is cut asunder and we are free*, while the smell of beer and wine issues from their drunken mouths and noses Anyone if he can but read this *distich*, if he live ever so carnally, is a good evangelical man and a fine brother. And should someone come who would in true and sincere love admonish or reprove them and direct them to Jesus Christ, to His doctrine, sacraments and unblamable example, and show that it does not become a Christian to carouse and drink, and to revile and curse, etc., he must from that hour hear that he is a legalist *(Werkheiliger)*, a heavenstormer or a factionist, a fanatic or hypocrite, a defamer of the sacrament or an Anabaptist *(Works,* I, 112).

Menno listed six earmarks by which the true church of Christ may be known:

1. By an unadulterated, pure doctrine . . 2. By a scriptural use of the sacramental signs . . 3 By obedience to the Word . . 4 By unfeigned brotherly love . . . 5. [By] an unreserved confession of God and Christ . . . 6. By oppression and tribulation for the sake of the Lord's Word . . *(Works,* II, 83)

Again Menno wrote to his "true brethren and sisters in Jesus Christ":

. . You must be conformed unto Christ in mind, spirit, courage and will, both in doctrine and life, as Christ Jesus is conformed unto the nature and image of His blessed heavenly Father, to which He was so conformed that He did nothing but what His Father did, Jn. 5; that He taught nothing but the word of His Father, Jn. 7. In the same manner with those who are begotten of the living, saving Word of our beloved Lord Jesus Christ; they are by virtue of their new birth so conformed unto Christ, so like unto Him, so really implanted into Him, so converted into His heavenly nature, that they do not teach nor believe any doctrine but that which conforms unto the

THE CHURCH AS A FELLOWSHIP

doctrine of Christ; do not make use of any religious ceremonies but Christ's ceremonies which He has taught and commanded in Holy gospel. . . .

. . . Such regenerated and godly minded live unblamably, even according to the measure of the rule of the holy gospel of Jesus Christ and His apostles. Therefore He kisses them as His beloved chosen ones with the mouth of His peace, Cant. 1, and calls them His church, His bride, flesh of His flesh, and bone of His bone . . . (*Works*, II, 443).

In other words, for the Anabaptists it was impossible to accept the idea of a provincial church which embraced the entire population of the land, reckoning them all as Christians because they were *christened* as babes. The only people the Anabaptists could consider members of the church were *those who had made a personal commitment to Christ*. Let the indifferent and the carnal know where they are; let them be outside the church, lost and in need of evangelization. It was because of this conception of church membership as a commitment to an earnest Christian life that the Brethren insisted on believers' baptism. No infant could make a personal commitment to Christ nor assume the obligations of church membership. It does not follow however that the Anabaptists regarded infants as lost. Menno protested thus:

. . . If it should be said that we rob the children of the promise and of the grace of God you will observe that they contradict us out of hatred and envy and do not tell the truth. Say, who has the strongest ground and hope of the salvation of their children? Is it he who places his hopes upon an outward sign [infant baptism]? Or is it he who bases his hopes upon the promise of grace given and promised of Christ Jesus? (*Works*, II, 226).

Menno believed in the salvation of children because of,

. . . The word of the Lord that the kingdom is promised them by grace, by the election of God our heavenly Father through the merits of Jesus Christ, as He says, "Suffer little children and forbid them not, to come unto me; for of such is the kingdom of heaven" . . . not the baptism of antichrist [infant baptism] but the promise of Jesus Christ assures us of the salvation of our little children if they die and depart from here. But if the good Father suffer them to grow up and grant them His grace, then we would educate them in the instruction and fear of the Lord as much as we are able. When they can understand God's Word and believe it the Scripture directs them to be baptized [Matt. 28:19; Mark 16:16] (*Works*, II, 318).

. . . For Jesus' sake sin is not imputed to infants that are innocent and incapable of understanding. [Eternal] life is promised not through any one ceremony but out of pure grace through the blood of the Lord. . . (*Works*, I, 33).

On the subject of adult baptism Menno pleaded:

True Christians believe and obey. Are you a sincere Christian, born of God? Then why do you dread baptism which is among the least that God commanded you? . .

He then made an extensive list of the demands which God makes upon His children to conform to Him in heart and life, and added:

We think that these and the like commands are more painful and difficult to perverse flesh, which is naturally so prone to follow its own way, than to have a handful of water applied, and a sincere Christian must be ready to do all this; if he is not, he is not born of God, for the regenerated are of one mind with Christ Jesus (*Works*, I, 38)

Kept Pure by Discipline

The necessity of church discipline is the negative counterpart of the high calling of the church. If the church is composed of born-again, obedient disciples of the Lord Jesus, then any who grow cold and revert to a life of sin must be regarded as in need of restoration. The church must put forth every effort to win the backslider to a renewal of his Christian life. But if in spite of earnest entreaty and prayer the offender insists on continuing in his sin it becomes obligatory for the church to make known to him that he has placed himself outside the pale of the church. This is well set forth in Article XVI of the Dordrecht Confession of Faith, which should be consulted at this point (page 87 of this book).

The reformers ridiculed the Anabaptists for exercising church discipline, claiming that it was practiced in violation of the teaching not to uproot the tares until the harvest (Matt. 13:24-30, 37-43). They also accused the Brethren of considering themselves an assembly of absolutely perfect Christians—an odd charge to bring against a group which insisted on dealing with its transgressors!

Menno Simons made it abundantly clear that church discipline did not apply to every kind of transgressions; only open transgressions are to be dealt with by the church.

> . . . Should it ever happen that anyone should sin against God in private, from which may His power preserve us all, and should the Spirit of grace which works repentance again operate upon his heart and cause genuine repentance, of this we have not to judge, for it is a matter between him and God. For since it is evident that we do not seek our righteousness and salvation, the remission of our sins, satisfaction, reconciliation and eternal life in or through excommunication but alone in the righteousness, intercession, merits, death and blood of Christ There are but two objects and ends why the ban [excommunication] is commanded in the Scriptures, which can have no reference to such an one Because in the first place his sins are private, hence no offence can follow And secondly because he is in deep contrition and is penitent in life; therefore he has no need then of being brought to repentance. Nor are we anywhere commanded of Christ to put him to open shame before the church. Reflect on these things *(Works,* I, 254; repeated, I, 283).
>
> Not the weak but the corrupt members are cut off lest they corrupt the others. . . . I desire that excommunication be practiced in a sincere, paternal spirit, in faithful love, according to the doctrine of Christ and His apostles. . . *(Works,* I, 284).
>
> . . . None is cut off by us or ejected from the communion of the brethren . . . but those who have already ejected themselves either by false doctrine or by a blamable life from Christ and His communion For we do not wish to eject any but to accept them; not to cut them off but to restore them: not to reject but to win them back, not to afflict but to console them, not to condemn but to save them. . . .
>
> But those whom we cannot raise up and admonish unto repentance by tears, threatening, reproving, or by any other Christian service and divine means, we should reluctantly separate from us, sincerely deploring the fall and damnation of such erring brethren. . . *(Works,* II, 446).

Pertinent Biblical Passages

1. On the Membership of the Church:
    Acts 2:47: "And the Lord was adding together the ones being saved, day by day." Greek.
    Acts 5:14: "Believers were the more added to the Lord. . . ."
    Acts 6:7. "The number of the disciples multiplied . . . greatly."
2. On the Characteristics of Church Members:
    Acts 6:7: "Obedient to the faith."
    Acts 11:24: "Full of the Holy Ghost and of faith."
    Acts 9:31: "Walking in the fear of the Lord. . . ."

THE CHURCH AS A FELLOWSHIP

3. On the Divine Head of the Church:
    Matt. 16:18: "Upon this rock I will build my church...."
    I Cor. 3:11: "Other foundation can no man lay than that is laid, which is Jesus Christ."
    Eph. 5:23: "Christ is the head of the church: and He is the Saviour of the body."

4. On the Discipline of the Church:
    Rom. 16:17: "Now I beseech you, brethren, mark them which cause divisions and offences contrary to the doctrine which ye have learned; and avoid them."
    Titus 3:11: "A factious man, after a first and second admonition refuse...."
    I Cor. 5:13: "Therefore put away from among yourselves that wicked person."

5. On the Great Commission Given to the Church:
    Matt. 28:19f: "Go ye therefore, and teach all nations, baptizing them in the name of the Father, and of the Son, and of the Holy Ghost: teaching them to observe all things whatsoever I have commanded you: and, lo, I am with you alway, even unto the end of the world."
    John 20:21: "Then said Jesus to them again, Peace be unto you: as my Father hath sent Me, even so send I you."
    Acts 1:8. "Ye shall receive power, after that the Holy Ghost is come upon you: and ye shall be witnesses unto Me both in Jerusalem, and in all Judea, and in Samaria, and unto the uttermost part of the earth."

Reading References in the Confessions and Catechism

Schleitheim Confession, Articles I, II, III.
Dordrecht Confession, Article VIII.
Christian Fundamentals, Article IX.
Shorter Catechism, Questions 11-17.
Waldeck Catechism, Part Third, Chapter III, Questions 18-26.
Roosen's Catechism, Questions 75-99.

Study Questions

1. Why did the Anabaptists reject the state church system of their day?
2. Are infants saved by baptism? without baptism? How are infants saved?
3. What does baptism symbolize? Are infants capable of this?
4. What is involved in uniting with the church?
5. Of whom does the church consist?
6. What is meant by calling the church a fellowship rather than an organization or a hierarchy?

Chapter X
The High Calling of the Church of Christ

The Anabaptist concept of the church composed of individual souls who were saved by accepting the Lord Jesus Christ as their Saviour, and who were glorifying God by a holy walk and a life of Christian witnessing, was only one aspect of their view of the church. *They also thought of the church as a corporate body achieving the will of God for society.* This doctrine distinguished them more sharply than any other from the large Protestant groups. They held that the state had to live its life on a sub-Christian level, restraining unregenerate men by the employment of police force and the magistracy. But when a person became a Christian and accepted baptism he was lifted up into the society of the redeemed, a body of people who loved one another and were mutually concerned for the welfare of their fellow believers and for the corporate witness of the brotherhood, a society in which there was no need of force and coercion. Church discipline aided in keeping this society holy. Here Jesus Christ was sovereign, directing His people by His Word, in the power of the Holy Spirit. His servants, the ministers or teachers in the congregations, were confident that the Holy Spirit would so bless their teaching of the Word that the members of Christ's body, being regenerated believers, would seek to conform themselves to Christ and His Word.

Needless to say, this vision, if the state churchmen had it at all, was an empty dream for a people's (provincial) church. Such a body did not achieve a high ethical level in Christ. In the state churches one could think of the vertical relation only, the individual soul reaching up to God. It was the Anabaptists who sought earnestly to build Christ's *kingdom* here and now. And that kingdom was not a theoretical concept for them, but a glorious reality, composed, as it was, of their fellow believers, the members of their congregations. The Lutherans thought of individual believers forsaking a sinful society and finding forgiveness and grace, (Pietism is Lutheranism at its highest level of devotion). The Reformed dreamed of Christianizing the social order: Christian mayors, Christian magistrates, Christian policemen, Christian soldiers; but they had to be dual personalities, faithfully bearing the sword of the Spirit as believers and (in violation of the Christian ethic) bearing the sword of steel as citizens of this world. The Anabaptists with their conception of separation of church and state agreed with the Lutherans that the social order could not be Christianized, and they agreed with the Reformed in desiring to create a Christian society—*but they sought to do this only in the*

THE HIGH CALLING OF THE CHURCH OF CHRIST 57

church. This involved a certain "withdrawal" from one sector of the life of society, not a physical withdrawal into monasteries, but a certain "abandonment" of non-Christian society to its own management and a concentration on the evangelization of individuals from that non-Christian society. The church of Christ was therefore the society in which Christ exercised His glorious reign. The highest achievement of this life was to participate in extending that kingdom of glory. The statements of the Anabaptists on the subject of the kingdom will therefore help us to see their vision of the nature, place and function of the church. Here are some extracts from Menno Simons' writings:

... Spiritually we acknowledge no king, neither in heaven above nor upon earth beneath, [other] than the only, eternal and true King, spiritual David, Christ Jesus who is Lord of lords and King of kings ..

But according to the flesh we teach and exhort to be obedient to the emperor, kings, lords and princes, yea, to all in authority in all their transactions and civil regulations so far as they are not contrary to the Word of God ..

We teach and confess that we know of no sword nor commotion in the kingdom or church of Christ other than the sharp sword of the Spirit, God's Word , which is sharper and more piercing than any two-eged sword ... But the sword of worldly policy we leave with those to whom it is committed...

We acknowledge, teach and seek no other kingdom than that of Christ which shall endure for ever, in which there is no pomp, splendor, gold, silver, meat and drink, but righteousness, peace and joy in the Holy Ghost; we confess with Christ that our kingdom is not of this world... *(Works,* I, 82, 83, cf I, 95).

... We know that all the promises to the fathers, the waiting of the patriarchs, the whole figurative law, and all the predictions of the prophets, are fulfilled *in* Christ, *with* Christ, and *through* Christ; that Christ is our King, Prince, Lord, Messiah, the promised David... *(Works,* I, 116).

... All those who are born of God with Christ, who thus conform their weak life to the gospel, are thus converted and follow the example of Christ, hear and believe His holy Word, follow His commands which He in plain words commanded us in the holy Scriptures, form the holy, Christian church which has the promise, the true children of God, brothers and sisters of Christ, for they are born with Him of one Father and of the new Eve, the pure, chaste bride They are flesh of Christ's flesh, and bone of His bone, the spiritual house of Israel, the spiritual city, Jerusalem, temple and Mount Zion . . . .

These regenerated have a spiritual King over them who rules them by the unbroken scepter of His mouth, namely with His Holy Spirit and Word He clothes them with the garment of righteousness, of pure white silk, He refreshes them with the living water of His Holy Spirit, and feeds them with the bread of life His name is Christ Jesus .. *(Works,* I, 170).

... Now the bright light of the holy Gospel of Christ shines again in refulgent splendor in these vexatious times of all anti-Christian abominations, God's own and first-begotten Son, Christ Jesus, is gloriously revealed, His good will and pleasure and holy Word concerning faith, regeneration, repentance, baptism, the Lord's Supper, and the whole saving doctrine, life and ordinance, have again come to light through much seeking, prayer, reading, teaching and writing, ... now all things—God be praised for His grace—proceed according to the true, apostolic rule in the church, whereby the kingdom of Christ rises in honor, and the kingdom of antichrist is sinking. .. *(Works,* I, 242).

... We do not teach and practice the doctrine of having goods in common But we teach and maintain by the Word of the Lord that all truly believing Christians are members of one body and are baptized by one Spirit into one body. , that they are partakers of one bread .., that they have one Lord and one God .

... All those who are born of God, who are gifted with the Spirit of the Lord, and who according to the Scriptures are called into one body of love in Christ Jesus, are prepared by ... love to serve their neighbors, not only with money and goods but also after the example of their Lord and Head, Jesus Christ, in an evangelical manner with life and blood They show mercy and love as much as they can; suffer no beggars among them, take to heart the need of the saints, receive the miserable; take the stranger into their houses; console the afflicted, assist the needy; clothe the naked, feed the hungry; do not turn their face from the poor; and do not despise their own flesh . . . (*Works*, II, 309).

. . . I beseech you as my sincerely beloved brethren by the grace of God, nay I command you with holy Paul, by the Lord Jesus Christ who at His coming will judge the living and the dead, diligently to observe each other unto salvation in all becoming ways, teaching, instructing, admonishing, reproving, threatening and consoling each other as occasion requires, not otherwise than in accordance with the Word of God, and in unfeigned love, that we may all grow up in God and become united in faith and in the knowledge of the Son of God into one perfect man, and according to the measure of the gift of Jesus Christ. . . .

Therefore take heed. If you see your brother sin, then pass not by him as one that does not prize his soul; but if his fall be curable, from that moment endeavor to raise him up by gentle admonition and brotherly instruction before you eat, drink, sleep or do anything else, as one who ardently desires his salvation, lest your poor, erring brother harden and corrupt in his fall, and perish in his sin (*Works*, II, 444, 445).

In view of the emphasis of the Brethren on need for the grace of God and on the necessity of fraternal helpfulness in spiritual matters it is clear that the Anabaptists did not claim to be morally perfect, a church without spot or wrinkle,—though indeed that was their goal, and toward it they pressed earnestly.

Menno held that there are four kinds of sin: (1) The corrupt nature or inherent sin, which "for Christ's sake . . . is not accounted as sin." (2) Acts of sin, such as "adultery, fornication, avarice, debauchery, hatred, envy, lying, theft, murder and idolatry;" for which there is no forgiveness apart from repentance. "If this inherent sin is to lose its effect and actual sin be forgiven, then we must believe the word of the Lord, be regenerated by faith, and thus by virtue of the new birth, by true repentance resist the inherent sin, die unto actual sin and be pious." (3) "The third kind are human frailties, errors and stumblings which are yet daily found among the saints and regenerated, such as untempered thoughts, careless words and rashness in our actions . . . . The unbelieving . . . . commit sin unrestrainedly and fearlessly. . . .

"But those who are born from above are fearful of all sin; they know by the law that all which is contrary to the first righteousness is sin, be it inwardly or outwardly, important or trifling; and therefore they daily fight in spirit and faith with their weak flesh; sigh and lament about their errors . . . they daily approach the throne of grace with contrite hearts and pray: Holy Father, forgive us our trespasses as we forgive those that trespass against us. And thus they are not rejected by the Lord on account of such transgressions which are not committed willfully and intentionally, but contrary to their will out of mere thoughtlessness and frailty."

(4) The fourth type of sin is connected with becoming an apostate (*Works*, II, 312-314).

It is evident that the moral earnestness of the Brethren and their vision of the high calling of the church were both derived from the New Testament; they were sorely needed in the world four centuries ago; and

THE HIGH CALLING OF THE CHURCH OF CHRIST 59

even the Christian world of today could profitably follow the Brethren as they sought to follow Christ.

Pertinent Biblical Passages

1. On Christians Constituting a Divine Kingdom:
    Col. 1.13: God "hath delivered us from the power of darkness, and hath translated us into the kingdom of His dear Son."
    Acts 14:22: "We must through much tribulation enter into the kingdom of God."
2. On the Holy Character of Kingdom Members:
    I Cor. 6:9f: "Be not deceived: neither fornicators, nor idolators, nor adulterers, . . . nor thieves, nor covetous, nor drunkards, nor revilers, nor extortioners, shall inherit the kingdom of God."
    Gal. 5:19f: "Now the works of the flesh are manifest, which are these: fornication, uncleanness, lasciviousness, idolatry, sorcery, enmities, strife, jealousies, wraths, factions, divisions, parties, envyings, drunkenness, revellings, and such like; of which I forewarn you, even as I did forewarn you, that they who practise such things shall not inherit the kingdom of God." A.S.V.
    Gal. 5:22f: "But the fruit of the Spirit is love, joy, peace, longsuffering, kindness, goodness, faithfulness, meekness, self-control; against such there is no law." A.S.V.
    Rom. 14:17: "The kingdom of God is not eating and drinking, but righteousness and peace and joy in the Holy Spirit." A.S.V.
3. On the Corporate Witness of Christians:
    I Pet. 2.9: "Ye are an elect race, a royal priesthood, a holy nation, a people for God's own possession, that ye may show forth the excellencies of Him who called you out of darkness into His marvellous light." A.S.V.
    II Cor. 3:2: "Ye are our epistle written in our hearts, known and read of all men."
4. On the Christian's Relation to the State:
    Rom. 13:1, 5: "Let every soul be subject to the higher authorities. For there is no authority except of God: the ones existing are ordered of God. . . . Wherefore it is necessary to be in subjection, not only on account of the wrath, but also on account of the conscience." Greek.
    Rom. 13:6: "For for this cause pay ye tribute also: for they are God's ministers. . . ."
    I Pet. 2:17: "Honor the king."
    I Tim. 2·1f: "I exhort therefore, that, first of all, supplications, prayers, intercessions, and giving of thanks, be made for all men; for kings, and for all that are in authority; that we may live a quiet and peaceable life in all godliness and honesty."

Reading References in the Confessions and Catechisms

Schleitheim Confession, Articles III, IV.
Dordrecht Confession, Articles VIII, XIII.
Shorter Catechism, Questions 11-17, 28, 29.
Waldeck Catechism, Part Third, Chapter IV, 1-10; II, 26, 27.
Roosen's Catechism, Questions 75-99; 132-138.

Study Questions

1. How may we acquire a vision of the high calling of the church, and at the same time avoid pride?
2. Compare the concept of the church as held by the Lutherans, the Reformed, and the Anabaptists.
3. Does the doctrine of nonresistance for Christians condemn the state as a curse, and make anarchists of those who hold to nonresistance?
4. Can the church do the work of the state or the state do the work of the church?
5. Summarize the differences in (a) function; (b) personnel; (c) head; (d) methods; (e) sanctions; and (f) means of entrance, as between the church and the state.
6. What are the obligations of the Christian to the state?
7. What attitudes and activities best enable the church to reflect the glory of Jesus to non-Christian society? What would hinder?
8. How would the Christian life suffer if one were to think only of his individual relation to God rather than also of his kingdom membership?

Chapter XI
The Heart of the Christian Life

It was pointed out above that the Anabaptists were simple Biblicists, little concerned with systems of theology. Neither were the Anabaptists sacramentarians. They did not teach that baptism effected regeneration, nor did they base their hope of salvation on baptism. It was Luther who fell back on his baptism when his faith wavered; but never did an Anabaptist make such a statement. Both Pilgram Marpeck and Menno Simons lamented the fact that professing Christians, however careless in their life, claimed to be Christians because of having been baptized as infants. For the Brethren there was no divine efficacy in the ceremony of baptism; rather, baptism was the external seal of having espoused discipleship; it was the sign of the covenant between the new disciple and God (cf. I Peter 3:21 in the German Bible). In commenting on Peter's statement that baptism was "the covenant of a good conscience with God" Menno writes:

> Here Peter teaches us how the inward baptism saves us, by which the inner man is washed, and not the outward baptism by which the flesh is washed; for only this inward baptism . . . is of value in the sight of God, while outward baptism follows only as an evidence of [the] obedience which is of faith. For could outward baptism save without the inward washing, the whole Scriptures which speak of the new man would be spoken to no purpose, the kingdom of heaven would be bound to elementary water, the blood of Christ would be shed in vain, and no one that is baptized could be lost. No, no! Outward baptism avails nothing so long as we are not inwardly renewed, regenerated, and baptized of God with the heavenly fire and the Holy Ghost. But when we receive this baptism from above we will be constrained through the Spirit and Word of God by a good conscience . . . to believe sincerely in the merits of the death of the Lord, and in the power and benefits of His resurrection. And henceforth . . . we submissively covenant with the Lord through the outward sign of baptism, which is enjoined on all the believers in Christ . . that we will no longer live according to the evil, unclean lusts of the flesh but walk according to the witness of a good conscience before Him
>
> . . Baptism is a sign of obedience, commanded of Christ, by which we testify when we receive it that we believe the Word of the Lord, that we are sorry for and repent of our former life and conduct, that we desire to rise with Christ unto a new life, and that we believe in the forgiveness of sin through Jesus Christ Not, my beloved, that we believe in the remission of sins through baptism; by no means Because by baptism we cannot obtain faith and repentance, neither do we receive the forgiveness of sins, nor peace, nor liberty of conscience. But we testify thereby that we have repented, received pardon and faith in Christ . . In short, had we forgiveness of sins and peace of conscience through outward ceremonies and elements then the REALITY would be superseded and His merits made of no effect. *(Works, I, 28)*

Baptism was for the Brethren merely an outward testimony to their inner experience of salvation and to their intention to live the Christian life. It is therefore wholly wrong to state that the Anabaptists placed much stress on baptism. Indeed they placed little stress on any external ordinances. Everywhere they baptized believers, observed the Lord's

Supper, and exercised church discipline—and in some communities they practiced feet washing as an ordinance—but that was the extent of their church ceremonies (cf. Menno's *Works*, II, 242-244). Menno Simons wrote a vigorous reply to the charge that the Brethren were "new monks" (*Works*, II, 316ff).

Not only did the Brethren refuse to rely on the observance of ordinances for their salvation; they did not consider regeneration or even faith, as the final essence of Christianity. They believed in and stressed both the new birth and saving faith, to be sure, but they were only the indispensable foundation of the Christian life, not ends in themselves. *The essence of Christianity was thought of as discipleship,* as a faithful "following-after" (*Nachfolge*) of Christ, a resolute obedience to the ethical demands of the New Testament. The Brethren were sharply critical of hearing people boast of baptism, of theology and faith while they lived in the lusts of the flesh. Baptism has its place, of course, but not to confer supernatural grace. Doctrine has its place, but not as a substitute for life. It is faith that saves, and faith alone, *but where there is no discipleship there is no saving faith.* Menno's outburst is typical of the attitude of the Brethren four centuries ago:

> ... The reckless people are chained to and consoled in their unbelief and licentious, carnal life by their light minded doctrine, sacraments and easy life, for they preach and teach you, "There are none that can truly believe; we are all sinners—therefore none can rightly keep the commandments of God In your baptism (they say) you became a regenerated Christian and received the Holy Ghost. Although you could not understand the Word, although you have no faith in Christ Jesus nor knowledge of good or evil, nor any change or renewing of heart, because you were an unconscious child,"—and similar false consolations You hear their absolutions and receive their bread, as if that were sufficient, and never mind that you are yet an impenitent, avaricious, proud, drunken, unclean, envious and idolatrous man .. (*Works*, II, 265).

In another treatise Menno says succinctly:

> Verily they are not the church of Christ who merely boast of His name. But those are the true church of Christ who were converted, who are born from above of God, who are of a regenerated mind, and by the operation of the Holy Spirit from the hearing of the divine Word have become children of God, who obey Him and live unblamably in His holy commandments and according to His holy will all their days, or after their calling (*Works*, II, 241).

There is abundant evidence, even from the pens of the most bitter opponents of the Anabaptists, that *the Brethren did succeed in reaching a distinctly higher level of Christian living than the state church groups of the sixteenth century.* This was the result of their insistence that the essence of Christianity was the realization of God's will in the lives of Christian disciples, that redemption must inevitably bear rich fruit in daily life. Without holiness of life and effective witnessing there is no real Christianity. The new life must be *in evidence* for the glory of God and the salvation of the lost.

Pertinent Biblical Passages

1. On the Absolute Importance of the Fruit of Faith:
    Matt. 7:15-19: "Beware of false prophets ... Ye shall know them by their fruits .... A good tree cannot bring forth evil fruit,

THE HEART OF THE CHRISTIAN LIFE 63

neither can a corrupt tree bring forth good fruit . . . . Wherefore by their fruits ye shall know them."

Rom. 6:16. "Know ye not, that to whom ye yield yourselves servants to obey, his servants ye are to whom ye obey; whether of sin unto death, or of obedience unto righteousness?"

James 2:14: "What doth it profit, my brethren, if a man say he hath faith, but have not works? Can that faith save him?" A.S.V. Read the entire discussion, Jas. 2.14-26, a passage which declares the same truth as Rom. 6.

2. On the Life as a Test of Saving Faith:

Matt. 7:21: "Not every one that saith unto me, Lord, Lord, shall enter into the kingdom of heaven; but he that doeth the will of My Father which is in heaven."

Jas. 1:22: "Be ye doers of the Word, and not hearers only, deceiving your own selves."

Rev. 22:14: "Blessed are they that do His commandments, that they may have right to the tree of life, and may enter in through the gates into the city."

Reading References in the Confessions and Catechisms

Schleitheim Confession: Read the last three paragraphs of the introdutory discussion, beginning, "A very great offense . . . ." Also Articles I, IV.

Dordrecht Confession, Article VI.
Shorter Catechism, Questions 3-6, 19.
Waldeck Catechism, Part Third, Chapter III, 1-34; IV, 1, 34-36.
Roosen's Catechism, Questions 99, 100.

Study Questions

1. What is the relation between faith and life?
2. Distinguish between true faith and "dead faith."
3. Are people saved by keeping ordinances?
4. Can a man be saved without holiness? How is holiness obtained?
5. What does it mean to follow Jesus? to take up one's cross?
6. What is the basis of salvation? who will be saved?

Chapter XII
Taking Up the Cross

The Anabaptists emphasized separation from the "world," meaning the mass of unregenerate men together with all their sinful ways and life. And they expected a certain amount of opposition and persecution from the world. They spoke much of bearing "the cross," of being faithful unto death, of being willing to shed their blood for their testimony to the truth. Menno described true Christians as "prepared to take upon themselves the cross of Christ, and to forsake father, mother, husband, wife, children, possessions and self, for the sake of the testimony of His holy Word when the honor and praise of God require it" (*Works*, II, 110). This did not indicate an unhealthy desire for martyrdom. But when they lay in prison with no hope of release they naturally turned their minds toward their eternal Home. Yet even then they did not forget their families and congregations. In 1567 Christian Langedul, a Dutch Mennonite imprisoned for his faith, wrote the following in one of his letters to his wife:

> I must stop since my paper is used up Greet all the friends much in the Lord whenever you have a proper opportunity, as also all friends according to the flesh; especially greet grandmother and comfort her as best you can since I have great anxiety for her sake, and for you and my children I often think of my sweet P., but I am glad when he is out of my thoughts Do the best in everything. I greet you with a holy kiss of peace I hope the Lord will shorten my days, because He loves me. To L. E. I hope to write yet when I get time, greet her much in my name Herewith I commend you to the Lord. . . .
>
> By me your very weak husband, Christian Langedul, from prison in which I am for the testimony of the Lord

After being sentenced to death he wrote the following to his wife:

> Grace and peace from our heavenly Father through Christ Jesus, this I wish you my dear and chosen wife and sister in the Lord. And may the comforter, the Holy Ghost, comfort you in your tribulation as He will do according to His promise . . I expect to inherit salvation through the grace of the Lord and am of good cheer herein. I will therefore thank the Lord forever for His love O my love, the winepress must now be trodden and I am quite ready for it · the Lord be praised. Truly He is a God of all comfort. . . Oh, that I could fully thank the Lord for all the comfort and strength He grants to me, unworthy one . . .
>
> Herewith I commend you to the Lord and to the Word of His grace. Greet all the friends most cordially with the peace of the Lord Greet warmly R. Langedul, also your sister and all the friends whenever it is convenient, and bid them all adieu Adieu my dear lamb, adieu Written on the twelfth of September, 1567, by me, Christian Langedul, your husband and weak brother in the Lord, imprisoned and sentenced to death for the testimony of Christ and for our conscience. . .

In 1573 a young man and his wife, John and Janneken van Munstdorp, were seized in a meeting of Dutch Mennonites and imprisoned at Antwerp in the first year of their marriage. Here are some extracts from his letter to his wife, written in prison:

An affectionate greeting to you my beloved wife whom I love from the heart and greatly cherish above every other creature, and must now forsake for the truth for the sake of which we must count all things loss and love Him above all. I hope though men separate us here that the Lord will again join us together in His eternal kingdom where no one will be able to part us and we shall reign forever in the heavenly abode. . . .

. . . adieu and farewell, my lamb, my love; adieu and farewell to all that fear God; adieu and farewell until the marriage of the Lamb in the New Jerusalem. Be valiant and of good cheer; cast the troubles that assail you upon the Lord and He will not forsake you; cleave to Him and you will not fall Love God above all, have love and truth, love your salvation and keep your promises to the Lord (*Martyrs' Mirror*, 984).

John was executed first, by burning. Soon after his martyrdom Janneken bore a little daughter to whom she gave her own name. Before her death at the stake Janneken wrote a long letter to her month-old child, which letter was preserved and incorporated in the *Martyrs' Mirror*. Parts of the letter set forth the sixteenth century Mennonite belief in the cross of the Christian. After reporting to the child how her parents had died, and entreating her not to be ashamed of her executed parents, she continued:

Hence, my young lamb for whose sake I still have and have had great sorrow, seek when you have attained your understanding this narrow way though there is sometimes much danger in it according to the flesh as we may see and read if we diligently examine and read the Scriptures, that much is said concerning the cross of Christ. And there are many in this world who are enemies of the cross, who seek to be free from it among the world and to escape it. But, my dear child if we would with Christ seek and inherit salvation we must also help bear His cross And this is the cross which He would have us bear: to follow His footsteps and to help bear His reproach, for Christ Himself says: "ye shall be persecuted, killed, and dispersed for my name's sake." Yea, He Himself went before us in this way of reproach and left us an example that we should follow His steps, for His sake all must be forsaken, father, mother, sister, brother, husband, child, yea, one's own life . . .

. . . And, my dear child, this is my request of you since you are still very little and young—I wrote this when you were but one month old—, as I am soon now to offer up my sacrifice by the help of the Lord I leave you this "That you fulfill my request, always uniting with them that fear God, and do not regard the pomp and boasting of the world, nor the great multitude whose ways lead to the abyss of hell, but look at the little flock of Israelites who have no freedom anywhere and must always flee from one land to the other as Abraham did, that you may hereafter obtain your fatherland. For if you seek your salvation it is easy to perceive which is the way that leads to life, or the way that leads into hell ."

. . . I leave you here, Oh, that it had pleased the Lord that I might have brought you up I should so gladly have done my best with respect to it, but it seems that it is not the Lord's will And though it had not come thus, and I had remained with you for a time, the Lord could still take me from you; and then too you should have to be without me,—even as it has now gone with your father and myself· that we could live together but so short a time when we were so well joined, since the Lord had so well mated us that we would not have forsaken each other for the whole world. And yet we had to leave each other here for the Lord's sake So I must also leave you here, my dearest lamb, the Lord that created and made you now takes me from you it is His holy will. I must now pass through this narrow way which the prophets and martyrs of Christ passed through and many thousands who put off the mortal clothing, who died here for Christ, and now they wait under the altar till their number shall be fulfilled, of which number your dear father is one And I am now on the point of following him . .

. I herewith commend you to the Lord and to the comforting Word of His grace, and bid you adieu once more I hope to wait for you, follow me, my dearest child.

Once more adieu, my dearest upon earth, adieu and nothing more, adieu, follow me, adieu and farewell . . (984-987)

The Brethren read in the Scriptures the words of Christ that "Ye shall be hated of all nations for my name's sake" (Matt. 24:9); "If they have persecuted me, they will also persecute you" (John 15:20); and Paul's testimony that "all that will live godly in Christ Jesus shall suffer persecution" (II Tim. 3:12). Consequently *the only way to glory is the way of the cross.* Menno wrote:

> Yea, this is and remains the only narrow and straight way and door through which we must all enter, neither can we ever desire in any other way to enter with the saints into eternal life, rest and peace .... Yes, my brethren, would you be the people and disciples of the Lord you must also bear the cross of Christ ... (*Works*, I, 192).

The world pressed the heavy cross on the shoulders of the Christians because it could not bear their testimony of the truth and their protest against its sin. Because of the separation of the Brethren from the world the wicked were convicted of their sin and persecuted them. Therefore the bearing of the cross became the earmark of the true children of God. *Only those who were truly saints excited the opposition of the world.* And only those who were born of the Spirit were willing to bear the cross. Menno expressed it thus:

> ... Forasmuch as we thus separate ourselves from them and testify by word and deed even unto death that their works are evil, therefore they are filled with the most inhuman rancor and indignation ....
> ... Our actual confession, that is to say, our separation from them is the sole reason why the blind, blood-thirsty world, frantic with rage, tyrannizes over us with so much cruelty, and why we must suffer and bear so much ....
> ... Our separation has no other foundation nor design than this, that we desired in our weakness to observe with all our heart the Word of God and keep His commandments, and that we might in real charity and in fact show to the whole world that they lie in wickedness and are strangers to God and His Word,—to the end that they may in due time awake and turn from iniquity ... (*Works*, I, 202f).

But the cross which the witness of Christ brings is no mere human arrangement; God has ordained it for the good of His saints. The cross plays a significant role in the sanctification of Christians. In his treatise on *The Cross* Menno sets forth the place of the Christian's cross in the crucifixion of the believer's affection for the things of time and sense. "The gracious God and Father," says Menno,

> has prepared and left in His house an excellent remedy therefor, namely the oppressive cross of Christ, so that we who in unbounded mercy are received through Christ Jesus to the glory of the Father, believing in pureness of heart on Christ Jesus, and [who] love Him in our weakness may through the aforesaid cross, that is, through much affliction, oppression, anxiety, apprehension, bonds, robbery, etc, forsake all the transitory delights and enjoyments of earth, die unto the world and the flesh, love God alone, [and] set our affections on things above, where Christ sitteth on the right hand of God ... (*Works*, I, 205f).
> Forasmuch as eternal Wisdom recognizes an extreme weakness, and since earthly ease, peace and prosperity have so great a tendency to ruin and undo us before our God and to render us careless, refractory, lukewarm, and drowsy, He has appointed His cross as an awakening rod for the use of all His followers... (*Works*, I, 206).

Menno believed that the number of the true saints would always remain comparatively small, for the world does not relish the heavy cross and the narrow way (I, 100; II, 75, 307). But he was not certain whether persecution unto martyrdom would always be the lot of the saints. Indeed he would have accepted gratefully a cessation of bloodshed in matters of faith, and for such cessation he pleaded eloquently (*Works,* 84-87).

A Life of Penitence

The Swiss Brethren had a tremendous emphasis on what they called *Bussfertigkeit,* a rather difficult term to translate. John Horsch suggests "penitence and contrition" as a translation. The Brethren felt that just as faith had to be in evidence, so repentance was not a matter of lip profession but had to be manifested in humility of heart, sorrow for sin, and positive holiness. Although the Brethren were in earnest about living the Christian life and seeking to keep all the commandments of the Lord, they realized that in themselves they were undone, and their consciousness of falling short of God's glory pained their consciences and made them contrite. They felt that they were needy creatures spiritually, hungering and thirsting after righteousness. Instead of comforting themselves that all men are by nature sinners they were broken in heart, sincerely sorry for their imperfection and failure. This emphasis on a life of penitence, of continually seeking for a deeper holiness of life, came to be a distinguishing characteristic of the Anabaptists, causing them to be maligned as "works-saints" and fanatics, "perfectionists." In 1538 a spokesman for the Brethren reported:

While yet in the national [Reformed] church we obtained much instruction from the writings of Luther, Zwingli, and others concerning the mass and other papal ceremonies, that they are vain Yet we recognized a great lack as regards repentance, conversion, and the true Christian life Upon these things my mind was bent I waited and hoped for a year or two, since the minister had much to say of amendment of life, of giving to the poor, loving one another, and abstaining from evil But I could not close my eyes to the fact that the doctrine which was preached and which was based on the Word of God, was not carried out No beginning was made toward true Christian living, and there was no unison in the teaching concerning things that were necessary And although the mass and the images were finally abolished, true repentance and Christian love were not in evidence Changes were made only as concerned external things . . . . Then God sent His messengers, Conrad Grebel and others, with whom I conferred about the fundamental teachings of the apostles and the Christian life and practice I found them men who had surrendered themselves to the doctrine of Christ by *Bussfertigkeit* With their assistance we established a congregation in which repentance was in evidence by newness of life in Christ.

* * *

The Anabaptists may never rate as outstanding and erudite theologians, but they did have sound principles of interpretation, as well as the determination to make the Bible alone the norm of their faith and practice. They held to Biblical doctrines of God, man, sin and salvation. They had a high view of the place and calling of the church, a view which has even today not been realized by Christendom as a whole. Their ethic of love and nonresistance is sorely needed in a world of wars and rumors of war. Upon the Mennonite Church of today rests the responsibility of holding aloft the Anabaptist torch of truth, a lamp which burns with the light of divine revelation, and a beacon which can give guidance to thousands of souls as they grope for the light of life.

Pertinent Biblical Passages

1. On the Cost of Discipleship:
    Luke 9:23f: "And He used to say to them all, If any one wishes to come after Me, let him deny himself, and let him take up his cross daily, and let him be following Me. For whoever would wish to save his life shall lose it, but whoever would lose his life for My sake,—this one shall find it." Greek. Cf. Matt. 16:24-26; Mark 8.34-38.
2. On the Test of Discipleship:
    Matt. 10:38f: "He that taketh not his cross, and followeth after Me is not worthy of Me. He that findeth his life shall lose it; and he that loseth his life for My sake shall find it."
    Luke 14:26f: "If any man come to Me, and hate not his father, and mother, and wife, and children, and brethren, and sisters, yea, and his own life also, he cannot be My disciple. And whosoever doth not bear his cross, and come after Me, cannot be My disciple."
    Luke 14:33: ". . . So likewise, whosoever he be of you that forsaketh not all that he hath, he cannot be My disciple." Read the preceding verses.
3. On Pauline Encouragements to a Suffering Discipleship:
    II Tim. 2:3: "Thou therefore endure hardness, as a good soldier of Jesus Christ."
    I Tim. 1:18: "This charge I commit unto thee, son Timothy, . . . that thou . . . mightest war a good warfare."
4. On Paul's Experiences:
    I Cor. 15:31: ". . . I die daily."
    Read what discipleship to Jesus cost Paul. II Cor. 11:23-28.

Reading References in the Confessions and Catechisms

Waldeck Catechism, Introduction, Question 5.
Roosen's Catechism, Questions 99, 100.

Study Questions

1. What did Jesus mean by the believer's cross?
2. What blessings does the bearing of one's cross bring?
3. Why does following Christ involve reproach and suffering?
4. Can one be a Christian without taking up his cross?
5. Are Christians to go out of their way to seek suffering?
6. Ought Christians become weary or discouraged if they suffer as believers?
7. Distinguish between the cross of Jesus and that of His followers.

Appendixes

Appendix I
The Schleitheim Confession

Adopted by a Swiss Brethren Conference, February 24, 1527

The Seven Articles of Schleitheim were written with Michael Sattler of Stauffen, Germany, as the chief author, it is believed Sattler was originally an officer in a Roman Catholic monastery. He early embraced the faith of the Swiss Brethren and served until his early martyrdom (May 1527) as an outstanding leader. Van Braght lists the nine charges on which Sattler was sentenced to death, together with Sattler's reply He also gives a brief account of his trial and a copy of a letter from "Brother Michael Sattler of Staufen" to "the Church of God at Horb" (1933 *Martyrs' Mirror*, 416-420) In his farewell pastoral letter Sattler wrote, "Remember our assembly, and strictly follow that which was resolved on therein," an undoubted reference to the Seven Articles and a hint as to his own leadership in the meeting.

The Schleitheim Confession was widely circulated. Ulrich Zwingli translated it into Latin and attempted to refute it already in 1527 It was in print in its original German form as early as 1533. John Calvin used a now-lost French translation of the Seven Articles in his refutation of Anabaptism published in 1544. By 1560 there was also a Dutch translation of the confession The English translation in W. J. McGlothlin's *Baptist Confessions of Faith*, Philadelphia, 1911, 3-9, was made from Zwingli's Latin translation. For an excellent survey of known manuscript copies and printed editions of the Schleitheim Confession, see Robert Friedmann's article in *The Mennonite Quarterly Review*, XVI, 2 (April, 1942), 82-87

The Seven Articles are not at all a full statement of Christian doctrine. They were written in days of fierce persecution when there was little interest in or possibility of erecting a grand system of Christian theology. Sattler wished only to set up certain pillars of truth against the unsound teachings of that period He seems in particular to be setting up a defense against the doctrines of some "false brethren" with antinomian tendencies

Along with the writings of Conrad Grebel (very limited in extent) and Pilgram Marpeck (extensive, but not of the quality of the Dutch Menno Simons) the Schleitheim Confession is of great significance for the determination of the teaching of the first Swiss Brethren.

The following is my translation of the full text of the pastoral letter, apparently from "Brother Michael Sattler," and which includes the Seven Articles of faith For the German text used, see Walther Kohler · *Bruderlich Vereinigung etzlicher Kinder Gottes sieben Artikel betreffend* . (*Flugschriften aus der ersten Jahren der Reformation*, 2 Band, 3 Heft), Leipzig, 1908, 305-316, also Heinrich Bohmer: *Urkunden zur Geschichte des Bauernkrieges und der Wiedertaufer*, Bonn, 1910, second edition, 1921; reprint, Berlin, 1933, 27-33. The translation is somewhat free in places, particularly in the citation of Bible verses where the King James Version was followed unless the German text deviated too markedly. Here is the translation, reprinted from *The Mennonite Quarterly Review*, XIX, 4 (October, 1945), 247-253·

BROTHERLY UNION OF A NUMBER OF CHILDREN OF GOD CONCERNING SEVEN ARTICLES

May joy, peace and mercy from our Father through the atonement of the blood of Christ Jesus, together with the gifts of the Spirit—who is sent from the Father to all believers for their strength and comfort and for their perseverance in all tribulation until the end, Amen—be to all those who love God, who are the children of light, and who are scattered everywhere as it has been ordained of God our Father, where they are with one mind assembled together in one God and Father of us all: Grace and peace of heart be with you all, Amen

Beloved brethren and sisters in the Lord: First and supremely we are always concerned for your consolation and the assurance of your conscience (which was previously misled)* so that you may not always remain foreigners to us and by right almost completely excluded, but that you may turn again to the true implanted members of Christ, who have been armed through patience and knowledge of themselves, and have therefore again been united with us in the strength of a godly Christian spirit and zeal for God.

It is also apparent with what cunning the devil has turned us aside, so that he might destroy and bring to an end the work of God which in mercy and grace has been partly begun in us But Christ, the true Shepherd of our souls, Who has begun this in us, will certainly direct the same and teach [us]* to His honor and our salvation, Amen

Dear brethren and sisters, we who have been assembled in the Lord at Schleitheim on the Border, make known in points and articles to all who love God that as concerns us we are of one mind to abide in the Lord as God's obedient children, [His] sons and daughters, we who have been and shall be separated from the world in everything, [and] completely at peace. To God alone be praise and glory without the contradiction of any brethren. In this we have perceived the oneness of the Spirit of our Father and of our common Christ with us For the Lord is the Lord of peace and not of quarreling, as Paul points out. That you may understand in what articles this has been formulated you should observe and note [the following].

A very great offense has been introduced by certain false brethren among us, so that some have turned aside from the faith, in the way they intend to practice and observe the freedom of the Spirit and of Christ. But such have missed the truth and to their condemnation are given over to the lasciviousness and self-indulgence of the flesh. They think faith and love may do and permit everything, and nothing will harm them nor condemn them, since they are believers.

Observe, you who are God's members in Christ Jesus, that faith in the heavenly Father through Jesus Christ does not take such form. It does not produce and result in such things as these false brethren and sisters do and teach. Guard yourselves and be warned of such people, for they do not serve our Father, but their father, the devil.

But you are not that way. For they that are Christ's have crucified the flesh with its passions and lusts. You understand me well and [know] the brethren whom we mean. Separate yourselves from them for they are perverted. Petition the Lord that they may have the knowledge which leads to repentance, and [pray] for us that we may have constancy to persevere in the way which we have espoused, for the honor of God and of Christ, His Son, Amen.

* * *

The articles which we discussed and on which we were of one mind are these: 1. Baptism, 2. The Ban [Excommunication]; 3. Breaking of Bread; 4. Separation from the Abomination, 5. Pastors in the Church; 6. The Sword; and 7. The Oath.

First. Observe concerning baptism: Baptism shall be given to all those who have learned repentance and amendment of life, and who believe truly that their sins are taken away by Christ, and to all those who walk in the resurrection of Jesus Christ, and wish to be buried with Him in death, so that they may be resurrected with Him, and to all those who with this significance request it [baptism] of us and demand it for themselves This excludes all infant baptism, the highest and chief abomination of the pope. In this you have the foundation and testimony of the apostles Matt. 28, Mark 16, Acts 2, 8, 16, 19. This we wish to hold simply, yet firmly and with assurance

Second. We are agreed as follows on the ban: The ban shall be employed with all those who have given themselves to the Lord, to walk in His commandments, and with all those who are baptized into the one body of Christ and who are called brethren or sisters, and yet who slip sometimes and fall into error and sin, being inadvertently overtaken The same shall be admonished twice in secret and the third time openly disciplined or banned according to the command of Christ. Matt. 18. But this shall be done

---

*The words in brackets are inserted by the translator to clarify the text. The words in parentheses are a part of the original text. [J C. W.]

according to the regulation of the Spirit (Matt. 5) before the breaking of bread, so that we may break and eat one bread, with one mind and in one love, and may drink of one cup

Third. In the breaking of bread we are of one mind and are agreed [as follows]: All those who wish to break one bread in remembrance of the broken body of Christ, and all who wish to drink of one drink as a remembrance of the shed blood of Christ, shall be united beforehand by baptism in one body of Christ which is the church of God and whose Head is Christ. For as Paul points out we cannot at the same time be partakers of the Lord's table and the table of devils, we cannot at the same time drink the cup of the Lord and the cup of the devil. That is, all those who have fellowship with the dead works of darkness have no part in the light Therefore all who follow the devil and the world have no part with those who are called unto God out of the world All who lie in evil have no part in the good

Therefore it is and must be [thus]: Whoever has not been called by one God to one faith, to one baptism, to one Spirit, to one body, with all the children of God's church, cannot be made [into] one bread with them, as indeed must be done if one is truly to break bread according to the command of Christ.

Fourth We are agreed [as follows] on separation: A separation shall be made from the evil and from the wickedness which the devil planted in the world, in this manner, simply that we shall not have fellowship with them [the wicked] and not run with them in the multitude of their abominations This is the way it is: Since all who do not walk in the obedience of faith, and have not united themselves with God so that they wish to do His will, are a great abomination before God, it is not possible for anything to grow or issue from them except abominable things For truly all creatures are in but two classes, good and bad, believing and unbelieving, darkness and light, the world and those who [have come] out of the world, God's temple and idols, Christ and Belial, and none can have part with the other

To us then the command of the Lord is clear when He calls upon us to be separate from the evil and thus He will be our God and we shall be His sons and daughters.

He further admonishes us to withdraw from Babylon and the earthly Egypt that we may not be partakers of the pain and suffering which the Lord will bring upon them.

From this we should learn that everything which is not united with our God and Christ cannot be other than an abomination which we should shun and flee from. By this is meant all popish and antipopish works and church services, meetings and church attendance,* drinking houses, civic affairs, the commitments [made in] unbelief and other things of that kind, which are highly regarded by the world and yet are carried on in flat contradiction to the command of God, in accordance with all the unrighteousness which is in the world From all these things we shall be separated and have no part with them for they are nothing but an abomination, and they are the cause of our being hated before our Christ Jesus, Who has set us free from the slavery of the flesh and fitted us for the service of God through the Spirit Whom He has given us

Therefore there will also unquestionably fall from us the unchristian, devilish weapons of force—such as sword, armor and the like, and all their use [either] for friends or against one's enemies—by virtue of the word of Christ, Resist not [him that is] evil.

Fifth. We are agreed as follows on pastors in the church of God: The pastor in the church of God shall, as Paul has prescribed, be one who out-and-out has a good

---

* This severe judgment on the state churches must be understood in the light of sixteenth century conditions The state clergymen were in many cases careless and carnal men All citizens in a given province were considered members of the state church because they had been made Christians ("christened") by infant baptism. Also, in 1527 Zurich had begun to use capital punishment on the Swiss Brethren, with the full approval of the state church leaders. Sattler himself was burned at the stake less than three months after the Schleitheim conference.

report of those who are outside the faith. This office shall be to read, to admonish and teach, to warn, to discipline, to ban in the church, to lead out in prayer for the advancement of all the brethren and sisters, to lift up the bread when it is to be broken, and in all things to see to the care of the body of Christ, in order that it may be built up and developed, and the mouth of the slanderer be stopped.

This one moreover shall be supported of the church which has chosen him, wherein he may be in need, so that he who serves the Gospel may live of the Gospel as the Lord has ordained. But if a pastor should do something requiring discipline, he shall not be dealt with except [on the testimony of] two or three witnesses. And when they sin they shall be disciplined before all in order that the others may fear.

But should it happen that through the cross this pastor should be banished or led to the Lord [through martyrdom] another shall be ordained in his place in the same hour so that God's little flock and people may not be destroyed.

Sixth. We are agreed as follows concerning the sword: The sword is ordained of God outside the perfection of Christ. It punishes and puts to death the wicked, and guards and protects the good. In the Law the sword was ordained for the punishment of the wicked and for their death, and the same [sword] is [now] ordained to be used by the worldly magistrates.

In the perfection of Christ, however, only the ban is used for a warning and for the excommunication of the one who has sinned, without putting the flesh to death —simply the warning and the command to sin no more.

Now it will be asked by many who do not recognize [this as] the will of Christ for us, whether a Christian may or should employ the sword against the wicked for the defence and protection of the good, or for the sake of love.

Our reply is unanimously as follows. Christ teaches and commands us to learn of Him, for He is meek and lowly in heart and so shall we find rest to our souls. Also Christ says to the heathenish woman who was taken in adultery, not that one should stone her according to the law of His Father (and yet He says, As the Father has commanded me, thus I do), but in mercy and forgiveness and warning, to sin no more. Such [an attitude] we also ought to take completely according to the rule of the ban.

Secondly, it will be asked concerning the sword, whether a Christian shall pass sentence in worldly disputes and strife such as unbelievers have with one another. This is our united answer. Christ did not wish to decide or pass judgment between brother and brother in the case of the inheritance, but refused to do so. Therefore we should do likewise.

Thirdly, it will be asked concerning the sword, Shall one be a magistrate if one should be chosen as such? The answer is as follows: They wished to make Christ king, but He fled and did not view it as the arrangement of His Father. Thus shall we do as He did, and follow Him, and so shall we not walk in darkness. For He Himself says, He who wishes to come after me, let him deny himself and take up his cross and follow me. Also, He Himself forbids the [employment of] the force of the sword saying, The worldly princes lord it over them, etc., but not so shall it be with you. Further, Paul says, Whom God did foreknow He also did predestinate to be conformed to the image of His Son, etc. Also Peter says, Christ has suffered (not ruled) and left us an example, that ye should follow His steps.

Finally it will be observed that it is not appropriate for a Christian to serve as a magistrate because of these points: The government magistracy is according to the flesh, but the Christians' is according to the Spirit; their houses and dwelling remain in this world, but the Christians' are in heaven; their citizenship is in this world, but the Christians' citizenship is in heaven; the weapons of their conflict and war are carnal and against the flesh only, but the Christians' weapons are spiritual, against the fortification of the devil. The worldlings are armed with steel and iron, but the Christians are armed with the armor of God, with truth, righteousness, peace, faith, salvation and the Word of God. In brief, as is the mind of Christ toward us, so shall the mind of the members of the body of Christ be through Him in all things, that there may be no schism in the body through which it would be destroyed. For every kingdom divided against itself will be destroyed. Now since Christ is as it is written of Him, His members must also be the same, that His body may remain complete and united to its own advancement and upbuilding.

Seventh. We are agreed as follows concerning the oath· The oath is a confirmation among those who are quarreling or making promises. In the Law it is commanded to be performed in God's Name, but only in truth, not falsely. Christ, who teaches the perfection of the Law, prohibits all swearing to His [followers], whether true or false—neither by heaven, nor by the earth, nor by Jerusalem, nor by our head—and that for the reason which He shortly thereafter gives, For you are not able to make one hair white or black. So you see it is for this reason that all swearing is forbidden: we cannot fulfill that which we promise when we swear, for we cannot change [even] the very least thing on us.

Now there are some who do not give credence to the simple command of God, but object with this question: Well now, did not God swear to Abraham by Himself (since He was God) when He promised him that He would be with him and that He would be his God if he would keep His commandments,—why then should I not also swear when I promise to someone? Answer: Hear what the Scripture says· God, since He wished more abundantly to show unto the heirs the immutability of His counsel, inserted an oath, that by two immutable things (in which it is impossible for God to lie) we might have a strong consolation. Observe the meaning of this Scripture: What God forbids you to do, He has power to do, for every thing is possible for Him God swore an oath to Abraham, says the Scripture, so that He might show that His counsel is immutable. That is, no one can withstand nor thwart His will; therefore He can keep His oath. But we can do nothing, as is said above by Christ, to keep or perform [our oaths]: therefore we shall not swear at all [*nichts schweren*].

Then others further say as follows: It is not forbidden of God to swear in the New Testament, when it is actually commanded in the Old, but it is forbidden only to swear by heaven, earth, Jerusalem and our head. Answer: Hear the Scripture, He who swears by heaven swears by God's throne and by Him who sitteth thereon. Observe: it is forbidden to swear by heaven, which is only the throne of God· how much more is it forbidden [to swear] by God Himself! Ye fools and blind, which is greater, the throne or Him that sitteth thereon?

Further some say, Because evil is now [in the world, and] because man needs God for [the establishment of] the truth, so did the apostles Peter and Paul also swear. Answer: Peter and Paul only testify of that which God promised to Abraham with the oath. They themselves promise nothing, as the example indicates clearly. Testifying and swearing are two different things For when a person swears he is in the first place promising future things, as Christ was promised to Abraham Whom we a long time afterwards received. But when a person bears testimony he is testifying about the present, whether it is good or evil, as Simeon spoke to Mary about Christ and testified, Behold this [child] is set for the fall and rising of many in Israel, and for a sign which shall be spoken against.

Christ also taught us along the same line when He said, Let your communication be Yea, yea; Nay, nay; for whatsoever is more than these cometh of evil. He says, Your speech or word shall be yea and nay. [However] when one does not wish to understand, he remains closed to the meaning. Christ is simply Yea and Nay, and all those who seek Him simply will understand His Word. Amen.

* * *

Dear brethren and sisters in the Lord: These are the articles of certain brethren who had heretofore been in error and who had failed to agree in the true understanding, so that many weaker consciences were perplexed, causing the Name of God to be greatly slandered Therefore there has been a great need for us to become of one mind in the Lord, which has come to pass. To God be praise and glory!

Now since you have so well understood the will of God which has been made known by us, it will be necessary for you to achieve perseveringly, without interruption, the known will of God. For you know well what the servant who sinned knowingly heard as his recompense.

Everything which you have unwittingly done and confessed as evil doing is forgiven you through the believing prayer which is offered by us in our meeting for all our shortcomings and guilt [This state is yours] through the gracious forgiveness of God and through the blood of Jesus Christ. Amen

Keep watch on all who do not walk according to the simplicity of the divine truth which is stated in this letter from [the decisions of] our meeting, so that everyone among us will be governed by the rule of the ban and henceforth the entry of false brethren and sisters among us may be prevented.

Eliminate from you that which is evil and the Lord will be your God and you will be His sons and daughters.

Dear brethren, keep in mind what Paul admonishes Timothy when he says, The grace of God that bringeth salvation hath appeared to all men, teaching us that, denying ungodliness and worldly lusts, we should live soberly, righteously, and godly, in this present world, looking for that blessed hope, and the glorious appearing of the great God and our Saviour Jesus Christ, Who gave Himself for us, that He might redeem us from all iniquity, and purify unto Himself a people of His own, zealous of good works. Think on this and exercise yourselves therein and the God of peace will be with you.

May the Name of God be hallowed eternally and highly praised, Amen May the Lord give you His peace, Amen.

The Acts of Schleitheim on the Border [Canton Schaffhausen, Switzerland], on Matthias' [Day],* Anno MDXXVII.

* February 24

Appendix II
The Dordrecht Confession

Adopted by a Dutch Mennonite Conference April 21, 1632

Mennonites are not a creedal church. No human system of doctrine stands between them and the Word of God It is to the Scriptures that they are bound. Yet it must also be stated that Mennonites actually hold to rather well defined doctrinal views Many confessions of faith were produced beginning with the Schleitheim articles of 1527. The best of these confessions, although they all resemble each other rather closely, is undoubtedly the one adopted at Dordrecht, Holland, in 1632

In the days of Menno Simons, 1496-1561, the Mennonites of the Netherlands were one brotherhood. But beginning in 1567 a number of schisms occurred Bishop Dirck Philips, 1504-68, the great co-worker of Menno, affiliated himself with the Flemish Mennonites, while Bishop Peter Janz Twisck, 1565-1636, who was married to Menno's granddaughter, adhered to the Frisians Hendrik Roosevelt, a Flemish bishop, and others, labored unsuccessfully for union.

About 1630 another series of efforts were made to unite various Mennonite groups The "Olive Branch" confession of 1627 (printed on pages 27-33 of the 1938 *Martyrs' Mirror*) was an effort to provide a basis for union between the Friesian and Flemish churches The Jan Cents' Confession of 1630 (pages 33-38, *Martyrs' Mirror*) was subscribed to by fourteen Friesian and High German ministers

The Dordrecht Confession of 1632 was written in the first draft by Adrian Cornelis, bishop of the Flemish Mennonite Church in Dordrecht About the middle of April 1632 a number of Mennonite ministers assembled in Dordrecht in spite of the protest of the Reformed clergy against "this extraordinary gathering of Anabaptists from all provinces." The conference was successful in forming a union, a united brotherhood At the close of the sessions the ministers extended to each other the right hand of fellowship, greeted each other with the holy kiss, and observed the Lord's Supper together Of the fifty-one Flemish and Frisian ministers who signed this confession of faith, two were of Crefeld, Germany and two represented "the upper country" (central or south Germany).

The Alsatian Mennonites adopted the Dordrecht Confession in 1660, when thirteen ministers and deacons subscribed to it The Palatine and German Mennonite Churches also subsequently adopted it. However, the Swiss Mennonite churches never subscribed to it In 1725 the Pennsylvania Mennonites, mostly Swiss, of what are now the Franconia and Lancaster Conferences, adopted the Dordrecht Confession, undoubtedly through the influence of the Dutch Mennonites of Germantown, near Philadelphia Sixteen ministers signed a statement of adoption A number of the more conservative Mennonite bodies of America, including the *Mennonite Church,* now recognize the Dordrecht Confession as the official summary of their doctrinal beliefs Historically this confession of faith was used as a basis of instruction to classes of young people who were being prepared for baptism and church membership. At the present time in the *Mennonite Church* the chief significance of the Dordrecht Confession is undoubtedly its value as a symbol of the Mennonite heritage of faith and way of life.

The text of the Dordrecht Confession printed below is basically that which is now in circulation in the Mennonite Church in America It is apparently a translation of a German translation of the Dutch original In Van Braght's *Bloedigh Tooneel* of 1660 the Dordrecht Confession is printed in the unpaginated introduction. The names of the signers given below were taken from the 1660 edition For an English translation made directly from the original Dutch, see the 1938 edition of the *Martyr's Mirror,* pages 38-44 The *Martyr's Mirror* text of the Dordrecht Confession was used to correct the text which is in common circulation among American Mennonites The corrections were merely a matter of wording, not a change in sense

The Alsatian Mennonite statement which follows the Dordrecht Confession was corrected from the *Christliche Glaubens-Bekentnos* . , Amsterdam, 1664, pages 35, 36.

Article I
Of God and the Creation of all Things

Whereas it is declared, that "without faith it is impossible to please God" (Heb. 11:6), and that "he that cometh to God must believe that He is, and that He is a rewarder of them that diligently seek Him," therefore we confess with the mouth, and believe with the heart, together with all the pious, according to the Holy Scriptures, that there is one eternal, almighty, and incomprehensible God, Father, Son, and the Holy Ghost, and none more and none other, before whom no God existed, neither will exist after Him. For from Him, through Him, and in Him are all things. To Him be blessing, praise, and honor, for ever and ever. Gen. 17:1; Deut. 6.4; Isaiah 46:9; I John 5:7.

In this one God, who "worketh all in all," we believe Him we confess as the creator of all things, visible and invisible; who in six days created and prepared "heaven and earth, and the sea, and all things that are therein" And we further believe, that this God still governs and preserves the same, together with all His works, through His wisdom, His might, and the "word of His power." Gen. 5:1, 2; Acts 14:15; I Cor. 12.6; Heb 1 3.

When He had finished His works and, according to His good pleasure, had ordained and prepared each of them, so that they were right and good according to their nature, being and quality, He created the first man, Adam, the father of all of us, gave him a body formed "of the dust of the ground, and breathed into his nostrils the breath of life," so that he 'became a living soul," created by God "in His own image and likeness," in "righteousness and true holiness" unto eternal life He also gave him a place above all other creatures and endowed him with many high and excellent gifts, put him into the garden of Eden, and gave him a commandment and an interdiction. Thereupon He took a rib from the said Adam, made a woman out of it, brought her to him, and gave her to him as a helpmate and housewife Consequently He has caused, that from this first man, Adam, all men who "dwell on the face of the earth," have been begotten and have descended Gen 1.27; 2.7, 15-17, 22; 5.1; Acts 17.26.

Article II
Of the Fall of Man

We believe and confess, that, according to the purport of the Holy Scriptures, our first parents, Adam and Eve, did not long remain in the happy state in which they were created, but did, after being seduced by the deceit and subtilty of the serpent, and envy of the devil, violate the high command of God, and became disobedient to their Creator; through which disobedience "sin entered into the world, and death by sin," so that "death passed upon all men, for that all have sinned," and thereby incurred the wrath of God and condemnation For which reason our first parents were, by God, driven out of Paradise, to cultivate the earth, to maintain themselves thereon in sorrow, and to "eat their bread in the sweat of their face," until they "returned to the ground, from which they were taken." And that they did, therefore, through this one sin, so far apostatize, depart, and estrange themselves from God, that they could neither help themselves, nor be helped by any of their descendants, nor by angels, nor by any other creature in heaven or on earth, nor be redeemed, or reconciled to God; but would have had to be lost forever, had not God, who pitied His creatures, in mercy, interposed in their behalf and made provision for their restoration. Gen. 3:6, 23, Rom. 5:12-19; Ps. 47:8, 9; Rev. 5:3; John 3:16.

Article III
Of the Restoration of Man through the Promise of the Coming of Christ

Regarding the restoration of our first parents and their descendants, we believe and confess: That God, not withstanding their fall, transgression and sin, and although they had no power to help themselves, He was nevertheless not willing that they should

THE DORDRECHT CONFESSION 79

be cast off entirely, or be eternally lost; but again called them unto Him, comforted them, and showed them that there were yet means with Him for their reconciliation; namely, the immaculate Lamb, the Son of God; who "was fore-ordained" to this purpose "before the foundation of the world," and who was promised to them and all their descendants, while they (our first parents) were yet in paradise, for their comfort, redemption, and salvation, yea, who was given to them thenceforward, through faith, as their own; after which all the pious patriarchs, to whom this promise was often renewed, longed and searched, beholding it through faith at a distance, and expecting its fulfillment—expecting that He (the Son of God), would, at His coming, again redeem and deliver the fallen race of man from their sins, their guilt, and unrighteousness John 1:29, 11 27, I Pet. 1.18, 19, Gen. 3 15; I John 2.1, 2, 3.8, Gal 4.4, 5.

Article IV

OF THE ADVENT OF CHRIST INTO THIS WORLD, AND THE REASON OF HIS COMING

We believe and confess further: That "when the fulness of the time was come," after which all the pious patriarchs so ardently longed, and which they so anxiously awaited—the previously promised Messiah, Redeemer, and Saviour, proceeded from God, being sent by Him, and according to the prediction of the prophets and the testimony of the evangelists, came into the world, yea, into the flesh—, so that the Word itself thus became flesh and man, and that He was conceived by the Virgin Mary (who was espoused to a man named Joseph, of the house of David), and that she bare Him as her first-born son at Bethlehem, "wrapped Him in swaddling clothes, and laid Him in a manger." John 4·25, 16 28, I Tim. 3 16; Matt. 1.21, John 1·14, Luke 2.7.

Further we believe and confess, that this is the same One, "whose goings forth have been from of old, from everlasting," who has "neither beginning of days, nor end of life" Of whom it is testified, that He is "Alpha and Omega, the beginning and the end, the first and the last." That this is also He—and none other—who was chosen, promised, and sent; who came into the world, and who is God's only, first, and proper Son, who was before John the Baptist, before Abraham, before the world; yea, who was David's Lord, and who was God of the "whole earth," "the first-born of every creature", who was sent into the world, and Himself delivered up the body prepared for Him, as "an offering and a sacrifice to God for a sweet smelling savour," yea, for the comfort, redemption, and salvation of all—of the human race. Micah 5 2; Heb. 7 3; Rev. 1:8; John 3·16; Rom. 8 32, Col. 1.15; Heb. 10·5.

But how, or in what manner, this worthy body was prepared, or how the Word became flesh, and He Himself man, we content ourselves with the declaration which the worthy evangelists have given and left in their description thereof, according to which we confess with all the saints, that He is the Son of the living God, in whom exist all our hope, comfort, redemption, and salvation, and which we are to seek in no one else. Luke 1:31-35; John 20 31.

Further, we believe and confess by authority of scripture, that when He had ended His course, and "finished" the work for which He was sent into the world, He was, by the providence of God, delivered into the hands of the unrighteous, suffered under the judge, Pontius Pilate, was crucified, died, was buried, rose again from the dead on the third day, and ascended into heaven, where He now sits at the right hand of the Majesty of God on high; from whence He will come again to judge the living and dead Luke 23·1, 52, 53, 24.5, 6, 51.

Thus we believe the Son of God died—"tasted death for every man," shed His precious blood, and thereby bruised the head of the serpent, destroyed the works of the devil, "blotted out the hand-writing," and purchased redemption for the whole human race; and thus He became the source of eternal salvation to all who from the time of Adam to the end of the world, shall have believed in Him, and obeyed Him. Gen. 3 15, I John 3 8; Col 2:14, Rom. 5·18.

Article V

Of the Law of Christ, which is the Holy Gospel, or the New Testament

We also believe and confess, that Christ, before His ascension, established and instituted His New Testament and left it to His followers, to be and remain an everlasting testament, which He confirmed and sealed with His own precious blood; and which He has so highly commended to them, that neither men or angels may change it, neither take therefrom nor add thereto. Jer. 31:31, Heb. 9:15-17; Matt. 26:28; Gal. 1:8; I Tim. 6:3-5; Rev. 22:18, 19; Matt. 5:18; Luke 21:33.

And that He has caused this Testament (in which the whole counsel and will of His heavenly Father, so far as these are necessary to the salvation of man, are comprehended), to be proclaimed, in His name, through His beloved apostles, messengers, and servants (whom He chose and sent into all the world for this purpose)—to all nations, people and tongues; these apostles preaching repentance and remission of sins; and that He, in said Testament, caused it to be declared, that all men without distinction, if they are obedient, through faith, follow, fulfill and live according to the precepts of the same, are His children and rightful heirs; having thus excluded none from the precious inheritance of eternal salvation, except the unbelieving and disobedient, the headstrong and unconverted, who despise such salvation; and thus by their own actions incur guilt by refusing the same, and "judge themselves unworthy of everlasting life." Mark 16 15, Luke 24 46, 47; Rom. 8 17; Acts 13 46.

Article VI

Of Repentance and Amendment of Life

We believe and confess, that, as the "imagination of man's heart is evil from his youth," and consequently inclined to all unrighteousness, sin, and wickedness, that, therefore, the first doctrine of the precious New Testament of the Son of God is, Repentance and amendment of life. Gen 8·21, Mark 1·15

Therefore those who have ears to hear, and hearts to understand, must "bring forth fruits meet for repentance," amend their lives, believe the Gospel, "depart from evil and do good," desist from wrong and cease from sinning, "put off the old man with his deeds and put on the new man," which after God is created in "righteousness and true holiness." For neither *Baptism, Supper, nor church-fellowship,* nor any other external ceremony, can, without faith, the new birth, and a change or renewal of life, help, or qualify us, that we may please God, or receive any consolation or promise of salvation from Him. Luke 3 8; Eph. 4:22-24, Col. 3:9, 10.

But on the contrary, we must go to God "with a sincere heart in full assurance of faith," and believe in Jesus Christ, as the Scriptures speak and testify of Him. Through which faith we obtain the pardon of our sins, become sanctified, justified, and children of God; yea, partakers of His mind, nature and image, as we are born again of God through His incorruptible seed from above. Heb. 10:21, 22; John 7.38; II Pet. 1 4.

Article VII

Of Holy Baptism

Regarding baptism, we confess that all penitent believers, who through faith, the new birth and renewal of the Holy Ghost, have become united with God, and whose names are recorded in heaven, must, on such Scriptural confession of their faith, and renewal of life, according to the command and doctrine of Christ, and the example and custom of the apostles, be baptized with water in the ever adorable name of the Father, and of the Son, and of the Holy Ghost, to the burying of their sins, and thus to become incorporated into the communion of the saints; whereupon they must learn to observe all things whatsoever the Son of God taught, left on record, and commanded His followers to do. Matt. 3 15, 28·19, 20; Mark 16·15, 16; Acts 2.38; 8·12, 38, 9·18, 10.47, 16 33, Rom. 6 3, 4; Col. 2.12.

Article VIII
OF THE CHURCH OF CHRIST

We believe in and confess a visible Church of God, consisting of those, who, as before remarked, have truly repented, and rightly believed, who are rightly baptized, united with God in heaven, and incorporated into the communion of the saints on earth I Cor 12:13

And these, we confess, are a "chosen generation, a royal priesthood, an holy nation," who have the testimony that they are the "bride" of Christ; yea, that they are children and heirs of eternal life—a "habitation of God through the Spirit," built on the foundation of the apostles and prophets, of which "Christ Himself is the chief cornerstone"—the foundation on which His church is built. John 3.29; Matt. 16 18; Eph. 2·19-21, Tit 3 7, I Pet. 1:18, 19; 2.9.

This church of the living God, which He has purchased and redeemed through His own precious blood, and with which He will be—according to His own promise—for her comfort and protection, "always, even unto the end of the world," yea, will dwell and walk with her, and preserve her, that no "winds" nor "floods," yea, not even the "gates of hell shall prevail against her"—may be known by her evangelical faith, doctrine, love, and godly conversation; also by her pure walk and practice, and her observance of the true ordinances of Christ, which He has strictly enjoined on His followers Matt 7 25, 16·18; 28.20, II Cor. 6.16

Article IX
OF THE ELECTION, AND OFFICES OF TEACHERS, DEACONS, AND DEACONESSES, IN THE CHURCH

Regarding the offices, and election of persons to the same, in the church, we believe and confess: That, as the church cannot exist and prosper, nor continue in its structure, without offices and regulations, that therefore the Lord Jesus has Himself (as a father in his house), appointed and prescribed His offices and ordinances, and has given commandments concerning the same, as to how each one should walk therein, give heed to His own work and calling, and do it as it becomes Him to do. Eph 4.11, 12

For He Himself, as the faithful and great Shepherd, and Bishop of our souls, was sent into the world, not to wound, to break, or destroy the souls of men, but to heal them; to seek that which is lost, and to pull down the hedges and partition wall, so as to make out of many one, thus collecting out of Jews and heathen, yea, out of all nations, a church in His name; for which (so that no one might go astray or be lost) He laid down His own life, and thus procured for them salvation, made them free and redeemed them, to which blessing no one could help them, or be of service in obtaining it I Pet. 2 25, Matt. 18:11, Eph. 2·13, 14, John 10 9, 11, 15

And that He, besides this, left His church before His departure, provided with faithful ministers, apostles, evangelists, pastors, and teachers, whom He had chosen by prayer and supplication through the Holy Spirit, so that they might govern the church, feed His flock, watch over, maintain, and care for the same yea, do all things as He left them an example, taught them, and commanded them to do, and likewise to teach the church to observe all things whatsoever He commanded them Eph. 4 11, 12, Luke 6·12, 13, 10 1, Matt. 28 20.

Also that the apostles were afterwards, as faithful followers of Christ and leaders of the church, diligent in these matters, namely, in choosing through prayer and supplication to God, brethren who were to provide all the churches in the cities and circuits, with bishops, pastors, and leaders, and to ordain to these offices such men as took "heed unto themselves and unto the doctrine," and also unto the flock; who were sound in the faith, pious in their life and conversation, and who had—as well within the church as "without"—a good reputation and a good report; so that they might be a light and example in all godliness and good works; might worthily administer the Lord's ordinances—baptism and supper—and that they (the brethren sent by the apostles) might also, at all places, where such were to be had, appoint faithful men as elders, who were able to teach others, confirm them in the name of the Lord "with the laying on of hands," and who (the elders) were to take care of all things of which the church stood in need, so that they, as faithful servants, might well "occupy" their Lord's money, gain thereby, and thus "save themselves and those who hear them" I Tim. 3:1; 4 14-16, Acts 1 23, 24; Tit. 1:5; Luke 19.13.

That they should also take good care (particularly each one of the charge over which he had the oversight), that all the circuits should be well provided with deacons, who should have the care and oversight of the poor, and who were to receive gifts and alms, and again faithfully to distribute them among the poor saints who were in need, and this is in all honesty, as is becoming. Acts 6 3-6.

Also that honorable old widows should be chosen as deaconesses, who, besides the deacons are to visit, comfort, and take care of the poor, the weak, afflicted, and the needy, as also to visit, comfort, and take care of widows and orphans; and further to assist in taking care of any matters in the church that properly come within their sphere, according to their ability. I Tim. 5 9, 10; Rom. 16 1, 2.

And as it further regards the deacons, that they (particularly if they are fit persons, and chosen and ordained thereto by the church), may also in aid and relief of the bishops, exhort the church (being, as already remarked, chosen thereto), and thus assist in word and doctrine; so that each one may serve the other from love, with the gift which he has received from the Lord, so that through the common service and assistance of each member, according to his ability, the body of Christ may be edified, and the Lord's vineyard and church be preserved in its growth and structure. II Tim. 2.2.

Article X

OF THE LORD'S SUPPER

We also believe in and observe the breaking of bread, or the Lord's Supper, as the Lord Jesus instituted the same (with bread and wine) before His sufferings, and also observed and ate it with the apostles, and also commanded it to be observed to His remembrance, as also the apostles subsequently taught and observed the same in the church, and commanded it to be observed by believers in commemoration of the death and sufferings of the Lord—the breaking of His worthy body and the shedding of His precious blood—for the whole human race So is the observance of this sacrament also to remind us of the benefit of the said death and sufferings of Christ, namely, the redemption and eternal salvation which He purchased thereby, and the great love thus shown to sinful man; whereby we are earnestly exhorted also to love one another —to love our neighbor—to forgive and absolve him—even as Christ has done unto us—and also to endeavor to maintain and keep alive the union and communion which we have with God, and amongst one another; which is thus shown and represented to us by the aforesaid breaking of bread. Matt. 26 26; Mark 14:22; Luke 22:19, 20; Acts 2·42, 46; I Cor. 10·16; 11·23-26.

Article XI

OF THE WASHING OF THE SAINTS' FEET

We also confess a washing of the feet of the saints, as the Lord Jesus did not only institute and command the same, but did also Himself wash the feet of the apostles, although He was their Lord and Master; thereby giving an example that they also should wash one another's feet, and thus do to one another as He did to them; which they also afterwards taught believers to observe, and all this is a sign of true humiliation; but yet more particularly as a sign to remind us of the true washing—the washing and purification of the soul in the blood of Christ. John 13.4-17; I Tim. 5:9, 10.

Article XII

OF MATRIMONY

We also confess that there is in the church of God an "honorable" state of matrimony between two believers of the different sexes, as God first instituted the same in

THE DORDRECHT CONFESSION

paradise between Adam and Eve, and as the Lord Jesus reformed it by removing all abuses which had crept into it, and restoring it to its first order. Gen. 1:27; 2:18, 21-24.

In this manner the Apostle Paul also taught and permitted matrimony in the church, leaving it to each one's own choice to enter into matrimony with any person who would unite with him in such state, provided that it was done "in the Lord," according to the primitive order; the words "in the Lord," to be understood, according to our opinion, that just as the patriarchs had to marry amongst their own kindred or generation, so there is also no other liberty allowed to believers under the New Testament dispensation, than to marry among the "chosen generation," or the spiritual kindred of Christ, that is, to such—and none others—as are already, previous to their marriage, united to the church in heart and soul, have received the same baptism, belong to the same church, are of the same faith and doctrine, and lead the same course of life, with themselves. I Cor. 7:39; 9:5, Gen. 24 4; 28 6, 7; Num. 36.6-9.

Such are then, as already remarked, united by God and the church according to the primitive order, and this is then called, "Marrying in the Lord." I Cor. 7.39.

Article XIII
Of the Office of Civil Government

We also believe and confess, that God has instituted civil government, for the punishment of the wicked and the protection of the pious; and also further, for the purpose of governing the world, countries and cities; and also to preserve its subjects in good order and under good regulations. Wherefore we are not permitted to despise, revile, or resist the same, but are to acknowledge it as a minister of God and be subject and obedient to it, in all things that do not militate against the law, will, and commandments of God, yea, "to be ready to every good work," also faithfully to pay it custom, tax, and tribute; thus giving it what is its due, as Jesus Christ taught, did Himself, and commanded His followers to do. That we are also to pray to the Lord earnestly for the government and its welfare, and in behalf of our country, so that we may live under its protection, maintain ourselves, and "lead a quiet and peaceable life in all godliness and honesty." And further, that the Lord would recompense them (our rulers), here and in eternity, for all the benefits, liberties, and favors which we enjoy under their laudable administration. Rom. 13:1-7; Titus 3 1, 2; I Pet. 2.17; Matt. 17:27; 22:20, 21; I Tim. 2·1, 2.

Article XIV
Of Defense by Force

Regarding revenge, whereby we resist our enemies with the sword, we believe and confess that the Lord Jesus has forbidden His disciples and followers all revenge and resistance, and has thereby commanded them not to "return evil for evil, nor railing for railing," but to "put up the sword into the sheath," or, as the prophet foretold, "beat them into ploughshares." Matt. 5 39, 44; Rom 12:14, I Pet. 3:9; Isa. 2:4; Micah 4 3.

From this we see, that, according to the example, life, and doctrine of Christ, we are not to do wrong, or cause offense or vexation to anyone, but to seek the welfare and salvation of all men; also, if necessity should require it, to flee, for the Lord's sake, from one city or country to another, and suffer the "spoiling of our goods," rather than give occasion of offense to anyone; and if we are struck in our "right cheek, rather to turn the other also," than revenge ourselves, or return the blow. Matt. 5.39; 10 23; Rom 12 19.

And that we are, besides this, also to pray for our enemies, comfort and feed them, when they are hungry or thirsty, and thus by well-doing convince them and overcome the evil with good Rom. 12 20, 21.

Finally, that we are to do good in all respects, "commending ourselves to every man's conscience in the sight of God," and according to the law of Christ, do nothing to others that we would not wish them to do unto us. II Cor. 4:2; Matt 7:12; Luke 6:31

Article XV
OF THE SWEARING OF OATHS

Regarding the swearing of oaths, we believe and confess that the Lord Jesus has dissuaded His followers from and forbidden them the same; that is, that He commanded them to "swear not at all," but that their "Yea" should be "yea," and their "Nay, nay." From which we understand that all oaths, high and low, are forbidden; and that instead of them we are to confirm all our promises and covenants, declarations and testimonies of all matters, merely with "Yea that is yea," and "Nay that is nay," and that we are to perform and fulfill at all times, and in all things, to every one, every promise and obligation to which we thus affirm, as faithfully as if we had confirmed it by the most solemn oath. And if we thus do, we have the confidence that no one—not even government itself—will have just cause to require more of us. Matt. 5:34-37; Jas. 5:12; II Cor. 1:17.

Article XVI
OF THE ECCLESIASTICAL BAN OR EXCOMMUNICATION FROM THE CHURCH

We also believe in and acknowledge the ban, or excommunication, a separation or spiritual correction by the church, for the amendment, and not for the destruction, of offenders; so that what is pure may be separated from that which is impure. That is, if a person, after having been enlightened, and received the knowledge of the truth, and has been received into the communion of the saints, does willfully, or out of presumption, sin against God, or commit some other "sin unto death," thereby falling into such unfruitful works of darkness, that he becomes separated from God, and is debarred from His kingdom—that such an one—when his works are become manifest, and sufficiently known to the church—cannot remain in the "congregation of the righteous;" but must, as an offensive member and open sinner, be excluded from the church, "rebuked before all," and "purged out as a leaven," and thus remain until his amendment, as an example and warning to others, and also that the church may be kept pure from such "spots" and "blemishes;" so that not for the want of this, the name of the Lord be blasphemed, the church dishonored, and a stumblingblock thrown in the way of those "without," and finally, that the offender may not be condemned with the world, but that he may again be convinced of the error of his ways, and brought to repentance and amendment of life. Isa. 59:2; I Cor. 5 5, 6, 12; I Tim. 5:20; II Cor. 13:10.

Regarding the brotherly admonition, as also the instruction of the erring, we are to "give all diligence" to watch over them, and exhort them in all meekness to the amendment of their ways (Jas. 5:19, 20); and in case any should remain obstinate and unconverted, to reprove them as the case may require In short, the church must "put away from among herself him that is wicked," whether it be in doctrine or life.

Article XVII
OF THE SHUNNING OF THOSE WHO ARE EXPELLED

As regards the withdrawing from, or the shunning of, those who are expelled, we believe and confess, that if any one, whether it be through a wicked life or perverse doctrine—is so far fallen as to be separated from God, and consequently rebuked by, and expelled from, the church, he must also, according to the doctrine of Christ and His apostles, be shunned and avoided by all the members of the church (particularly by those to whom his misdeeds are known), whether it be in eating or drinking, or other such like social matters. In short, that we are to have nothing to do with him; so that we may not become defiled by intercourse with him, and partakers of his sins, but that he may be made ashamed, be affected in his mind, convinced in his conscience, and thereby induced to amend his ways. I Cor. 5:9-11; Rom. 16:17; II Thess. 3 14; Tit. 3:10, 11.

That nevertheless, as well in shunning as in reproving such offender, such moderation and Christian discretion be used, that such shunning and reproof may not be conducive to his ruin, but be serviceable to his amendment. For should he be in need, hungry, thirsty, naked, sick or visited by some other affliction, we are in duty bound, according to the doctrine and practice of Christ and His apostles, to render him aid and assistance, as necessity may require, otherwise the shunning of him might be rather conducive to his ruin than to his amendment. I Thess. 5:14.

Therefore we must not treat such offenders as enemies, but exhort them as brethren, in order thereby to bring them to a knowledge of their sins and to repentance; so that they may again become reconciled to God and the church, and be received and admitted into the same—thus exercising love towards them, as is becoming. II Thess. 3:15

Article XVIII
OF THE RESURRECTION OF THE DEAD AND THE LAST JUDGMENT

Regarding the resurrection of the dead, we confess with the mouth, and believe with the heart, that according to the Scriptures all men who shall have died or "fallen asleep," will, through the incomprehensible power of God, at the day of judgment, be "raised up" and made alive; and that these, together with all those who then remain alive, and who shall be "changed in a moment, in the twinkling of an eye, at the last trump," shall "appear before the judgment seat of Christ," where the good shall be separated from the evil, and where "every one shall receive the things done in his body, according to that he hath done, whether it be good or bad"; and that the good or pious shall then further, as the blessed of their Father, be received by Christ into eternal life, where they shall receive that joy which "eye hath not seen, nor ear heard, nor hath entered into the heart of man." Yea, where they shall reign and triumph with Christ for ever and ever Matt. 22 30-32; 25:31, Dan. 12:2; Job 19 25, 26; John 5:28, 29; I Cor. 15 51, 52; I Thess. 4:13.

And that, on the contrary, the wicked or impious, shall, as the accursed of God, be cast into "outer darkness," yea, into eternal, hellish torments, "where their worm dieth not, and the fire is not quenched," and where—according to Holy Scripture—they can expect no comfort nor redemption throughout eternity. Isa. 66:24; Matt. 25:46; Mark 9 46, Rev. 14:10, 11.

May the Lord through His grace make us all fit and worthy, that no such calamity may befall any of us; but that we may be diligent, and so take heed to ourselves, that we may be found of Him in peace, without spot, and blameless. Amen

* * *

Now these are, as before mentioned, the chief articles of our general Christian Faith, which we everywhere teach in our congregations and families, and according to which we profess to live; and which, according to our convictions, contain the only true Christian Faith, which the apostles in their time believed and taught; yea, which they testified to by their lives and confirmed by their deaths, in which we will also, according to our weakness, gladly abide, live, and die, that at last, together with the apostles and all the pious we may obtain the salvation of our souls through the grace of God

Thus were the foregoing articles of faith adopted and concluded by our united churches in the city of Dordrecht, in Holland, on the 21st day of April, in the year of our Lord 1632, and signed by the following ministers and teachers:

DORDRECHT
Isaac de Koning, and in behalf of our minister, Jan Jacobs
Hans Cobryssz
Iacuis Terwen
Claes Dircksz
Mels Gysbertsz
Adriaen Cornelissz

MIDDELBURGH
Bastiaen Willemsen
Ian Winckelmans

VLISSINGEN
Oillaert Willeborts
Iacob Pennen
Lieven Marynesz

AMSTERDAM
Tobias Govertsz
Pieter Iantz Moyer
Abraham Dircksz
David ter Haer
Pieter Iantz van Singel

HAERLEM
　Ian Doom
　Pieter Gryspeert
　Dirck Woutersz Kolenkamp
　Pieter Ioosten
BOMMEL
　Willem Iansz van Exselt
　Gisbert Spiering
ROTTERDAM
　Balten Centen Schoenmaker
　M. Michielsz
　Israel van Halmael
　Hendrick Dircksz Apeldoren
　Andries Lucken, de jonge [Jr.]
FROM THE UPPER PART OF THE COUNTRY
　Peeter van Borsel
　Antony Hansz
KREVELT dito
　Harman op den Graff
　Weylm Kreynen
ZEELANDT
　Cornelis de Moir
　Isaac Claessz
SCHIEDAM
　Cornelis Bom
　Lambrecht Paeldinck
LEYDEN
　Mr. C de Kroninck
　Ian Weyns
BLOCKZIEL
　Claes Claessen
　Pieter Peters
ZIERICZEE
　Anthonis Cornelissz
　Pieter Iansz Timmerman
UTRECHT
　Herman Segers
　Ian Hendricksen Hooghvelt
　Daniel Horens
　Abraham Spronck
　Willem van Broeckhuysen
GORCUM
　Iacob van der Heyde Sebrechts
　Ian Iansz V. K.
AERNHEM
　Cornelis Iansz
　Dirck Rendersen

Besides this confession being adopted by so many churches, and signed by their ministers, all the churches in Alsace, in the Palatinate, and in Germany afterwards adopted it unanimously Wherefore it was translated from the Holland into the languages of these countries—into French and German—for the use of the churches there, and for others, of which this may serve as a notice.

The following attestation was signed by the brethren in Alsace, who examined this confession and adopted it as their own:

We, the undersigned, ministers of the word of God, and elders of the church in Alsace, hereby declare and make known, that being assembled this 4th of February in the year of our Lord 1660, at Ohnenheim in the principality of Rappoltstein, on account of the Confession of Faith, which was adopted at the Peace Convention of the *Tauffsgesinten* which are called the Flemish, in the city of Dort, on the 21st day of April in the year 1632, and which was printed at Rotterdam by Franciscus von Hochstraten, Anno 1658, and having examined the same, and found it in agreement with our judgment, we have entirely adopted it as our own. Which we, in testimony of the truth, and a firm faith, have signed with our own hands, as follows.

Ministers of the Word
Hans Muller of Magenheym
Hans Ringer of Heydelsheym
Jacob Schnewli of Baldenheym
Henrich Schneider of Isenheim
Rudolph Egli of Kunenheim
Adolph Schmidt of Markirch

Deacons
Jacob Schmidt of Markirch
Bertram Habigh of Markirch
Ulrich Husser of Ohnenheim
Jacob Gachnauwer of Ohnenheim
Hans Rudi Bumen of Jepsenheim
Jacob Schneider of Dursantzenheym
Henrich Frick of Kunenheym

POSTSCRIPT TO THE FOREGOING EIGHTEEN ARTICLES

From an authentic circular letter of the year 1557, from the Highland to the Netherland churches, it appears that from the Eyfelt to Moravia there were 50 churches, of which some consisted of from 500 to 600 brethren And that there were about that time, at a conference at Strasburg, about 50 preachers and elders present, who discoursed about matters concerning the welfare of the churches

THE DORDRECHT CONFESSION 87

These leaders of the nonresistant Christians endeavored earnestly to propagate the truth, so that like a "grain of mustard seed," of small beginning it grew against all bloody persecution, to the height in which it is to be seen in so many large churches in Germany, Prussia, the Principality of Cleves, &c, and particularly in the United Netherlands

But finally, alas! there arose disunion amongst them about matters of faith, which so deeply grieved the peaceably disposed amongst them, that they not only thought about means to heal the schism, and restore union, but did also take the matter in hand, and concluded at Cologne, in the year 1591, a laudable peace between the Highland and Netherland churches. Still the schism was not fully healed. Consequently in the years 1628 and 1630, it was deemed necessary at a certain conference, by some lovers of peace to appoint another conference, in order to see whether they could come to an understanding, and the schism be fully healed Consequently, in order to attain their object in the most effectual manner, there assembled at Dort, from many of the churches in Holland, on the 21st of April, 1632, fifty-one ministers of the word of God, appointed for said purpose, who deemed it advisable that a scriptural confession of faith should be drawn up, to which all parties should adhere, and on which this peace convention and the intended union should be founded and built Which was then accordingly drawn up, publicly adopted, confirmed, signed, the so much wished for peace obtained, and the light again put on the candlestick, to the honor of the nonresistant Christianity.

Appendix III
Christian Fundamentals

Adopted by Mennonite General Conference, 1921

In recent years conditions in the realm of Christian activity and doctrine are such that the Church must place a distinct emphasis on the principles of the Christian faith and Christian living. Particular doctrines of the Church have been attacked and there has been much compromising with the world on matters of Christian living.

Because of these conditions the Mennonite General Conference in session at Garden City, Missouri, August 24-26, 1921, gave expression to the faith of the Church in relation to these conditions in a statement of doctrine pertaining to the fundamentals of the Christian faith. This statement does not supersede the eighteen articles of the Dort Confession, which the Church still confesses and teaches. It is rather a restatement of that confession in the light of present religious contentions and teachings It gives expression to some of the doctrines and practices of the early Church which at that time were not a matter of difference, but have since the time of the Dort Confession been questioned or denied by many church organizations. For the sake of preserving the faith and teaching the Gospel as given by Christ and His apostles the Church has confessed in this formal manner her faith in and practice of the Gospel of salvation in Jesus Christ.

ARTICLES OF FAITH

Article I
OF THE WORD OF GOD

We believe in the plenary and verbal inspiration of the Bible as the Word of God; that it is authentic in its matter, authoritative in its counsels, inerrant in the original writings, and the only infallible rule of faith and practice. Ex. 4:12; II Sam. 23 2, Ps. 12 6, 119:150, Jer.1 9; Matt. 5:18; 24:35; II Tim. 3.16; II Pet. 1:20, 21.

Article II
OF THE EXISTENCE AND NATURE OF GOD

We believe that there is but one God, eternal, infinite, perfect, and unchangeable, who exists and reveals Himself in three persons—Father, Son and Holy Spirit. Deut. 6·4; Ps. 90·2, Gen 17 1; Ps 147 5, 139 7-12, Isa. 40:28, 57 15; Mal. 3 6; Gen 1 2, 18; Heb. 1.8

Article III
OF THE CREATION

We believe that the Genesis account of the Creation is an historic fact and literally true Gen. 1:1, 21, 27; Ex. 20:11; Mark 10:6-9; Heb. 1:10; 4:4; 11:13.

Article IV
OF THE FALL OF MAN

We believe that man was created by an immediate act of God, in His own image and after His likeness, that by one act of disobedience he became sinful in his nature, spiritually dead, subject to physical death and to the power of the devil, from which fallen condition he was unable to save himself. Gen. 1:26, 27; 2.7, 16, 17, 3:1-7; Eph. 2.1-3, 12; John 6.44; Rom. 5·6.

Article V
OF JESUS CHRIST

We believe that Jesus Christ is the eternal Son of God, that He was conceived of the Holy Spirit and born of a virgin—the perfect God-man, that He was without sin, the divinely appointed substitute and representative of sinful man, paying the penalty for man's sins by His death on the cross, making the only adequate atonement for sin by the shedding of His blood, thus reconciling man to God, that He was raised from the dead, ascended to glory, and "ever liveth to make intercession for us." John 1 1, 14, 18; Heb 1 8; 13 8, Gen 3 15; Isa 7:14, Luke 1:35, Matt. 1:20-25; Isa 53: 5, 6; II Cor. 5 14, 21, Gal. 3 13; I Pet 2 22, 24, 3 18, Rom 5 8-10, Matt 28:6; Acts 3·24, 10 39-41, 17 31; I Cor. 15 20, Acts 1 11; Eph 1 19, 20, Rev 1 18, Col. 3.1, Heb 6 20, I John 2·1, 2, Heb 7 25.

Article VI
OF SALVATION

We believe that man is saved alone by grace through faith in the finished work of Christ; that he is justified from all things on the ground of His shed blood, that through the new birth he becomes a child of God, partaker of eternal life and blessed with all spiritual blessings in Christ. Eph 2 8, Rom 3 20-26, Acts 13 38, 39; John 1·12, 13; 3:4, 8, 16, 5:24; Eph. 1:3.

Article VII
OF THE HOLY SPIRIT

We believe in the deity and personality of the Holy Spirit; that He convinces the world of sin, of righteousness, and of judgment, that He indwells and comforts the believer, guides him into all truth, empowers for service and enables him to live a life of righteousness. Acts 5:3, 4; II Cor. 3:3, 17, John 16.7, 8, 13, I Cor. 3 16; Gal. 4:6; Acts 1:8; Rom. 8.1-4.

Article VIII
OF ASSURANCE

We believe that it is the privilege of all believers to know that they have passed from death unto life; that God is able to keep them from falling, but that the obedience of faith is essential to the maintenance of one's salvation and growth in grace. I John 3:14; 5:13; Rom. 8:16; II Cor. 12.9; Jude 24, 25; Rom. 16.25, 26; 1:5; Gal. 3:11; John 8:31, 32; II eter 1 5-11.

Article IX
OF THE CHURCH

We believe that the Church is the body of Christ, composed of all those who through repentance toward God, and faith in the Lord Jesus Christ, have been born again and were baptized by one Spirit into one body, and that it is her divinely appointed mission to preach the Gospel to every creature, teaching obedience to all His commandments. Matt. 16·18; Eph. 1·23, Col. 1:18; Acts 20.21; Luke 24.47; Acts 17:30; 16:31; Gal. 3 26, I Cor. 12:13; Matt. 28:19, 20; Mark 16·15; Acts 1:8.

Article X
OF SEPARATION

We believe that we are called with a holy calling to a life of separation from the world and its follies, sinful practices, and methods; further that it is the duty of the Church to keep herself aloof from all movements which seek the reformation of society independent of the merits of the death of Christ and the experience of the new birth. I Pet. 2.9; Tit. 2:11-14; II Cor. 6 14-18; Rom. 12:1, 2; Eph. 5·11, I John 2:15-17; II Thess. 2 6; Acts 4:12; John 3:3, 6, 7.

Article XI
Of Discipline

We believe that the Lord has vested the Church with authority in accordance with Scriptural teaching (1) to choose officials, (2) to regulate the observance of ordinances, (3) to exercise wholesome discipline, and (4) to organize and conduct her work in a manner consistent with her high calling and essential to her highest efficiency. Acts 6 1-6, 13 1-3, II Tim 2 2, Tit 1 5-9, 2 15, Matt 28 19, 20, 18·15-18; Eph. 4·11-16; Heb 13 17; Acts 14 21-23, 2 15.

Article XII
Of Ordinances

We believe that Christian baptism should be administered upon confession of faith, that the Lord's Supper should be observed as a memorial of His death by those of like precious faith who have peace with God, that feetwashing as an ordinance should be literally observed by all believers; that Christian women praying or prophesying should have their heads covered; that the salutation of the holy kiss should be duly and appropriately observed by all believers, that anointing with oil should be administered to the sick who call for it in faith, that marriage between one man and one woman is a divine institution dissoluble only by death, that on the part of a Christian it should be "only in the Lord" and that consistency requires that the marriage relation be entered only by those of like precious faith. Luke 22 19, 20, I Cor 11·23-28, Acts 2 38, 8 12, 18 8, John 13 1-7, I Cor 11 2-16, 16 20; Jas 5 14-16, Mark 10.6-12, Rom 7 2, I Cor 7 39; Amos 3 3.

Article XIII
Of Restrictions

We believe that all Christian should honor, pray for, pay tribute to, and obey in all things those who are in authority in state and nation, provided however, that should instances arise in which such obedience would violate the higher law of God "we ought to obey God rather than man," that Church and State are separate, and while believers are to be subject to, they are not a part of the civil, administrative powers; that it is contrary to the teachings of Christ and the apostles to engage in carnal warfare; that Christians should "adorn themselves in modest apparel, . . . not with broided hair, or gold, or pearls, or costly array," that the swearing of oaths is forbidden in the New Testament Scriptures, that secret orders are antagonistic to the tenor and spirit of the Gospel, and that life insurance is inconsistent with filial trust in the providence and care of our heavenly Father[1] I Pet. 2:13, 14, 17; Rom. 13 1-7, I Tim 2 1, 2; Acts 5.29, Matt. 22:21, Mark 10·42-44; John 18 36; II Cor. 10 4, I Tim. 2 9, 10, I Pet. 3:3-5; Matt 5 34-37; Jas. 5.12; John 18 20; Eph. 5 11, 12, I John 3:17; Gal. 6.10, Jer 49.11, Eph. 1 22, 23.

Article XIV
Of Apostasy

We believe that the latter days will be characterized by general lawlessness and departure from the faith; that on the part of the world "iniquity shall abound" and "evil men shall wax worse and worse"; that on the part of the Church there will be a falling away and "the love of many shall wax cold", that false teachers shall abound, both deceiving and being deceived, and further, that present conditions indicate that we are now living in these perilous times I Tim 4:1, 2; Rom. 16 17, 18, II Tim 3:1-5, 13, II Pet 2 1, 2, 10, Matt 24 11, 12, II Thess. 2 3

---

[1] This refers to commercial life insurance only. The Brotherhood has a growing awareness of its obligation to make systematic provision for the economic needs of its members including financial assistance for the widows and orphans in event of serious incapacity or death

Article XV

OF THE RESURRECTION

We believe in the bodily resurrection of Jesus Christ and in the bodily resurrection of all men, both of the just and the unjust—of the just to the resurrection of life, and of the unjust to the resurrection of condemnation John 20 20, 24-29; Luke 24·30, 31; I Cor. 15 42-44, Acts 24 15; John 5 28, 29, I Cor 15·20-23.

Article XVI

OF THE COMING OF CHRIST

We believe in the personal, imminent coming of our Lord as the blessed hope of the believer, that we who are alive and remain, together with the dead in Christ who will be raised, shall be caught up to meet the Lord in the air and thus ever be with the Lord. John 14.2, 3, Acts 1.11, Matt. 24.44; Heb. 10 37; Tit 2 11-13; I Thess 4 13-18.

Article XVII

OF THE INTERMEDIATE STATE

We believe that in the interval between death and resurrection, the righteous will be with Christ in a state of conscious bliss and comfort, but that the wicked will be in a place of torment, in a state of conscious suffering and despair. Luke 16·19-31; 23 43, Phil 1:23, II Cor. 5.1-8, I Thess. 5·10, II Pet. 2 9 (R.V.).

Article XVIII

OF THE FINAL STATE

We believe that hell is the place of torment, prepared for the devil and his angels, where with them the wicked will suffer the vengeance of eternal fire forever and ever, and that heaven is the final abode of the righteous, where they will dwell in the fulness of joy forever and ever Matt. 25· 41, 46; Jude 7; Heb. 14 8-11; 20:10, 15; II Cor. 5:21; Rev 21:3-8; 22:1-5

Appendix IV
The Shorter Catechism

This catechism of thirty-five questions and answers appeared among the Prussian Mennonites as early as 1690 It was probably the first Mennonite catechism in the German language, and as Robert Friedmann adds,* it was "at the same time the most successful one, as the countless reprints up to the most recent times indicate This is also true for American Mennonitism, since all editions of the *Christliches Gemutsgesprach* [Roosen's catechism] in this country since 1769 have this handy and useful *Fragenbuchlein* as an appendix" The original Confession of Faith to which this catechism was added as early as 1690 was reprinted in Prussia in 1751, 1756, 1781, and 1854, in Russia in 1853, 1873, and 1912 It was reprinted at Elkhart, Indiana, in 1878 at the instance of the Mennonite Congregation of Turner County, Dakota The catechism, as was noted above, appeared in all editions of the *Conversation on Saving Faith* [*Christliches Gemutsgesprach von dem Geistlichen und Seligmachenden Glauben* .] of which at least eleven German and six English editions appeared in America between 1769 and 1941 This is evidence of its great popularity among Mennonites.

The original German title was *Kurze Unterweisung aus der Schrift* , wording which is still retained in the latest English edition of Roosen's *Gemutsgesprach,* "Brief Instruction for Youth From the Scriptures" However when J. S Coffman and J F. Funk issued their *Confession of Faith and Ministers' Manual* in 1890 they labeled the thirty-five questions and answers, "The Shorter Catechism" As such it has been widely known in the modern American Mennonite Church. In some districts, the Franconia Conference, for example, these questions and answers have been used traditionally to instruct converts preparatory to baptism It is an excellent though brief summary of Christian faith and life. It is anonymous, though certain writers such as Berend Karl Roosen seem to have thought that Gerrit Roosen had written it

BRIEF INSTRUCTION FOR YOUTH FROM THE SCRIPTURES

Question 1. The question is put to the disciple, the person desiring to unite with the church, as to what induces him to desire to unite with the communion of believers and be baptized?

Answer. I am impelled by faith, to separate myself from the world and its sinful lusts, and to submit in obedience to my Lord, Redeemer, and Saviour, for the salvation of my soul. Heb. 5:9.

2. What has induced you to do this?

The will and good pleasure of God, which were proclaimed and demonstrated to me through the preaching of the holy Gospel; in which were also revealed unto me the laws and commandments of Christ, which I am bound to receive and observe in true faith. Matt. 7:21; 19:17.

3. Do you then expect to be justified and saved through your good works and the keeping of the commandments of Christ?

No. For through our good works alone we cannot merit heaven, for salvation is the unmerited grace of God purchased for us by Jesus Christ Eph. 2:8.

4. For what purpose then are good works, or the keeping of the commandments of Christ necessary?

---

* Robert Friedmann · *Mennonite Piety Through the Centuries,* (Goshen, Indiana The Mennonite Historical Society, Goshen College), 1949, p. 129.

They are evidence of true faith in Jesus Christ; for obedience out of love to God, is the light and life of faith without which "faith is dead." Jas. 2 20.

5. Through what is man justified before God?

Through the Lord Jesus Christ alone, of whose righteousness we must become partakers through "faith which worketh by love." Gal. 5 6

6. What is true faith?

It is a certain knowledge, whereby we hold everything as true that is revealed to us in Holy Scripture, and whereby we cherish a full confidence that the pardon of our sins, righteousness, and eternal life are granted unto us by God, through our Lord Jesus Christ. Eph. 2:5.

7. What do you believe?

I believe in God the Father, Son, and Holy Ghost.

8. How do you believe in God the Father?

I believe with the heart, and confess with the mouth, that He is one, eternal, almighty, and just God the Creator and Preserver of heaven and earth, together with all things visible and invisible Gen. 14:17.

9. How do you believe in the Son?

I believe that He is Jesus Christ, the Son of the living God, our Saviour and Redeemer, who has been with the Father from eternity, and who, at "the fullness of time," was sent into the world; that He was conceived by the Holy Ghost, born of the blessed Virgin Mary; suffered for us under Pontius Pilate; was crucified, dead and buried, rose again from the dead on the third day, ascended into heaven, and sits at the right hand of God, the almighty Father, whence He will again come to judge the living and the dead. Matt. 25:31; John 17 5; Gal. 4:4.

10. How do you believe in the Holy Ghost?

I believe and confess that the Holy Ghost proceedeth from the Father and the Son, and is of a Divine nature; therefore I also believe in God, Father, Son, and Holy Ghost, as being one true God. Besides I also confess a general, holy Christian church, the communion of saints, the remission of sins, the resurrection of the flesh, and thereafter eternal life. I John 5:20; John 5:29.

11. What do you confess of the Christian church, or the congregation of the Lord?

I confess by my faith that there is a Church of God, which the Lord Jesus purchased with His own blood, and which He sanctified and cleansed with the washing of water by the Word, that He might present it to Himself a glorious church. Eph 5:26, 27.

12. In what does the Church of God consist?

In a number of persons, who, through faith in Jesus Christ, have withdrawn from a sinful world and submitted in obedience to the Gospel, not to live any more to themselves, but to Christ, in true humility; who also give diligence to exercise Christian virtues, by observing God's holy ordinances Such are members of the body of Christ, and heirs of eternal life. II Pet 1:11.

13. How, and through what, is the Church of God upheld?

Through the preaching of the holy Gospel and the instruction of the Holy Ghost, for the purpose of carrying on and maintaining which, teachers and ministers are elected by the church. Eph. 4:11.

14. Who has given power to the church to choose teachers?

I confess that, as the apostles were accustomed to do, so has God also given power to His church to do, namely, to elect teachers and ministers, that the body of Christ may be edified and preserved. Wherefore the election of such teachers and ministers also takes place according to the example which the apostles were accustomed to observe in such matters. Eph. 4 12, Acts 1 15-26

15. Whence comes the ordinance of the service to the poor?

Of this service we have an example in the Acts of the Apostles, where the apostles, when the "number of the disciples was multiplied," called together the multitude and caused to be "appointed from among them, seven men," who took charge of the necessary "business," which example is still observed, so that that which is contributed by Christian hearts is properly applied to the relief of the necessities of the poor members of the church Acts 6 1, Eph 4 28

16. How, and through what means, are the members of the body of Christ incorporated into the church?

Through the ordinance of Christian baptism, on confession of their faith and repentance of their past sins, whereupon they are baptized in the name of the Father, the Son, and the Holy Ghost Matt 28 19

17. What is baptism properly?

I confess that it is an external ordinance of Christ, a sign of a spiritual birth from God, a "putting on of Christ," and an incorporation into His church, an evidence that we have established a covenant with Christ Rom. 6 4, Gal. 3:27, I Pet 3·21.

18. Of what use is baptism?

It represents to true believers the washing away of the impurity of their souls through the blood of Christ, namely, the pardon of their sins, whereupon they console themselves with the hope of eternal salvation through Jesus Christ, whom they have "put on" in baptism. Gal. 3·27.

19. To what are the members of the church of Christ bound by baptism?

To the act of suffering their past sins to be buried into Christ's death by baptism, and of binding themselves to Christ in a new life and conversation—a life of obedience—in order that they may follow His will and do what He has commanded them to do Matt. 28 20

20. What is the Lord's Supper?

I confess that it is an external ceremony and institution of Christ, administered to believers in the form of bread and wine; in the partaking of which the death and sufferings of Christ are to be declared and observed to His memory I Cor. 11:26.

21. What purpose does the observance of this ordinance subserve?

It is thereby represented to us how Christ's holy body was sacrificed on the cross, and His precious blood shed for us for the pardon of our sins. I John 1·7.

22. What is the use of the observance of the Lord's Supper?

We thereby bear witness to our simple obedience to Christ, our Saviour and Redeemer; which has the promise of eternal salvation Further, it secures unto us, through faith, the communion of the body and blood of Christ, and comforts us with the benefit of His death, that is, the assurance of the pardon of our sins I Cor. 10:16, Heb. 5 9.

23. Is marriage also an institution of God?

Yes For it is instituted by God Himself, and confirmed in the case of Adam and Eve in the Garden of Eden. Gen. 1·27, 28.

24. For what purpose is marriage instituted?

For the purpose of increasing the human race, so that the earth may thereby be peopled with inhabitants; also, that fornication may be avoided. Therefore "every man" is to "have his own wife," and "every woman her own husband" (I Cor. 7·2)

25. How must such marriage be begun so that it does not clash with the institution?

Persons who are not too nearly related by consanguinity, may, after diligent prayer to God, enter into this state, and endeavor to live therein, in a Christian manner, to the end of their days, provided that they, as members of the Christian Church, enter into marriage only with members of the church Lev 18 6-17, I Cor 7.39; 9:5

26. Is a member of the church not at all allowed to enter into matrimony with a person who is not agreed with him in faith and doctrine?

No For this is contrary to the marriage institution; and he who thus enters into matrimony, acts contrary to the law of God, and the doctrine of the apostles Deut 7 3, 4, Judges 3 6, 7; I Cor. 1.10, 7:39, Phil 2· 1, 2

27. Can also a lawful marriage, for any cause, be divorced?

No For the persons united by such marriage are so closely bound to each other that they can in no wise separate, except in case of fornication. Matt 19 9

28. What do you confess in regard to the power of civil government?

I confess, from the testimony of Holy Scripture, that kings and governments are instituted by God for the welfare and common interest of the countries over which they rule; and that he who resists such authorities, "resists the ordinance of God" Rom 13 1 Wherefore we are under obligation to fear and honor government, and obey the same in all things that do not militate against the Word of God So we are also commanded to pray for the same I Tim 1 2

29. Is it allowed to swear an oath?

No For although this was allowed to the fathers of the Old Testament, yet has our Lord and institutor of the New Testament, Christ Jesus, expressly forbidden it, Matt 5:33-37, which is confirmed by the Apostle James, when he says: "Above all things, my brethren, swear not . but let your yea be yea; and your nay, nay; lest ye fall into condemnation" (James 5.12)

30. Is it allowed to take revenge?

No; although there was liberty to do so under the Old Testament dispensation But now that it is totally forbidden by Christ and His apostles, we must not lust after it, but in meekness do good unto our neighbor, yea also to our enemies Matt 5·38, 39, Rom. 12.19-21

31. If a member of the church fall into some sin or misdeed, what is to be done in such case?

I confess by virtue of the doctrine of Christ and His apostles that reproof and discipline must be fostered and maintained among believers, so that the headstrong, as well as such as have committed gross sins and works of the flesh, whereby they have separated themselves from God, may not be suffered in the communion of believers, but may, for their own amendment, be rebuked before all, "that others also may fear " Matt. 18:15-18, Isa. 59·2; I Tim. 5.20.

32. How must we demean ourselves towards such as are thus separated from the church?

According to the doctrine of the apostles, the true members of the church of Christ are to withdraw from such reproved and impenitent offenders, and have no spiritual communion with them, except by chance or occasion, when they may be exhorted in love, compassion, and Christian discretion again to rise from their fallen state, and return to the church Rom. 16.17; Tit 3:10

33. How long is the avoiding of such offenders to be observed?

Until they return again, give evidence of repentance—sorrow for their sins—and earnestly desire again to be admitted into the communion of the church

In such case they are, after solemn prayer to God, again to be received and admitted. II Cor. 2:6, 7.

34. What do you believe concerning the second coming of Christ, and the resurrection of the dead?

I believe that Christ, our Head, Lord and Saviour, will just as He visibly ascended to heaven, again appear from thence in great power and glory, "with a shout . . and with the trump of God" (I Thess. 4 16) "For the hour is coming, in the which all that are in the graves shall hear his voice, and shall come forth, they that have done good, unto the resurrection of life, and they that have done evil, unto the resurrection of damnation" (John 5:28, 29). "For we must all appear before the judgment seat of Christ; that every one may receive the things done in his body, according to that he hath done, whether it be good or bad" (II Cor. 5.10).

35. Now as this confession agrees with the doctrine of Christ and His apostles, the question is finally put to the disciple: Whether he is inclined with his whole heart, to submit himself to the will of his Redeemer and Saviour, Jesus Christ, to deny himself together with all sinful lusts, and to strive by the grace of God, in true faith and heartfelt humility, to lead a pious and godly life and holy conversation, according to the commandments of God, as long as he lives?

Yes. To which are heartily wished God's grace and rich blessings, through the power of the Holy Spirit, to salvation, to whom be honor and praise for ever and ever. Amen.

Appendix V
The Waldeck Catechism

In 1778 there appeared at Elbing, Prussia, the *Kurze und einfaltige Unterweisung aus der Heiligen Schrift* (Brief and Simple Instruction from the Holy Scripture). It may have been reprinted at Elbing in 1783, since American reprints refer to the first edition as of 1783 In any case it is known to have been reprinted in Waldeck in 1797, in Strasburg, Alsace, in 1801, and at Giessen, Hesse, in 1834. The Amish of Zweibrücken adopted it in 1855. The Amish Mennonites of Montbeliard, France, published a French edition in 1822. In 1824 the Ontario, Canada, Mennonites had it published, in German of course, at Ephrata, Pennsylvania. German editions were published at Doylestown, Pennsylvania, in 1844, and at "Shippach" (Skippack, Pennsylvania) in 1848. I. Daniel Rupp's English translation was published at Lancaster, Pennsylvania, in 1849 for the use of the Oberholtzer Mennonites. (The General Conference of the Mennonite Church of North America has issued a number of editions) John F. Funk of Elkhart, Indiana, issued a German edition in 1869, and a revised English translation in 1874; this English translation was reprinted in 1883 and 1905 at Elkhart. The text given below is that of the 1905 reprint Although Funk's English edition contains the Waterloo preface, reprinted below, which reports the 1783 Elbing edition, and the 1797 Waldeck reprint, Funk nevertheless erroneously places on the title page, "Originally Published in the German Language, by the Mennonite Church in Waldeck." Because this confession has acquired the Waldeck appellation I have so labeled it in this book. All in all, at least seven German reprints of his catechism have appeared among American Mennonites, and many English reprint editions [1]

Robert Friedmann points out[2] that although this catechism in general seems to follow the arrangement of the Dutch Mennonite Confession of Faith of Minister Cornelis Ris, "the treatment of the catechism seems to be fully independent of the confession." He adds: "It is a very convenient textbook, short but precise and well articulated, much more effective than the other popular Mennonite catechism, Roosen's *Christliches Gemütsgesprach.*"[3]

The preface of the Ontario Mennonites to the 1824 German edition is herewith reprinted in English translation, also the Preface to Funk's English Edition.

PREFACE TO THE FIRST AMERICAN EDITION

To all the bishops, ministers, deacons, and members of our Mennonite Congregations, be abundant grace, peace, salvation and blessing, from God the Father, and Jesus Christ, our Lord, through the co-operating power of the Holy Ghost. Amen.

In compliance with the desire of many we have consented to reprint this little work which was first published in Elbing, in Prussia, in 1783; and in compliance with the desire of the churches in Hesse and Waldeck, reprinted in 1797

In its publication, however, nothing new is presented, but only the same old doctrine which Christ and His apostles taught, and which many of our fellow believers sealed with their blood, viz: The doctrines of the sacred Scriptures The book appears under the title of "Plain instructions from the sacred Scriptures," because the answers are generally given in the exact language of Scripture.

Our object is, that our beloved youth, in their tender years, might be taught and led to walk in the footsteps of Christ, our dear Redeemer. Let us give all

---

[1] Harold S. Bender *Two Centuries of American Mennonite Literature,* The Mennonite Historical Society, Goshen College, Goshen, Indiana, 1929, 12, 13, also Robert Friedmann *Mennonite Piety Through the Centuries,* 135
[2] *Op. cit.,* 135.
[3] *Ibid.,* 135.

diligence to the instruction of the young, and by the grace of God, labor for their souls; then we may expect that the Lord our God will bless our efforts, so that we may rejoice in the fruits of our labors in time and in eternity. Adult persons who are yet children in understanding may also be benefited by this work. May the Lord grant His blessings, that it may redound to His praise and honor.

PUBLISHER'S PREFACE TO THE FUNK EDITION

Two editions of this little work have already been issued in the German language and many inquiries having been made for it in the English, we herewith present this edition to the brotherhood, feeling that if the contents of the little work will be properly studied by the older members and diligently taught to the children and young people, under the blessing of God, it cannot fail to inculcate the principles of our religion into the minds of our people, so that they will manifest a deeper interest in the Word of God and in His church, and thus it may lead them to consecrate themselves more earnestly to His service, which is indeed a matter of the greatest importance and necessity in this present, evil time

May the blessing of God abide upon our efforts, and go with the little book, so that it may do much good to all into whose hands it may fall

MENNONITE PUBLISHING CO.

PLAIN INSTRUCTIONS FROM THE SACRED SCRIPTURES

IN QUESTIONS AND ANSWERS

Introduction

1. Question.—What is the most needful that we should seek for in this life?

Answer.—To live in communion with God, enjoy His favor and obtain eternal happiness hereafter. Matt. 6:33.

2. Have we not to care also for our temporal sustenance?

Yes. in a Christian manner, so that we seek first the kingdom of Christ and His righteousness Matt 6 31-34

3. What is the kingdom of God, or in what does it consist?

In this life it is within all believers, and is righteousness, and peace, and joy in the Holy Ghost, hereafter it is an eternal, blissful life with God and all the elect. Luke 17:21, Rom 14 17; Rev. 21.4.

4. How do we attain to it?

By faith in God and Jesus Christ, our Saviour John 17:3; Heb 11.6

5. Is it enough that we make a confession of our faith with the mouth only?

No· faith must work by love. Gal 5 6.

PART FIRST

OF THE CREATION

Chapter I

I God the Creator of All Things

1. Question.—Who created all things?

Answer.—God, the Lord In the beginning God created heaven and earth Gen. 1:1.

2. Who is God?

The only God, Father, Son and Holy Ghost Matt 28 18; I John 5 7

3. How can we know that there is a God?

Both nature and testimony of the sacred Scriptures teach us that there is a God Rom 1 19, 20; Deut 6:4, 5

II. THE KNOWLEDGE OF GOD FROM NATURE

4. How does nature teach us that there is a God?
All created things teach us that there must necessarily be a God who created all things. Job 12 7-10; Acts 17:24-28.

5. What does the Apostle Paul say on this subject?
He says, Because that which may be known of God is manifest, for the invisible things of Him from the creation of the world, are clearly seen, being understood by the things that are made, even His eternal power and Godhead Rom 1 19, 20

III. THE KNOWLEDGE OF GOD FROM THE SACRED SCRIPTURES

6. What are we taught in the sacred Scriptures of God?
That God is a Spirit John 4 24, II Cor. 3·17

7. What more do the sacred Scriptures testify of God?
That He is one everlasting, unchangeable, omnipresent, omniscient, omnipotent, holy, righteous, incomprehensible, benevolent, gracious, merciful and long-suffering God, etc Deut 6 4, Ps 90 2, Jas 1 17, Acts 10 33, Jer 23 23, 24; Ps 94 11; Rom 16 24, Gen 17.1; Isa 6 3, Deut 32 4; Rom 11 33; Ps 103 8

8. Do the sacred Scriptures tell us anything more concerning God?
Yes, they tell us a great deal more about Him, as may be seen by diligently reading them.

IV. THE INFALLIBILITY OF THE SACRED SCRIPTURES

9. What do we understand by the sacred Scriptures?
The writings of the Old and New Testaments, called the Bible.

10. Are these writings the Word of God?
Yes, all Scripture is given by inspiration of God II Tim 3.16

11. Were not the Scriptures written by the will of men?
By no means, but holy men of God spake, and also wrote, as they were moved by the Holy Ghost. II Pet 1 21; Rev. 1.11.

12. Are the sacred Scriptures the infallible truth?
Yes; for all things written therein, foretold of Christ, have been literally fulfilled Matt 26·56; Luke 24·26, 27.

13. Is it profitable for us diligently to read the sacred Scriptures?
Yes, for if we from childhood know the sacred Scriptures, they are able to make us wise unto salvation; but we must pray God for the influence of the Holy Spirit to enlighten our understanding II Tim 3.15, Eph 1 18

Chapter II

I OF THE TRINITY OF GOD

1. Question.—What do the sacred Scriptures teach us concerning the trinity of God?
Answer.—In them God has revealed Himself as the Triune God, Father, Son and Holy Ghost. I John 5·7.

2. What do the sacred Scriptures testify of God the Father?
That He is the true Father of the whole family in heaven and earth, that He is the Father of all believers, and especially that He is the Father of our Lord Jesus Christ. Eph. 3 15; I Cor 8 6; Gal. 4.6; Rom 8 15, II Cor 1 3.

3. What is taught in the sacred Scriptures about Christ, the Son of God?
That He is the true, own, and only begotten Son of God Ps 2 7; Rom 8 32, John 1:14.

4. Is Jesus Christ the Son of God from all eternity?
Yes; He had been with the Father before the world was; whose goings forth have been from of old, from everlasting. John 17·5; Micah 5 2.

5. Is He also true God?
Yes; He is the true God and eternal life. I John 5:20

6. What do the sacred Scriptures teach us concerning the Holy Ghost?
That He is a true Holy Ghost, proceeding from the Father, and sent by the Son, and thus proceedeth from the Father and the Son John 15:26

7. Is the Holy Ghost also called God?
Yes; when Ananias had lied against the Holy Ghost, Peter said, "Thou hast not lied unto men, but unto God." Acts 5:3, 4.

8. Are then the Father, Son and Holy Ghost three Gods?
No; there is only one God, for these three are one Mark 12 29, I John 5 7

Chapter III

I. How All Things Were Created by the Triune God

1. Question.—By whom did God create all things?
Answer.—He created all things by Jesus Christ, by whom also He made the worlds Eph 3·9; Heb 1 2.

2. Did the Holy Ghost also co-operate in the creation?
Yes, by the word of the Lord were the heavens made; and all the hosts of them by the breath of His mouth. Ps. 33·6

3. In how many days did God create all things?
In six days God made heaven and earth, and all things, and rested on the seventh day, and God blessed the seventh day and sanctified it Gen. 1 and 2

II The Creation of Man

4. What did the Lord God create in His own image?
God created man in His own image; in the image of God created He him Gen. 1:27.

5. How many human beings did God create in the beginning?
Only two; Adam and Eve, from whom all mankind descended. Acts 17 26

6. From what was Adam created?
From the dust of the ground: and God breathed into his nostrils the breath of life. Gen. 2:7.

7. How was Eve formed?
The Lord caused a deep sleep to fall upon Adam, and he slept; and he took one of his ribs and made a woman from it, and brought her unto him Gen 2·21, 22.

8. Where did the Lord place our first parents, Adam and Eve?
In the garden of Eden. Gen 2 8.

III. The Creation of Angels

9. Are there also created beings in heaven?
Yes; the angels. Heb. 1:6, 7; Col. 1·16

10. What are angels?
They are ministering spirits. Heb. 1:7-14.

11. To what end did God create the holy angels?
To praise and glorify God, and minister to the good of those who love and fear Him Isa 6 1-3; Matt 18·10; Ps. 34:7; Heb. 1·14

THE WALDECK CATECHISM, Part 1, Chapter III

12. Did any of the angels apostatize?
Yes; some of them left their own habitations, and are reserved in everlasting chains, under darkness, unto the judgment of the great day. Jude 6.

13. By what name are they called?
Evil spirits or devils [demons]. Luke 7:21; Mark 5:12

14. What are their nature and actions?
They are enemies of God, and seek the eternal destruction of mankind. I Pet 5 8

Chapter IV

IV. God's Providence and Government

1. Question.—Does God's providence extend to all things?
Answer.—Yes; He causes the grass to grow for the cattle, and herb for the service of man; He gives to all their meat in due season; He gives to all life and breath and all things. Ps. 104:14, 145 15; Acts 17 25

2. Can nothing exist without God's sustaining power?
No; for if He takes away their breath they die Ps 104·29.

3. Does God govern all things that He created?
Yes; He governs the nations upon the earth, and will reign forever and ever Ps. 67:1; Rev. 11·15.

4. Can we with our understanding comprehend God's providence and government?
No, God's ways are past finding out, and His judgments are unsearchable. Rom. 11.33; Ps. 147.5

5. What does this subject teach us?
That we should confide in God, our Creator, Preserver and Ruler, cast all our cares upon Him, and seek His kingdom and righteousness in the hope that all these things shall be added unto us. Matt. 6.33, I Pet 5.7.

PART SECOND

THE FALL OF MAN

Chapter I

V. Man's Condition Before the Fall

1. Question.—What was man's condition in Paradise, in the Garden of Eden?
Answer.—It was glorious and blessed. Gen. 1·27, 31.

2. Was man created good?
Yes; God made man upright—He created him in His own image Eccl 7 30; Gen 1:27.

3. In what does the image of God consist?
The image of God consists in this, that man is created after God in righteousness and true holiness. Eph. 4 24.

4. Did Adam and Eve abide in that blessed condition?
No; they sinned and apostatized from God; they and all their posterity Rom 5.12-19.

VI. The Fall of Man

5. By what act did our first parents sin against God?
They did eat of the tree of the knowledge of good and evil, which God had forbidden, and said, "Thou shalt not eat of it; for in the day that thou eatest thereof thou shalt surely die." Gen. 2 17, 3:3.

6. What induced them to commit this sin?
An evil spirit, called the serpent, deceived them. Gen. 3:5, 13.

7. Who is the serpent?
It is the Devil and Satan, who is a murderer from the beginning, and abode not in the truth. Rev. 12:9, John 8.44.

8. How did Satan deceive them?
He said, "Ye shall not surely die, ye shall be as gods, knowing good and evil" Gen. 3:1, 4, 5.

9. Why did they so readily believe the serpent?
Because they themselves had a desire for it, that they might be made wise and be as God Gen 3·6.

VII. Consequences of the Fall

10. What were the consequences of Adam's transgression?
He and his posterity became subject to sin and death Rom 5 12

11. To what kind of death did Adam and his posterity become subject?
To both spiritual and temporal death; the body must die and return to earth, and man became wholly incapable to that which is good, and liable to eternal punishment. Gen. 3 19, II Cor. 3 15; Rom 5 12-21

12. What happened to Adam's posterity?
All flesh had corrupted his way upon the earth so that the Lord determined to destroy them from the earth. Gen. 6 12, 13

13. Is there no one on the earth without sin?
That which is born of the flesh is flesh None are without sin except the Son of God, who is conceived by the Holy Ghost. John 3 6; Luke 1:35; Heb 7:26.

14. What do we learn from this?
From this we learn that by nature we are prone to evil, and children of wrath, and therefore being convinced of our miserable condition, we must seek God's grace and mercy. Eph. 2:2, 3.

PART THIRD

THE REDEMPTION OF MAN

Chapter I

I How Redemption Was Promised by God

1. Question.—Did the Lord God suffer man to remain in such a miserable condition?
Answer.—No, He redeemed His people. Luke 1 68

2. How did He redeem them?
By giving His only begotten Son John 3·16

3. How could He give His Son?
He had to assume human nature, that through death He might destroy him that had the power of death, that is, the devil Heb 2 14, 15

4. Was there no other way to redeem us?
No, none could by any means redeem his brother Ps 49 8, Rev 5 3, 4

5. Was only one, our Saviour, to die for all?
Yes, for as by one man's disobedience many were made sinners, so by the obedience of one shall many be made righteous. Rom 5 19

II The Promise to Adam and the Patriarchs Before the Giving of the Law

6. How could man know that a Redeemer was to come, and atone for our sins?
The Lord made this known to Adam; for He said to the serpent, "I will put enmity between thee and the woman, and between thy seed and her seed, it shall bruise thy head, and thou shalt bruise his heel" Gen. 3 15.

7. Has this promise reference to Christ?
Yes; it refers to Christ, who was crucified Col. 2:14; I John 3 8; Rev. 13 8.
8. Did the faithful before the flood believe in the promise?
Yes. by faith Abel offered burnt offerings unto God Enoch and Noah were also believers. Heb. 11:4-7
9. To whom did God make this promise more clearly?
To Abraham, Isaac, and Jacob, when He said, "In thee shall all families of the earth be blessed." Gen 12 2; 26:4, 28:14, Gal. 3 16.

III. OF THE LAW AS A GOVERNOR (SCHOOLMASTER) TO BRING US UNTO CHRIST

10. By what means did God discipline and instruct the people of Israel, before the advent of Christ?
By giving the law of Moses; especially the Ten Commandments given to him on Mount Sinai, written upon two tables of stone. Ex 20.
11. How do they read?
And God spake all these words, saying, I am the Lord thy God, which have brought thee out of the land of Egypt, out of the house of bondage Ex 20 1, 2.

FIRST TABLE

First Commandment
Thou shalt have no other gods before Me

Second Commandment
Thou shalt not make unto thee any graven image, or any likeness of any thing that is in heaven above, or that is in the earth beneath, or that is in the water under the earth: thou shalt not bow down thyself to them, nor serve them, for I the Lord thy God am a jealous God, visiting the iniquity of the fathers upon the children unto the third and fouth generation of them that hate Me, and shewing mercy unto thousands of them that love Me, and keep My commandments.

Third Commandment
Thou shalt not take the name of the Lord thy God in vain: for the Lord will not hold him guiltless that taketh His name in vain.

Fourth Commandment
Remember the sabbath day, to keep it holy Six days shalt thou labour, and do all thy work; but the seventh is the sabbath of the Lord thy God in it thou shalt not do any work, thou, nor thy son, nor thy daughter, nor thy man servant, nor thy maid servant, nor thy cattle, nor thy stranger that is within thy gates: for in six days the Lord made heaven and earth, the sea, and all that in them is, and rested the seventh day, wherefore the Lord blessed the sabbath day, and hallowed it

SECOND TABLE

Fifth Commandment
Honour thy father and thy mother, that thy days may be long upon the land which the Lord thy God giveth thee

Sixth Commandment
Thou shalt not kill.

Seventh Commandment
Thou shalt not commit adultery

Eighth Commandment
Thou shalt not steal

Ninth Commandment
Thou shalt not bear false witness against thy neighbour

Tenth Commandment

Thou shalt not covet thy neighbour's house, thou shalt not covet thy neighbour's wife, nor his man servant, nor his maidservant, nor his ox, nor his ass, nor any thing that is thy neighbour's.*

12. What is the sum of these Ten Commandments?
The first table commands us to love God with all the heart, with all the soul, and with all the mind.
The second table teaches us that we are to love our neighbor as ourselves Matt. 22:37, 39.

13. Has the law respect to the outward actions only?
No; it has special respect to the inward movings or desires of the heart. I Tim. 1·5.

14. Does the law forbid secret lusts?
Yes; for it is written, Thou shall not covet. Rom 7:7.

15. If an inclination or lust to sin is forbidden, has any one then ever fully kept the law?
No; for all mankind are under sin. Rom. 3:3, 19.

16. For what purpose was the law given?
That it should be our schoolmaster till Christ appeared, and that man might have a knowledge of sin. Gal. 3:24, Rom 3:20.

IV. The Promise Through the Prophets

17. Did the prophets prophesy concerning the coming of Christ?
Yes; and all the prophets from Samuel, and those that followed after, as many as have spoken, have likewise foretold of these days. Acts 3 24.

18. What did Moses say of the Saviour?
He said, "The Lord thy God will raise up unto thee a prophet from the midst of thee, of thy brethren, like unto Me; unto him ye shall hearken" Deut. 18 15

19. Are there any predictions in the psalms concerning Christ?
Yes, not only in the writings of Moses and the prophets; but also in the Psalms we find predictions concerning Christ. Luke 24:44.

Chapter II

I Christ's Appearance for Our Redemption

1. Question.—When did the Saviour appear in this world?
Answer.—When the time, which had been predicted, was fully come, God sent His Son. Gen. 49:10, Luke 2:1; Gal. 4:4.

2. How did His birth occur?
He was conceived of the Holy Ghost born of the pure virgin Mary; and His name was called Jesus Matt 1.18, 25; Luke 1:35.

3. Where was the Saviour born?
In Bethlehem, in Judea. Micah 5.1, Luke 2.4

4. What was the condition in which He was born?
Poor and despised; He was born in a stable in Bethlehem Luke 2 7

5. Where was He brought up?
At Nazareth Luke 14:16

---

*We have given the decalogue, unchanged, as Moses wrote it by divine command; and in the same order as it has at all times been received by our own fellow believers.

II. Christ's Baptism, and His Public Ministry

6. When was Christ proclaimed the Son of God?
When He was about thirty years of age, as He was baptized of John, a voice came from heaven, which said, "This is My beloved Son; in whom I am well pleased." Matt. 3:17; Luke 3:22.

7. Whereby did the Lord Jesus show that He is the Saviour of the world?
By His doctrine and miracles, for He taught as one that had authority and not as the scribes; and performed also many miracles. Mark 1 22; John 11:47

8. What was the substance of His preaching?
Repent ye, and believe the gospel. Mark 1:15.

9. What miracles did the Lord perform?
He opened the eyes of the blind, made the lame walk, cleansed the lepers, unstopped the ears of the deaf, made the dumb to speak, raised the dead, and performed many miracles. Luke 7:19-22.

III. The Sufferings and Death of Our Saviour

10. What did the Lord Jesus finally do for us?
He died for our sins according to the Scriptures. I Cor. 15:3.

11. What is properly the death of the Lord?
It is an offering for the sins of the whole world; and by which he hath perfected forever them that are sanctified. Heb. 10 14.

12. When did His sufferings begin?
In the night in which He was betrayed by Judas, in the garden of Gethsemane; His soul became exceeding sorrowful, even unto death. Matt. 26:36-38.

13. Why did He suffer such agony?
The Lord had laid on Him the iniquity of us all. Isa 53 6, 7

14. What followed His agony of soul?
He suffered Himself to be taken, condemned, and to be delivered over unto death, by Pontius Pilate, a Gentile judge. Matt 26 and 27 chapters

15. What death did the Saviour die?
He was crucified without the gates of Jerusalem, between two murderers. John 19:17, 18

16. Why had the Saviour to die on the cross?
Thereby to redeem us from the curse; for it is written, Cursed is every one that hangeth on a tree Gal. 3 13

17. Was the Lord Jesus also buried?
Yes: they laid Him in a new tomb hewn out in a rock. Matt. 27:60

IV. Christ's Resurrection and Ascension

18. Did the Saviour remain in the tomb?
No; He rose on the third day, according to the Scriptures Luke 24:34; I Cor 15:4; Ps. 16:10; John 20 and 21.

19. What does His resurrection assure us?
That we are justified through His blood; for He was delivered for our offenses, and was raised again for our justification. Rom. 4:25.

20. Where did the Lord Jesus remain after His resurrection?
He showed Himself alive to His disciples, being seen of them forty days, and speaking of the things pertaining to the kingdom of God Acts 1:3

21. What happened at the end of forty days?
Jesus led out His disciples as far as Bethany, on Mount Olivet, and there ascended into heaven. Luke 24:50, 51; Acts 1:9-11; Mark 16:19.

22. What did the Lord Jesus obtain for us by His ascension?
By His own blood He entered once into the holy place (heaven), having obtained eternal redemption for us. Heb. 9:12; I John 2:1, 2.

V. The Saviour's Threefold Office

23. The Lord Jesus having accomplished the work of redemption, in what offices are we to consider Him?
As our Prophet, High Priest, and King

24. In what does His prophetic office consist?
In this, that He teaches us the way of salvation, foretells future events, and confirms the same by miracles, for this was the office of a prophet under the Old Testament dispensation Deut 18 19; Matt 5 18, 19, 20 18, 19

25. What did the Saviour do as a High Priest?
As a High Priest He gave Himself for an offering, He intercedes for His people, and blesses His own Eph 5 2, Heb 9 26, John 17, Rom 8 34, Luke 24·50, Eph 1:3.

26. In what does Christ's office as a King consist?
He gives commands and laws; He governs His people; He puts all His enemies under His feet; He protects and rewards His own John 13 34, Jer 23 5, I Cor 15.5; Matt 25.34

27. What is the character of Christ's kingdom?
He has no temporal kingdom upon earth, but a spiritual kingdom in His believers; and possesses a heavenly kingdom of glory, into which He will eventually bring all His true followers John 18 36, Luke 1.33, 17 21, II Tim 4 18

VI The Sending of the Holy Ghost and Universal Grace

28. What gift did the Lord Jesus bestow upon His own, after His ascension?
He gave them the Holy Ghost according to His promise. John 14:16; Eph 4 8

29. When did this happen?
On the day of Pentecost Acts 2:1-4

30. Was the Holy Ghost given to the apostles only?
Peter said, "The promise is unto you, and to your children." God will give His Holy Ghost to them that ask Him. Acts 2 39; Luke 11.13.

31. What is the operation (office) of the Holy Ghost in believers?
He testifies of Jesus, He comforts believers, He sanctifies them, and leads them into all truth; and through the Holy Ghost, the love of God is shed abroad in the hearts of believers John 15 26, 16 7-14; I Cor. 6 11, Rom 5:5.

32. What especial work did the Holy Ghost enable the apostles to do?
He bestowed gifts upon them, which enabled them to preach the Gospel unto all nations, and to confirm it by miracles. Acts 2:4.

33. Were not the Jews only to be especially called?
No; the Word of God was first to be spoken to the Jews, but afterwards to the Gentiles also. Acts 13:46

34. Is it the will of God that all men should be saved?
Yes; God will have all men to be saved, and to come to a knowledge of the truth I Tim. 2 4.

35. Have all been redeemed?
Yes; Christ gave Himself a ransom for all. I Tim 2 6; Rom 5 18

36. Do all accept of this redemption?
No; all are not obedient to the Gospel Rom 2 8, II Thess 1.8

Chapter III

I Faith in Christ

1. Question.—Which is the true way to salvation?
Answer.—Faith in Jesus Christ our Saviour and His shed blood. John 20 31; Matt 16 16, 17; Rom. 3.25.

2. Does faith merit salvation?
No; but faith lays hold on the merits of Christ, whereby we obtain salvation and eternal life. John 3 36

3. What is true faith?
It is the substance of things hoped for, the evidence of things not seen Heb 11 1.

4. What does true faith require?
A sincere repentance or change of mind; that we become convinced of our depravity, and feel sorry for our sins Mark 1 15, John 3 3, Rom 12 2.

5. Is a believer changed in heart?
Yes; he is converted from the error of his way unto Christ, the Shepherd and Bishop of our souls. Jas 5.20, I Peter 2 25, Luke 15:17-19

II REGENERATION AND GOOD WORKS

6. What is the change of heart called in the New Testament?
Regeneration—a new creature John 3 3; Gal. 6.15; Titus 3:5

7. From whence cometh regeneration?
God Himself effects regeneration in us by His Word and Spirit, if we are obedient unto Him. I Peter 1 3; Jas. 1·17; John 3 5

8. Must every Christian needs be born again?
Yes; for without regeneration none can see the kingdom of God John 3 3, 5

9. Does regeneration produce a godly life?
Yes; whosoever is born of God doth not commit sin I John 3 9.

10. Can we not of our strength avoid sin and do good?
No; for Christ says, "Without Me ye can do nothing." John 15 5.

11. Does then a holy walk come alone from Christ and by His grace?
Yes; for Christ is made of God unto us, wisdom, and righteousness, and sanctification, and redemption. I Cor. 1:30.

III. JUSTIFICATION

12. What is justification?
It is the righteousness of Christ imputed to the penitent sinner, by faith. Rom 4:5, II Cor. 5.21.

13. Is then a sinner justified by grace?
Yes, we are justified without any merits, by His grace, through the redemption that is in Christ Jesus. Rom 3:24

14. What does justification avail us?
That we have peace with God, are His children, are made free from the law of sin, and thus become sanctified Rom. 5.1; 8 16, John 8 36

IV. SANCTIFICATION

15. What is it to be sanctified, or what is sanctification?
To be sanctified is to be freed from the dominion of sin, and to persevere in well doing Rom. 6 22.

16. Must a Christian be sanctified, or become holy?
Yes, for as He who has called us is holy, so we must be holy in all manner of conversation. I Peter 1 15

17. Who effects or works sanctification in us?
We are sanctified and justified in the name of the Lord Jesus, and by the Spirit of our God. I Cor 6.11

V. THE CHURCH OF GOD

18. What is the assembly (congregation) of believers called?
The church of God. I Cor. 1:2.

19. How does Christ view His church?
As His body. He is the head of the body—the church Col. 1:18.

20. Are all professing to belong to the church of God true members of the church of Christ?
No; they only are true members, who, by faith in Christ, have become the children of God. Gal. 3:26.

21. Are there to be teachers and ministers in the churches?
Yes; the ministers are to preach the Word diligently, and exhort; but the church is to hear and obey the Word. II Tim. 4:2. Titus 1:5; Heb. 13:17

VI. Holy Baptism

22. Did the Lord Jesus institute baptism, and command us to maintain and practice it?
Yes; He said to His disciples, "Go ye therefore, and teach all nations, baptizing them in the name of the Father, and of the Son, and of the Holy Ghost" Matt. 28:19.

23. Is baptism essential to salvation?
Yes; he that believeth and is baptized shall be saved. Mark 16:16.

24. Who are to be baptized?
All those who believe on the Lord Jesus Christ, repent and are converted unto Him. Acts 2.41; 8:37; 3 19; Matt. 3·8.

25. To what end was baptism instituted?
As a visible sign by which believers are united with the Lord Jesus and His Church. Gal. 3 26, 27; I Peter 3·21.

26. What does baptism teach us?
That we are buried with Christ by baptism into death; that like as Christ was raised up from the dead, by the glory of the Father, even so we also should walk in newness of life. Rom. 6:4, 5.

VII. The Lord's Supper

27. Who instituted the Lord's Supper?
The Lord Jesus Himself, in the night in which He was betrayed. Matt. 26:26-28.

28. With what did He institute it?
With bread and wine. I Cor 11.23-25.

29. For what purpose was the Lord's Supper instituted?
To commemorate the sufferings and death of Christ; and as a token of communion with Christ, and the communion of believers with each other Luke 22:19; I Cor. 11:26; 10.16, 17.

30. Is the Lord's Supper to be commemorated often?
Yes; according to the example of the first Christians it should be observed frequently. Acts 2.41, 42.

31. Who is to commemorate the Lord's Supper?
All baptized, penitent believers. Acts 2:41, 42.

32. What is required of those who wish to commemorate the Lord's Supper?
True examination. Let a man examine himself, and so let him eat of that bread, and drink of that cup. I Cor. 11:27, 28.

33. What do we thereby show forth?
We thereby show forth the Lord's death till He come. I Cor. 11:26.

34. What did the Lord Jesus do to His disciples after the Supper?
He washed their feet, and said, "If I then your Lord and Master, have washed your feet; ye also ought to wash one another's feet For I have given you an example, that ye should do as I have done to you" John 13 14, 15.

THE WALDECK CATECHISM, PART 3, CHAPTER IV

Chapter IV

I. THE LIFE AND DEPORTMENT OF BELIEVERS

1. Question.—How should believers conduct themselves in their walk and conversation?
Answer.—As the redeemed of the Lord they should serve God in holiness and righteousness which is acceptable to Him, and let their good works shine before men. Luke 1:74, 75; Matt 5:16.

2. Did the Lord Jesus also give us a command?
Yes; He said, "A new commandment I give unto you, That ye love one another; as I have loved you, that ye also love one another." John 13 34.

3. Shall we also love our enemies?
Yes; Christ says, "Love your enemies; bless them that curse you; do good to them that hate you, and pray for them which despitefully use you and persecute you, that ye may be the children of your Father which is in heaven " Matt. 5:44, 45.

II. NONRESISTANCE AND FORBEARANCE

4. What ought we to do when we are injured by any one?
We are not to render evil for evil, or railing for railing, but contrariwise blessing. I Peter 3:9.

5. Must all true Christians be willing to suffer patiently?
Yes; for it is written, "For even hereunto were ye called; because Christ also suffered for us, leaving us an example that ye should follow his steps." I Pet. 2 21. Matt. 10:22.

6. How does Christ comfort His followers in sufferings?
He says, "Blessed are ye when men shall revile you and persecute you—for great is your reward in heaven." Matt. 5.11, 12.

III. THE MAGISTRACY AND OATHS

7. How are we to deport ourselves toward the magistracy?
Let every soul be subject to the higher powers. For there is no power but of God; the powers that be are ordained of God. Rom. 13:1.

8. What does the Saviour tell us in regard to swearing oaths?
He says, "But I say unto you, Swear not at all let your communications be Yea, yea; Nay, nay: for whatsoever is more than these cometh of evil." Matt. 5:34, 37.

9. Is this said of all oaths?
Yes; for James says, "But above all things, my brethren, swear not; neither by heaven, neither by the earth, neither by any other oath." Jas. 5:12.

10. What did the Lord Jesus say of idle words?
But I say unto you, "That every idle word that men shall speak, they shall give an account thereof in the day of judgment." Matt. 12.36.

IV. MATRIMONY, DUTY OF PARENTS, CHILDREN, DOMESTICS, SUPERIORS

11. Who instituted matrimony?
The Lord God Himself, between Adam and Eve, in Paradise. Gen. 2:24.

12. What persons may enter the state of matrimony?
Those who are not too nearly related to each other, and who are of the same faith. Lev 18·6-20; I Cor. 7 29; 9·5.

13. May married persons be divorced?
No; they shall not be divorced saving for the cause of fornication. Matt. 5:32; 19:3, 9.

14. How are married persons to conduct themselves toward each other?

Husbands are to love their wives as their own bodies; and the women are to submit themselves unto their husbands. Eph 5 22-28

15. What are parents to do for their children?

They are to bring them up in the nurture and admonition of the Lord Eph 6.4

16. How are children to behave towards their parents?

They are to obey their parents in all things "Honour thy father and thy mother is the first commandment with promise" Col 3 20, Eph 6 1, 2

17. What have men servants and maid servants to observe towards their masters or superiors?

That they in all things obey their masters or superiors according to the flesh, not with eye-service, as men-pleasers; but in singleness of heart, fearing God, then they shall receive of the Lord the reward of the inheritance Col. 3 22-24

18. How are masters or superiors to treat their domestics?

They should forbear threatening, knowing that their master also is in heaven, with whom there is no respect of persons.

V. Church Discipline, or Excommunication of the Impenitent

19. If a brother or a sister of the church should be overtaken in a fault, how is such a one to be dealt with?

We are to restore such a one in the spirit of meekness. Gal. 6.1

20. But if the offender will not receive the admonition, what then is to be done?

He should be admonished a second time by two or three. Matt. 18.16.

21. But what are we to do with him who persistently refuses admonition, or who commits gross sin?

He must be excommunicated from the church, and we are to have nothing to do with him, that he may be ashamed Matt. 18 17; I Cor. 5.11, 13; II Thess. 3.6, 14.

22. But if he repent, how shall we deal with him?

We should forgive him and restore him Sufficient to such a man is the punishment which was inflicted of many; therefore, we must the more forgive and comfort him II Cor 2:5-7.

VI. Prayer

23. What is the true means by which we may obtain all things of God?

Prayer. Ask, and it shall be given unto you. Matt. 7.7.

24. Should we use many words in prayer?

No; we are not to use vain repetitions as the heathen do; for our Father in heaven knoweth what things we have need of before we ask Him. Matt 6:7, 8.

25. How do we call upon God the Father?

In the name of Jesus. For at His name every knee shall bow, that the Father may be glorified in the Son. John 14:13, Phil 2·10; Rom. 10 13.

26. How did the Lord Jesus teach us to pray?

Our Father which art in heaven, Hallowed be Thy name Thy kingdom come Thy will be done in earth, as it is in heaven Give us this day our daily bread And forgive us our debts, as we forgive our debtors. And lead us not into temptation, but deliver us from evil For Thine is the kingdom, and the power, and the glory, forever Amen Matt 6 9-13

27. Does God at all times hear our prayer?

Yes; this is the confidence that we have in Him, that if we ask anything according to His will, He heareth us Still He does sometimes delay to grant our petitions in order to test our faith I John 5 14, Matt 15 22, 28

28. Shall we also call upon the Lord Jesus?
Yes; they all shall honor the Son as they honor the Father, and call upon the name of our Lord Jesus Christ John 5 23, I Cor 1 2

29. How shall we call upon the name of the Lord Jesus?
As the Mediator between God and man, who gave Himself a ransom for all I Tim 2 5, 6

30. What should we bear in mind in prayer?
Thanksgiving But in every thing by prayer and supplication with thanksgiving, let your requests be made known unto God Phil 4 6, Eph 5 20

VII KNOWING AND DOING

31. Is it necessary that we should know what is good?
Yes, but knowledge (without charity) puffeth up I Cor 8 1

32. How are we, having knowledge, to demean ourselves?
We should be humble and diffident, for if a man think himself to be something when he is nothing, he deceiveth himself Gal 6 3

33. What does knowledge profit us?
Knowledge may teach us how we ought to conduct ourselves in the house of God. I Tim 3 15

34. Is then a mere knowledge of God's word not sufficient?
No, we must also be doers of the Word, and not hearers only Jas 1.22

35. What is the duty of Christians, in their whole walk and conversation?
All things whatsoever ye would that men should do to you, do ye even so to them And whatsoever ye do in word or deed, do all in the name of the Lord Jesus, giving thanks to God and the Father by Him Matt 7 12; Col 3 17.

36. What should we say when we have done all things?
We are unprofitable servants we have done that which was our duty to do Luke 17 10.

Chapter V

I. OF DEATH, THE RESURRECTION OF THE DEAD, AND THE DAY OF JUDGMENT

1. Question.—What is the end of this natural life?
Answer.—The end of life is death Sirach 14·18; Heb 9.27

2. Must all men die?
Yes; it is appointed unto men once to die Heb 9 27.

3. Does the soul die with the body?
No, the soul is immortal, which no man is able to kill Matt 10 28

4. What becomes of the soul after death?
This is shown unto us in the parable of the rich man and Lazarus Luke 16 19-26

5. Will there be any in the last day that will not die?
Yes, but they will be changed to immortality. I Cor 15 51.

II. THE RESURRECTION OF THE DEAD

6. Will the bodies of the dead rise again?
Yes, there will be a future resurrection of the just and unjust Acts 24·15

7. When will the dead rise?
At the last day For the trumpet shall sound, and the dead shall be raised incorruptible John 6.39; I Cor 15 51, 52

8. Who will raise the dead?
God will raise up the dead, by Jesus Christ II Cor 4.14

III. The Final Judgment

9. What will follow the resurrection of the dead?

There will be a day, in the which God will judge the world in righteousness. We must then all appear before the judgment seat of Christ. Acts 17:31; II Cor. 5 10.

10. Who will then be the judge?

Jesus Christ, the Son of God for the Father judgeth no man; but hath committed all judgment unto the Son John 5:22, 27.

11. How will this take place?

When the Son of Man shall come in His glory, and all the holy angels with Him, then shall He sit upon the throne of His glory; and before Him shall be gathered all nations, and He shall separate them one from another, as a shepherd divideth His sheep from the goats; and He shall set the sheep on His right hand, but the goats on the left. Matt. 25·31-33.

12. Will there be respect of persons?

No; for there is no respect of persons with God; He will reward every man according to his works. Rom. 2.6, 11.

13. Will men be judged only according to their works?

Men shall give account also, in the day of judgment, of every idle word that they speak. Matt. 12:36.

14. Will secret thoughts also be brought into judgment?

The Lord will bring to light the hidden things of darkness, and will make manifest the counsels of the hearts, and will judge the secrets of men. I Cor. 4:5, Rom. 2:16.

15. How will sentence then be pronounced?

Then shall the King say unto them on His right hand, Come, ye blessed of my Father, inherit the kingdom prepared for you from the foundation of the world. Then shall the King say also to them on the left hand, Depart from me, ye cursed, into everlasting fire, prepared for the devil and his angels. Matt. 25:34-41.

IV. The Reward of the Pious, and the Punishment of the Ungodly

16. What shall finally be the reward of the pious?

They shall enter into eternal life, and be free from all sin. There they shall be before the throne of God, and serve Him day and night in His temple; and He that sitteth on the throne shall dwell among them. They shall hunger no more, neither thirst any more; neither shall the sun light on them, nor any heat; for the Lamb which is in the midst of the throne shall feed them, and shall lead them into living fountains of waters: and God shall wipe away all tears from their eyes. Rev. 7:15.

17. What will become of the ungodly?

They shall be punished with everlasting destruction from the presence of the Lord and from the glory of His power. II Thess. 1.9.

18. What have we in conclusion to learn from all this?

We learn from all this that heaven and earth shall pass away, in a time and hour unknown to man; and that the Lord will then appear in judgment to give to every man according to his works. Therefore, we should always watch, and be ready, lest the day of judgment come upon us unawares, and always be ready to meet the Lord with joy, and to remain with Him unto all eternity. Amen.

Appendix VI
Roosen's Catechism

One of the outstanding elders and writers in German Mennonite history is Gerrit Roosen. He was born at Altona near Hamburg on February 25, 1612 At the age of twenty-six he founded a hosiery factory and business. He was also a prominent ship owner in his day. On August 28, 1640, he was united in marriage with Mayken or Maria Amoury. This union was graced with at least nine children. Mayken died September 18, 1695. Gerrit was ordained deacon in the year 1649 to succeed his father. On April 8, 1660, he was elected as a minister, preaching his first sermon the following Sunday, on the text, Micah 6 8. On June 12, 1663, he was ordained as an elder In the year 1702 he published two books: (1) a vindication of Mennonitism entitled, *Unschuld und Gegenbericht* . . . ; and (2) his catechism of 148 Questions and Answers entitled, *Christliches Gemutsgesprach* . . . , the full title of which in English translation reads thus: "Christian Spiritual[1] Conversation on Saving Faith and the Knowledge of the Truth which Leads to Godliness in the Hope of Eternal Life, Tit. 1.2."

No copy of the 1702 edition is today available in America, but the 1727 reprint contains the 148 Questions and Answers, as well as the Shorter Catechism of 1690, and another catechism of twenty-two questions and answers by "A. Z." (identity unknown), also twenty-eight prayers. At least six European editions have been catalogued by Robert Friedmann.[2] 1702, 1727, 1766, 1783, 1816 and 1838, none of which indicates the place of printing. American reprints are as follows: Ephrata, 1769 and 1770; Germantown, 1790; Lancaster, 1811, 1836, and 1869; Berlin (Kitchener) Ontario, 1839 and 1846; Doylestown, Pennsylvania, 1848; and Elkhart, 1868 and 1873. English editions: Lancaster, 1857, 1870, 1878, and 1892; Union Grove, Pennsylvania, 1921; Scottdale, Pennsylvania, 1941. The ninety-year-old patriarch surely produced a popular catechism.

At the age of ninety-seven Roosen administered his last baptismal and communion services. On November 20, 1711, at the age of ninety-nine, he died of a wound he had suffered while chopping wood, and was buried on November 26.

Concerning Roosen's large catechism, Robert Friedmann writes.[3] "Few books have met with such general approval among Mennonites everywhere as the *Gemutsgespräch*, the outstanding catechism of the church as a whole " Nevertheless there is a somewhat mediocre quality to the book. Roosen devotes a huge section to the doctrine of God, although he was not a great theologian. It is the extensiveness and Biblicism of his work which has undoubtedly contributed to its popularity among Mennonites While it is true that Roosen knew his aged grandmother, and heard her often, and although she had herself known Menno Simons, 1496-1561, nevertheless he seems to lack something of the vigor and decisiveness of the Anabaptists, Dr. Friedmann suggests that although Roosen had not become a Pietist, his position might be characterized by the phrase, "Mennonitism in minor key." Roosen betrays a feeling of greater spiritual nearness to the Protestants of his day than had been the case with the Anabaptists. He spends much more time on the truths upon which Christians agree, and correspondingly less than did the Anabaptists on the unique emphases of the Mennonites.

The text given below is that of the 1941 English edition, Scottdale, Pennsylvania

---

1 'Spiritual" is only an approximate equivalent for *Gemüt* Dr. Friedmann suggests that *Gemüt* refers to "emotional inwardness" (*Op cit.*, 235).
2 Robert Friedmann: *Mennonite Piety Through the Centuries*, (Goshen, Indiana: 1949), Goshen College, 144
3 *Op. cit.*, 144

HOW TO ATTAIN TRUE GODLINESS, DOCTRINE, AND PRACTICE

Question 1. Should man besides the necessary cares belonging to his bodily wants, also observe and consider more; so that he may keep his mind in a good state of rest?

Answer. Yes, certainly, as he would otherwise live like a brute in the world; wherefore he should, as a reasonable being, consider this well, and maintain his proper position among other creatures, which live along with him, and also receive their nourishment from the earth, whereby he will then find that he does not only surpass the creatures in many things in knowledge,—but also, that he is possessed of a much higher spirit than creatures

2. Are there also men who are not conscious of possessing a higher spirit than brutes, who yet maintain, that they can keep their minds in a good state of rest in this life?

Of such men there are more than enough in the world, who show not only by their words, but also by their actions, course of life, and countenance, that they know nothing of their salvation, much less that they are concerned about it. They know neither themselves nor their condition and live worse than the brutes But whenever any of these men become of another and a better mind, and get into other reflections—which cannot take place, however, without divine agency—and continue in them they will come not only to a knowledge of the nature of their condition, but also to a knowledge of themselves, and their higher spirit Many wise heathen came to great knowledge, through which they endeavored to bring other men, who from inattention forgot themselves, and lived more like brutes than men, to a better and higher knowledge by their ingenious sayings, among which the best and most useful is considered to be the one. "Know thyself"

3. Are there also men who do not know themselves as such?

Not only have wise heathen found this by examination, but experience teaches daily, that there are men who, like blind heathen, have no knowledge of themselves, but live more brutish than human, from which it is evident, that they neither know themselves, their Creator, nor the spirit that is in them

4. In what, then, does man's true knowledge of himself consist?

This knowledge consists in two things (1) to know that of and from himself, he has no power to do or understand anything, either in matters external or spiritual, (2) to have a knowledge of his transitory and troublesome state of life

5. Did the wise heathen obtain the knowledge of themselves, wherewith they could teach others with their sayings?

The wise heathen obtained a knowledge of themselves through the light of nature, a diligent observation of their mind, as well as that of external nature, in regard to other living creatures, also by observing the glorious firmament and the active power visible in all creatures By this means they came to still higher knowledge, namely that there can be nothing of itself, but that there must be a First Cause, a Head and Being, in which, and through which, all things are, and through whose power everything is kept in state and being

First Article, of Faith of God

6. What First Cause then, is that, in which, from which, and through which, we and all things are, and are kept in being?

This First Cause is the Great and Incomprehensible God, who has created everything in heaven above, on earth beneath, and in the water He is the Creator and Preserver of all things, and keeps everything by the power of His word From this God man has received a much higher spirit than other creatures, as he has been "created in His own image" (Gen 1 2, 7), and has also been appointed by Him, lord over all things

7. Are the sayings of the wise heathen sufficient whereby to come to this high knowledge of God?

The sayings of the wise heathen are not sufficient for this purpose, although we may learn something from them, but the Holy Scriptures teach us this knowledge with much clearness and many particulars

8. In what respect, then, are the Holy Scriptures preferable to other writings?

The Holy Scriptures are Scriptures given by inspiration of God, "profitable for doctrine, for reproof, for correction, for instruction in righteousness" (I Tim 3: 16) They are given through highly enlightened, holy men, who were gifted by the Spirit of God above other men, and who spake these Scriptures by inspiration of God, "as they were moved by the Holy Ghost" (II Pet 1 21) Cp II Sam 23.2

9. Do the Holy Scriptures also teach that we should come to a knowledge of ourselves?

Of this we have so much information in the Holy Scriptures that it would be superfluous to quote it here. The holy men of God among whom was the king and prophet David, saw that many men forgot themselves, and did not discern the glory of their Creator He says, "Know ye that the Lord He is God, it is He that made us, and not we ourselves" (Ps 100 3) And again, "Verily every man at his best state is altogether vanity. Surely every man walketh in a vain shew: surely they are disquieted in vain" (Ps 39 5, 6). Again, "For if a man think himself to be something, [understand, of himself] when he is nothing, he deceiveth himself" (Gal. 6.3) Further, "What hast thou that thou didst not receive? now if thou didst receive it, why dost thou glory, as if thou hadst not received it?" (I Cor. 4 7)

10. Is it enough for man to come to a knowledge of himself and of God, in order that he may thereby, in this life, have a mind and conscience at rest?

That is not sufficient He must go further in his knowledge in order that he may obtain still more knowledge of the Great God, through whom and from whom he himself and everything exists, as the Holy Scriptures also testify of God, that He is He who upholds "all things by the word of His power" (Heb 1·3).

11. Did those who had not the Holy Scriptures not come to a true knowledge of God through a consideration of their condition and the observation of created things?

Neither the one nor the other was sufficient; for, while they saw and knew from created things that there is and must be a God who created such things; they did not glorify Him "as God, neither were thankful; but became vain in their imaginations, and their foolish heart was darkened Professing themselves to be wise, they became fools" (Rom 1·21, 22) Cp Eph 4 18 For "that which may be known of God" (Rom 1 19) God had revealed to them And what they further came to, is added or explained in the same chapter (v 28).

12. Is it sufficient that we absolutely believe and hold that there is a God, who created the heavens, the earth, and the water, together with all things that are on and in them?

It is certainly not sufficient for us merely to believe and hold that there is a God, leaving Him as such, without conforming to His Holy Word, for, " it is written, The just shall live by faith For the wrath of God is revealed from heaven against all ungodliness and unrighteousness of men, who hold the truth in unrighteousness" (Rom 1 17, 18) And it is also testified of such men. "They profess that they know God; but in work they deny Him, being abominable, and disobedient, and unto every good work reprobate" (Tit 1 16).

13. What more, then, must be observed and done by man, besides having faith in and knowledge of God, in order that he may have a mind at rest, and hope in God in this life?

Man must by faith entirely submit and give himself up to the Great God, and show himself in all things obedient to Him He must honor, praise, serve, and fear Him, as is much required of us in Holy Scripture, in which God represents Himself to man as a Lord and Father when He says "A son honoureth his father, and a servant his master; if then I be a father, where is Mine honour? and if I be a master, where is My fear? saith the Lord of Hosts" (Mal. 1:6). So also Moses taught the children of Israel to know their God, who brought them out of the land of Egypt, in the following sentiment: Now Israel! What doth the Lord thy God require of thee but that thou love Him "with all thine heart, and with all thy soul, and with all thy might" (Deut. 6:6), honoring, fearing and serving Him, and walking in His ways, that it may be well with thee and thy children forever.

14. Is the acceptable and perfect will of God sufficiently made known to us in Holy Scripture, namely, as to how we may live and walk acceptably before Him?

It is incontrovertible that the perfect and acceptable will of God is sufficiently made known to us in Holy Scripture; inasmuch as it is frequently represented as the inspired word of God throughout its contents; and amongst others by Isaiah when he says: "Seek ye out of the book of the Lord, and read: no one of these shall fail, none shall want her mate: for my mouth it hath commanded, and His Spirit it hath gathered them" (Isa 34:16) And again by Paul to Timothy, when he says: "All Scripture is given by inspiration of God, and is profitable for doctrine, for reproof, for correction, for instruction in righteousness, that the man of God may be perfect, throughly furnished unto all good works" (II Tim. 3:16, 17)

15. Which is the chief article taught in Holy Scripture which we are to observe and consider and from which we may hope in God to have eternal life?

This chief article is, as has already been observed in part, faith in God and His holy Word, accompanied by a pure and fervent love; so that faith and love work together; for where true faith in God exists love is its companion. Now out of this faith, hope is born, so that one springs from the other, for, "without faith it is impossible to please Him" (Heb. 11:6). For when the Lord Jesus was once asked which was the great commandment in the law He answered: "Thou shalt love the Lord thy God with all thy heart, and with all thy soul, and with all thy mind. This is the first and great commandment. And the second is like unto it, Thou shalt love thy neighbour as thyself. On these two commandments hang all the law and the prophets" (Matt. 22:37-40). Therefore Paul also says, "Now the end of the commandment is charity out of a pure heart, and of a good conscience, and of faith unfeigned" (I Tim. 1:5). "For in Jesus Christ neither circumcision availeth any thing, nor uncircumcison; but faith which worketh by love" (Gal. 5:6). "And now abideth faith, hope, charity, these three; but the greatest of these is charity" (I Cor. 13:13).

16. Are then these two articles, namely, hope and love, so connected with faith, that without them, we can have no hope in God and eternal life?

Yes, certainly; it is faith, from which true love has its origin and through which our hope is strengthened, that is so necessary a thing. Without it it is impossible to please God, as we have just seen from Heb. 11:6. "But he that believeth not shall be damned" (Mark 16:16).

17. What then is faith properly in itself?

Faith is to accept and receive as truth that which has been propounded to us from Holy Scripture by devout men; which we should hold and believe as being as infallible, as if we had seen it ourselves, or heard it from the mouth of God. In accordance with this also is the testimony of Paul, "Now faith is the substance of things hoped for, the evidence of things not seen" (Heb 11:1). As we also read of Moses, "By faith he forsook Egypt, not fearing the wrath of the king: for he endured, as seeing Him who is invisible" (Heb. 11:27).

18. What then must we properly and chiefly believe of God, and how must we believe in Him, and be steadfast in such faith, inasmuch as a proper faith in

Him, is frequently called a saving faith, and which is the foundation of a happy hope in Him?

Besides faith in God, as already mentioned, we must also believe the testimony of the Holy Gospel of Jesus Christ, the living Son of God "And this is life eternal, that they might know Thee the only true God, and Jesus Christ, whom Thou hast sent" (John 17 3) Paul also says, "If thou shalt confess with thy mouth the Lord Jesus, and shalt believe in thine heart that God hath raised Him from the dead, thou shalt be saved For with the heart man believeth unto righteousness; and with the mouth confession is made unto salvation" (Rom. 10.9, 10).

19. On what must saving faith be grounded or built?

Not on man's wisdom or enticing, pretty words, proceeding out of his own heart, but on the infallible word of God alone, to which the Scriptures of the Old and New Testaments are serviceable, being written and produced by holy men, "moved by the Holy Ghost" (II Pet. 1 21) Faith is confirmed by signs and wonders. Thereon Paul grounded his faith when he said that he believed all things written in the law and in the prophets Acts 24 14 This he said, because the Gospel was not yet then written. To this Christ also directs, when He says, "He that believeth on Me, as the Scripture hath said, out of his belly shall flow rivers of living water" (John 7 38).

20. Is the general description of faith called Symbolum Apostolorum, or Apostolic Faith, or Apostolic Confession of Faith, not the true Formulary of the Christian Faith; and has he who confesses it not the true Confession of the Christian Faith?

The so-called Symbolum Apostolorum contains, it is true, the chief articles of the Christian Faith, and may, in so far, be regarded as a Confession of the same, inasmuch as it agrees with the writing of the apostles. But it is not to be received as truth that, as some pretend, the twelve apostles brought into its present form, each of them composing an article of it. It is, however, not on this account in itself objectionable, but saving evangelical faith requires yet more particulars to a full instruction in it.

21. Is then the foregoing Formulary of Faith, when expressed according to the words it contains, not the right Confession of the Christian Faith, which is required of a Christian and which is necessary to salvation?

Saving faith does not consist in the production of an article thus composed, which is conceived by the memory, and brought forth by the mouth; or else school children would have saving faith, as they can readily express this article No. The right and full faith to salvation must be planted and conceived in the hearts and minds of men by reading and hearing the Word of God. When this has taken root it will by its efficacious power produce fruits of faith which will be seen by others, as has already been said in Question 15 and answer to the same, and proved from Gal 5 6, I Tim 1 5 That true faith to salvation does not merely rest in the heart but must also be increased in the same and brought forth, is also proved from Rom 10 10 That we are justified if we believe with the heart and saved if we make confession with the mouth was the reason that Philip said to the eunuch, "If thou believest with thine heart ." (Acts 8 37) And that faith comes into the heart of man by hearing the Word of God, or by reading and reflecting on the same, is seen not only from this example of the eunuch, and in the same chapter from that of the people of Samaria but also from the sending of the apostles to preach the Gospel Acts 8 14, 17; Mark 16:15, 16 For this reason Paul also says, "How shall they believe in Him of whom they have not heard?" (Rom. 10.14) And lastly he says, "So then faith cometh by hearing, and hearing by the Word of God" (Rom 11.17)

22. Has then the requisite faith also certain signs whereby it may be known to be saving faith, as a good tree is known by the fruit which it brings forth?

Where no fruit of faith is shown or to be seen, there the full and true faith in the great and true God does not exist whereby the promised salvation by grace is obtained, for thus it is testified of faith, "The just shall live by his faith" (Hab 2:4) And "Now the just shall live by faith; but if any man draw back, my soul shall have no pleasure in him" (Heb. 10:38). The same is to be inferred from the word of Peter, "And beside this, giving all diligence, add to your faith virtue; and to virtue knowledge, and to knowledge temperance; and to temperance patience, and to patience godliness, and to godliness brotherly kindness; and to brotherly kindness charity For if these things be in you, and abound, they make you that ye shall neither be barren nor unfruitful in the knowledge of our Lord Jesus Christ But he that lacketh these things is blind, and cannot see afar off" (II Pet. 1:5-9). And James says, "For as the body without the spirit is dead, so faith without works is dead also" (Jas. 2 26), which agrees with the words of Christ, "Let your light so shine before men, that they may see your good works, and glorify your Father which is in heaven" (Matt. 5 16)

23. Is not that a perfect faith, if we believe in the Great God of heaven who rules with power and glory over everything in heaven and on earth, like a king and emperor over their dominions?

The Great God of heaven and earth is represented to us as being in heaven, as He also is, but He is so represented to us, because we are on earth The Lord God, although He created the earth and yet does not need it, is represented as being locally separated from us by being in heaven, as is taught in the Lord's Prayer, "Our Father which art in heaven . ." (Matt 6·9) We must not, however, therefore imagine that the Lord God is confined to heaven and separated from earth, as, for instance, a king resides in his capital, separated from the rest of his country and subjects The Lord God is a God everywhere present, as David amply testifies in his 139th Psalm; and as the Lord Himself speaks through Isaiah: "The heaven is My throne, and the earth is my footstool" (Isa. 66.1) The wise king Solomon expresses himself likewise in dedicating the temple, when he says, "The heaven and heaven of heavens cannot contain Thee" (I Kings 8 27). Although God is frequently represented as being in heaven, yet He is "not far from every one of us" (Acts 17·27).

Article First, of the Divine Attributes

24. Is God as well present with us on earth as He is with angels in heaven?

Certainly the Lord God is as well present with us on earth as He is with the angels in heaven; and we people on earth are as well in His presence as the angels in heaven are in His presence. For thus says the Lord through Jeremiah, "Am I a God at hand, and not a God afar off? . Do not I fill heaven and earth?" (Jer. 23 23, 24). And through Isaiah He says, "For thus saith the high and lofty One that inhabiteth eternity, whose name is Holy; I dwell in the high and holy place, with him also that is of a contrite and humble spirit, to revive the spirit of the humble, and to revive the heart of the contrite ones" (Isa. 57:15). The same is confessed by the king and prophet David, when he says, "Whither shall I go from Thy Spirit? or whither shall I flee from Thy presence? If I ascend up into heaven, Thou art there, If I make my bed in hell, behold Thou art there" (Ps 139 7, 8).

Article Second, of the Divine Attributes

25. Is there anything more to be believed and confessed of God, than that He is as well present on earth as in heaven, and is consequently everywhere present?

There are yet more and different attributes in God, who is God of heaven and earth, to be believed and confessed, namely, such as these That He is a

Great Lord, yea, a Lord of lords, and a King of kings, who has not only created heaven and earth, and the water, and everything that is in and on them, but also, that everything belongs to Him, for thus it is testified of Him, "The earth is the Lord's, and the fulness thereof; the world, and they that dwell therein" (Ps 24:1). And further: "For the Lord is a great God, and a great King above all gods. In His hand are the deep places of the earth: the strength of the hills is His also. The sea is His, and He made it and His hands formed the dry land" (Ps. 95:3-5).

Article Third, of the Divine Attributes

26. Does saving faith yet imply some particular divine attributes, if it is to be a perfect, evangelical faith?

In order that we may stand well and perfect in our faith in God, it must, according to Holy Scripture, also contain and imply a knowledge of the divine attributes, as made known to us in Holy Scripture, so that we believe as well that the Lord God is a God of such attributes as that we believe that He is God, inasmuch as from such faith, as well as from a knowledge of the divine attributes alone, obedience to, and the fear of God follow; in which attributes God is said to be excellent, as testified by Jeremiah when he says, "There is none like unto Thee, O Lord; Thou art great, and Thy name is great in might Who would not fear Thee, O King of nations?" (Jer. 10.6, 7). His greatness and power David also expresses, "Our God shall come, and shall not keep silence· a fire shall devour before Him, and it shall be very tempestuous round about Him He shall call to the heavens from above, and to the earth, that He may judge His people Gather My saints together unto Me; those that have made a covenant with Me by sacrifice" (Ps. 50.3-5) This knowledge also induced David to say· "My flesh trembleth for fear of Thee, and I am afraid of Thy judgments" (Ps 119 120)

27. What divine attributes are those revealed to us in Holy Scripture which it is as necessary for us to believe of God, as to believe that there is a God?

The divine attributes revealed to us in Holy Scripture, and which we should firmly believe, are the following· That the Lord God is One God, who is eternal, almighty, true, just, holy, and omniscient. in which attributes He exists as well in Himself, as in exercising them over man He shows mercy to all who fear Him, and listen to Him, as a gracious, merciful, long-suffering God, showing "mercy unto thousands of them that love Me and keep My commandments" (Ex. 20.6). But the seven first spiritual attributes, which serve as a caution to the pious in their pilgrimage through this world, redound to the fear and terror of the wicked and ungodly; inasmuch as they abuse and despise the goodness of God; and after their hardness and impenitent hearts treasure up unto themselves "wrath against the day of wrath and revelation of the righteous judgment of God; who will render to every man according to his deeds" (Rom 2.5, 6). On the contrary, however, the goodness of God is at all times over them that fear and love Him, and they can comfort themselves with David that the Lord "knoweth our frame; He remembereth that we are dust" (Ps 103:14)

28. Why is it so necessary to believe that the Lord God is a God of such divine attributes?

It is so necessary to believe this for the reason, that such belief serves to increase holy adoration, esteem, and veneration for the divine majesty among men. It is an active inducement to the attentive to fear God, for if the divine attributes were not incorporated in the Christian faith, men would again easily fall into errors of the heathen, who had all kinds of unmovable, dead images, and held them as their gods; which had indeed hands, feet, eyes, ears, and mouths made for them, but could therewith neither handle, walk, see, hear, nor speak. Ps 115:5-7. And each held in his imagination his own god as greater than all others, as they also judged of the God of heaven, whom Paul preached. Acts

19·27, 28 So it may also be seen in the adventure of Jonah that each man cried to his god Jonah 1:5 But our God "is over all" and "blessed forever" (Rom. 9·5).

29. What evidence have we in Holy Scripture that the Lord God is a God of such divine attributes and to what is it serviceable?

Of such evidence we have plenty in Holy Scripture, and among those who first gave evidence to this effect was Moses, with whom the Lord spake "face to face" (Ex 33·11), who received the first words of God on tables of stone, and delivered them to man, who also testifies of the oneness of God, as follows "Hear, O Israel: the Lord our God is one Lord" (Deut 6·4). And again, "Unto thee it was shewed, that thou mightest know that the Lord He is God; there is none else beside Him" (Deut. 4 35). And through the prophet Isaiah God testifies of Himself, when He says "I am the Lord, and there is none else, there is no God besides Me " "I am God, and there is none else, I am God, and there is none like Me" (Isa 45:5; 46 9) And Solomon says at the close of his prayer, "That all the people of the earth may know that the Lord is God, and that there is none else" (I Kings 8.60).

30. To what may the knowledge be serviceable that the Lord God is One God?

Such knowledge may be serviceable to us in many respects. First, if we should come into strange countries among heathen people where strange gods, or the sun, moon, or stars were worshiped, and we were urged to do the same, we might then think of the doctrine of Christ when He says, "Thou shalt worship the Lord thy God, and Him only shalt thou serve" (Matt 4 10), and of the angel who said to John, "worship God" (Rev. 19.10). For though we were at the ends of the earth, in Asia, Africa, Europe, or America, or elsewhere we would still have our God there to worship, as was the case with Daniel in the lions' den, and the three young men in the fiery furnace, who, although they were in a strange land among heathen people, still worshiped the God of heaven, and were heard, as is to be seen in Daniel 3 See also the case of Jonah in the fish's belly. Jonah 2 2

31. How and where is it certified and proved, that the Lord God is One God?

It is declared by and proved from the works of creation, as well as from Scripture, that the Lord God was before all visible and invisible things were created, and although these, namely, heaven and earth, and all things visible, will pass away, He will remain the same God as He was before, as the pious king David testifies of Him through the Spirit of God, "Lord, Thou hast been our dwelling place in all generations. Before the mountains were brought forth, or ever Thou hadst formed the earth and the world, even from everlasting to everlasting, Thou art God" (Ps 90 1, 2). And again, "Of old hast Thou laid the foundation of the earth and the heavens are the work of Thy hands. They shall perish, but Thou shalt endure yea, all of them shall wax old like a garment; as a vesture shalt Thou change them, and they shall be changed. But Thou art the same, and Thy years shall have no end" (Ps 102·25-27). This was also acknowledged by Abraham, who "planted a grove in Beersheba, and called there on the name of the Lord, the everlasting God" (Gen 21:33)

32. To what purpose is this knowledge of the eternity of God serviceable?

This knowledge is in many respects serviceable to the comfort of the pious, and to the strengthening of their faith, particularly to the comfort of themselves and children, when they consider that they have the Lord God as well with and about them, as He was from the beginning with all the pious ancient fathers to the enlightening of their understanding, their help and protection, when they walked in His fear, and continued in the right faith; as did the ancient fathers; of which Isaiah testifies when he says, "Hast thou not known? hast thou not heard, that the everlasting God, the Lord, the Creator of the ends of the earth, fainteth not, neither is weary? there is no searching of His understanding. He giveth power to the faint; and to them that have no might He increaseth strength" (Isa. 40:28, 29) Thus have the pious not only such a kind God over them during their lifetime; but also a God to whom they may at their death confidently give in charge their children, with a similar assurance, if they only fear God. As an example may be taken the children of Jonadab, son of Rechab (Jer 35). As David also assures, for, after speaking of the eternity of God, he says, "The children of Thy servants shall continue, and their seed shall be established before Thee" (Ps 102·28) And in Psalm 115, and 125.1, he says in substance that the Lord will abide with the pious forever, that He is "their hope and their shield," and that those who fear Him, also hope in Him, not only for this life, but for a happy existence in the life to come; so that even as they are from the eternal God, so they must also abide eternally The same is confirmed in substance in Rev. 22:3-6.

33. By what do we perceive and know, that the Lord God is an almighty God, and can so firmly believe the same?

God's almightiness or omnipotence may especially be seen in the great and incomprehensible works of creation, and in the preservation of all visible things, which have been in a state of operation for many hundreds of years, and all this by the "word of His power," as the pious king David also acknowledges, "For He spake, and it was done, He commanded, and it stood fast" (Ps 33.9) So God also spake to Abraham: "I am the Almighty God; walk before Me, and be thou perfect" (Gen. 17.1).

34. In what respect can the knowledge be serviceable to our faith, that the Lord God is an almighty God?

The knowledge may be serviceable to man for good in many respects, when he perceives and believes that God has power over everything, to do and carry out what He has promised in His Word. 1. First indeed it is serviceable in reminding him of his due obedience, to live piously and righteously, as said before, that God said to Abraham, "Walk before Me, and be thou perfect" (Gen 17:1). And Peter says, "Humble yourselves therefore under the mighty hand of God, that He may exalt you in due time" (I Pet 5 6) 2 It is serviceable to the pious and godly as a great and sure consolation in all their necessities and tribulations, that God is mighty to preserve, to help, and to save them; as also David speaks of the ways of the Lord, "Call upon Me in the day of trouble I will deliver Thee, and thou shalt glorify Me" (Ps. 50 15). And God Himself speaks through Isaiah, "When thou passest through the waters, I will be with thee; and through the rivers, they shall not overflow thee: when thou walkest through the fire, thou shalt not be burned; neither shall the flame kindle upon thee" (Isa. 43.2). Of all this we have sufficient examples and proof in the case of the children of Israel in the Red Sea, the prophet Jonah, the three young men in the fiery furnace, Daniel in the lions' den, Joseph in Egypt, and David in the persecution of Saul, who all felt and experienced God's omnipotence in their time of need; as is to be seen in Psalm 50·15, as already mentioned

35. Is this knowledge of the omnipotence of God also of use or service to those who do not live piously?

As excellent and wholesome as it is for the believing and pious, so dreadful it is to the profligate, and to those who live on so securely in disobedience and sin. They will be frightened and tremble when they shall hear of God's threatenings against and punishments of their ungodly lives, and how God has shown His power in the execution of His judgments, as is manifest in the case of Sodom, Gomorrah, Pharaoh and his host, Korah, Dathan, and Abiram, Jezebel, Absalom, and Jerusalem.

36. Is it also necessary that we believe and confess that God is a true God?

It is necessary to believe, that God is a true God, not only for the sake of the truth, that there is a God; but also that God Himself is the Truth; and that all that His servants, the prophets and apostles, have brought forth of Him, is firm, sure and infallible truth, as Paul testifies· "Let God be true, but every man a liar" (Rom 3:4). As also Moses says, "God is not a man, that He should lie; neither the son of man, that He should repent: hath He said, and shall He not do it? or hath He spoken, and shall He not make it good?" (Num 23.19).

37. To what then is it especially serviceable to believe that the Lord God is a true God?

It is serviceable not only to the pious as a special consolation, but also to sinners, when they hear the Word of God propounded to them for their conversion and reformation Still more especially is it serviceable to the pious as a consolation in all occurring events, that they can firmly depend on God's Word and promises, as to what He has promised to give them, as well in this life, as in the life to come. Therefore they can place their hope and confidence firmly thereon, as David says· "For the word of the Lord is right, and all His works are done in truth" (Ps 33:4). "For all the promises of God in Him are yea, and in Him Amen, unto the glory of God by us" (II Cor 1.20) "He is a buckler to all those that trust in Him" (Ps. 18:30)

38. Is it also serviceable to anything else to believe that God is true in His Word?

It has been noted that such faith is a great consolation to the pious. Now just as it serves the pious as a consolation, so it is on the contrary to ungodly, wilful and impenitent sinners a certain assurance of their punishment, if they continue and persist in their sinful course of life; for it is to be known that what God has pronounced concerning such in His Word will certainly come over them, as Paul says, "Despisest thou the riches of his goodness and forbearance and longsuffering; not knowing that the goodness of God leadeth thee to repentance? But after thy hardness and impenitent heart treasurest up unto thyself wrath against the day of wrath and revelation of the righteous judgment of God; who will render to every man according to his deeds" (Rom. 2:4-6). Therefore it serves sinners as a fear and dread, as Solomon says: "The wicked flee when no man pursueth" (Prov. 28.1).

39. Whence are we to believe that the Lord God is a holy God?

This is not only made known to us in His Word, but if we ponder in our minds over the divine perfections and majesty, we may therefrom comprehend and judge of His holiness, for Paul was even permitted to say of that which is human. "If the firstfruit be holy, the lump is also holy: and if the root be holy, so are the branches" (Rom 11:16). Now if that was holy which was sacrificed according to the law of the Lord, it follows that He also must be holy to whom such sacrifice was made, namely, God Besides, His angels are holy, as may be seen from Matt 25 31; then how much more is God holy who created them, so that the angels may of right cry out. "Holy, holy, holy, is the Lord of hosts. the whole earth is full of His glory" (Isa 6 3) And this the Lord God also speaks of Himself through Moses, "Ye shall . . be holy; for I am holy." Lev. 11·44, 45. Cp. Lev. 19·2; I Pet. 1 16

40. To what is the knowledge serviceable that the Lord God is a holy God?

It is serviceable to awaken and incite all pious and true Christians to a holy life and conversation, wherewith they show themselves to be children of their heavenly Father, and that they belong through faith in Jesus Christ to the family of God, and can call Him "Father" in their prayers Matt. 6 9 This, Peter says, is their calling: "But as He which hath called you is holy, so be ye holy in all manner of conversation" (I Pet. 1:15). And Paul also writes, "You hath He reconciled in the body of His flesh through death, to present you holy and unblameable and unreproveable in His sight" (Col. 1·21, 22). Even as the holy Zacharias prophesied: "That we being delivered out of the hand of our enemies might serve Him [God] without fear, in holiness and righteousness before Him, all the days of our life" (Luke 1:74, 75))

41. Whereby can we know that we should believe that the Lord God is a just God?

That we must also understand and conclude from His divine majesty and perfections, besides that it is declared to us in His holy Word, that He is just in His judgments on all the doings of men, whether they be good or evil (1) In this life; (2) After this life at the day of judgment, as David testifies of both when he says, "For the righteous Lord loveth righteousness, His countenance doth behold the upright" (Ps 11.7) "God judgeth the righteous, and God is angry with the wicked every day If he turn not, He will whet His sword, He hath bent His bow, and made it ready" (Ps. 7 11, 12) The Lord God also says Himself "I . . . give every man according to his ways, and according to the fruit of his doings" (Jer 17.10) And as the Lord God is just in the doings of men in this life, so will He also "judge the world in righteousness" at the day of judgment. Acts 17 31. This is also declared by Malachi (Mal 4 1-3) and by Matthew (Matt 25:34, 41)

42. To what may the knowledge be serviceable that the Lord God is a just God?

It is indeed serviceable to all men in many respects for good, if they would only always think about it and consider that God is a just God It is first serviceable to the pious as a precaution to administer justice and right in all their doings, their business and conversation, trade and profession, and that no one does in any wise oppress, take the advantage of, or "defraud his brother"; for the Lord, says Paul, "is an avenger of all such" (I Thess. 4 6). As God also speaks through Zechariah: "These are the things that ye shall do; speak ye every man the truth to his neighbour, execute the judgment of truth and peace in your gates" (Zech. 8·16) "Whosoever doeth not righteousness is not of God, neither he that loveth not his brother" (I John 3 10) Secondly, it may serve as a particular consolation to the pious, when they do their duty in their calling in justice and righteousness, but are nevertheless oppressed, persecuted, ill treated, slandered and ridiculed, on account of their piety; as was Joseph by his brethren. Gen. 37. It serves them as a consolation, when they thus see how the Lord carries out and defends the cause of the innocent, for, says Solomon, "the integrity of the upright shall guide them" (Prov 11 3). Thus the pious may and shall be happy in God in persecution, inasmuch as they know that God knows and judges them differently from what men do For, "the innocent shall stir up himself against the hypocrite. The righteous also shall hold on his way" (Job 17:8, 9). Of this we have an example in the case of David in the persecution of Saul I Sam. 19.10.

43. Is the knowledge of God's justice also in any way serviceable to sinners?

A consideration of God's justice may serve to inspire profligate and wilful sinners with fear and terror, as it does the pious with consolation, when they hear of God's justly threatened punishments, which God remembers "Woe unto the wicked! it shall be ill with him for the reward of his hands shall be given him" (Isa 3 11) And on those on whom God Himself will pass the heavy sentence of woe, on them it will remain. "For the wrath of God is revealed from heaven against all ungodliness and unrighteousness of men, who hold the truth in unrighteousness" (Rom 1·18) Now if such sinners see God's justice in the punishment of sin it may awaken in them repentance and sorrow for sin and a **reformation of life**, as may be seen in the case of those who became converted at Pentecost Acts 2. For if God's Word, God's omniscience, omnipotence, and justice, are discerned by sinners, sorrow for sin is not far off, and which awakens an internal sorrow and fear, as David says, "My flesh trembleth for fear of Thee; and I am afraid of Thy judgments" (Ps 119:120).

44. Is God also an omniscient God, to whom everything is known that men do?

That the Lord God is an omniscient God must follow from His omnipotence, even if it were not made known or revealed to us in Holy Scripture, but it is made known to us in Scripture, "He that planted the ear, shall He not hear? He that formed the eye, shall He not see?" (Ps 94 9) "Can any hide himself in secret places that I shall not see him? says the Lord" (Jer. 23 24) And Paul testifies of this when he says, "Neither is there any creature that is not manifest in His sight. but all things are naked and opened unto the eyes of Him with whom we have to do" (Heb 4 13).

45. How may this knowledge of the omniscience of God be serviceable to us if we believe and confess the same?

This knowledge of and belief in the omniscience of God is a chief article of the Christian faith inasmuch as man is thereby incited and animated to obedience towards God, the leaving off of evil, and reformation of life; for if God were an almighty and just God only, and not also an omniscient God, He would be circumstanced like a potentate who could not exercise his power and execute his judgments, because the misdeeds of his subjects could be hidden from him But as we know that the Lord God is omniscient, we must ever confess with David. "O Lord, Thou hast searched me, and known me. Thou knowest my downsitting and mine uprising, Thou understandest my thoughts afar off" (Ps 139.1, 2). And this belongs to the omniscience of God, that the prayers of the pious, although they are performed in secret, by each person according to his concerns, are known to and heard by Him, as David again says. "There is not a word in my tongue, but lo, O Lord, Thou knowest it altogether" (Ps 139 4) And this was the consolation of the pious Hezekiah when he thought he had to die, that all his doings were known to the Lord He says. "Remember now, O Lord, I beseech Thee, how I walked before Thee in truth and with a perfect heart, and have done that which is good in Thy sight" (Isa 38:3).

46. Is this knowledge of God's omniscience also in any way serviceable to profligate sinners?

As long as such sinners live on in unbelief and say in their hearts, with all the ungodly: "There is no God," and "God is not in all their thoughts" (Ps. 10.4) such knowledge is of no use to them· But if they are not yet wholly sunk in infidelity, nor avow such sentiments, and then come to think of the omniscience of God, it may serve them as a beginning to cease from and leave off their wicked and sinful course of life, or else they have to fear and dread God's threatened punishment, as Isaiah says, "Woe unto them that seek deep to hide their counsel from the Lord, and their works are in the dark, and they say, Who seeth us? and who knoweth us?" (Isa 29 15). And David confesses the same before the Lord when he says "If I say, Surely the darkness shall cover me, even the night shall be light about me Yea, the darkness hideth not from Thee, but the night shineth as the day· the darkness and the light are both alike to Thee" (Ps 139 11, 12)

47. Are there also attributes in the Lord God which are particularly exercised towards those who fear Him?

Yes, certainly As we have said before, and as is testified in many places in Holy Scripture, the Lord God is a gracious, merciful, longsuffering, and meek God towards all pious and godly persons who honor, serve, and love Him; even as we may see and read here and there in Holy Scripture: He shows mercy unto thousands of them that love Him, and keep His commandments Ex 20 6 And again, "The Lord, the Lord God, merciful and gracious, longsuffering, and abundant in goodness and truth, keeping mercy for thousands, forgiving iniquity and transgression and sin, and that will by no means clear the guilty" (Ex 34 6, 7) This also David testifies when he says "The Lord is merciful and gracious, slow to anger, and plenteous in mercy He will not always chide, neither will He keep His anger forever He hath not dealt with us after our sins, nor rewarded us according to our iniquities For as the heaven is high above the earth, so great is His mercy toward them that fear Him As far as the east is from the west, so far hath He removed our transgressions from us" (Ps 103 8-12).

48. May then the pious sin against God's grace, since they know that they have a merciful God?

No, since they would in this manner abuse the grace of God, and turn it into lasciviousness, as Jude says (Jude 4), and Paul corroborates, "What shall we say then? Shall we continue in sin, that grace may abound? God forbid. How shall we, that are dead to sin, live any longer therein?" (Rom 6 1, 2)

49. How then must the grace, mercy, and goodness of God be understood, so that they may be of use to the pious and godly?

For the pious and godly the grace and mercy of God are the main work in which they may have comfort in their pilgrimage and spiritual warfare, for thereby they are supported, if they peradventure err or stumble in their good intention. Without these they would have to despair, when they consider the great demand which God has made on them and all mankind, namely "Ye shall . . . be holy; for I am holy" (Lev. 11 44) "Be ye therefore perfect, even as your Father which is in heaven is perfect" (Matt. 5 48).

50. On what does the consolation of the pious rest in respect of the grace and mercy of God?

On the unspeakable and unfathomable love wherewith He has loved the whole world. John 3 16 God is "rich in mercy, for His great love wherewith He loved us" (Eph 2 4) But the pious, who feel their imperfection, sigh unto their God, for He knows what kind of creatures we are, and remembereth that we are dust" (Ps 103 14) Especially do they comfort themselves with the words of Peter, that the Lord "is longsuffering to usward, not willing that any should perish, but that all should come to repentance" (II Pet 3 9) This then awakens in the pious, in their sorrow over their sins, a hope in God's mercy, until they say, "I have trusted in Thy mercy, my heart shall rejoice in Thy salvation" (Ps 13 5). And David says therefore in his heart "I will love Thee, O Lord, my strength. The Lord is my rock, and my fortress, and my deliverer; my God, my strength, in whom I will trust" (Ps 18 1, 2) Besides this, see the Lord's promise and assurance, made through Isaiah, "They that wait upon the Lord shall renew their strength . . ." (Isa 40·31)

51. Is then this faith in and knowledge of the grace, meekness, longsuffering, and mercy of God, serviceable to no others, than mercy to those who endeavor to serve and fear the Lord in obedience?

It is serviceable not only to these, but also to those who, like the prodigal son, see the miserable and dangerous condition in which they stand towards God in respect of their souls, namely, how they abused the "grace and goodness of God, and turned them into lasciviousness" (Jude 4), and thus feel and are sensible of the burden of their sins, and sigh and speak with David "Mine iniquities are gone over mine head as an heavy burden they are too heavy for me My wounds stink and are corrupt because of my foolishness" (Ps. 38 4, 5). These may come t o God and say. "Have mercy upon me, O God, according to Thy lovingkindness according unto the multitude of Thy tender mercies blot out my transgressions Wash me thoroughly from mine iniquity, and cleanse me from my sin: For I acknowledge my transgressions and my sin is ever before me. Against Thee, Thee only, have I sinned, and done this evil in Thy sight" (Ps. 51:1-4) To those who thus draw nigh unto God, God will draw nigh (Jas. 4:8), especially when they follow the counsel which He has given through Isaiah, "Wash you, make you clean, put away the evil of your doings from before Mine eyes; cease to do evil; learn to do well" (Isa 1:16, 17)) Then comes He to meet them whom God the Father hath sent, to call sinners to repentance, and stands with outstretched arms, and says, "Come unto Me, all ye that labour, and are heavy laden, and I will give you rest" (Matt. 11 28) The sinner coming to God with such lamentation, and also with a contrite heart and a fixed purpose to reform his life, evidences true godly sorrow which "worketh repentance to salvation not to be repented of" (I Cor. 7 10). To such a sinner the door of mercy stands open, as is to be seen, with many particulars, in the case of the prodigal son, and his sins shall be remembered no more Jer. 31:34, Ezek 33 16

52. Is then the Lord God not also merciful to impenitent sinners?

As long as men continue in their profligate, carnal, and wicked course of life and conduct they cannot console themselves with the meekness, grace, and mercy of God, for, "there is no peace, saith the Lord, unto the wicked" (Isa 48:22). "For the wrath of God is revealed from heaven against all ungodliness and unrighteousness of men, who hold the truth in unrighteousness" (Rom. 1:18). And this sentence on the ungodly stands fixed: "Woe unto the wicked! it shall be ill with him; for the reward of his hands shall be given him" (Isa 3:11).

53. Are then such people called ungodly or godless, because God has nothing to do with them, and they nothing with God, and they are therefore godless, that is, without God?

They are not called godless, because they are without God, or because God has nothing to do with them, but because they are not willing to bear the Lord's easy yoke and light burden (Matt. 11:30), and follow their own will contrary to the will of God, and pursue their affairs with all kinds of crafty artifices, and without any fear of God, as David says, "The wicked boasteth of his heart's desire .... The wicked, through the pride of his countenance, will not seek after God: God is not in all his thoughts" (Ps. 10:3, 4). "The wicked are like the troubled sea, when it cannot rest, whose waters cast up mire and dirt" (Isa. 57:20). Therefore David speaks further rightly of them when he says, "The transgression of the wicked saith within my heart, that there is no fear of God before his eyes" (Ps. 36 1). For they turn themselves from God's commandments as if there were no God.

54. Is there then for such people no more hope of salvation? Must they remain banished from the Lord's countenance?

There is no hope for the salvation of such people, as long as they continue in their ungodliness, and wickedness, and reject the counsel of God against themselves; for, although they know "the judgment of God, that they which commit such things are worthy of death, not only do the same, but have pleasure in them that do them" (Rom. 1:32), and are "abominable, and disobedient, and unto every good work reprobate" (Tit 1:16). Therefore Scripture says unto them "After thy hardness and impenitent heart treasurest up unto thyself wrath against the day of wrath and revelation of the righteous judgment of God; who will render to every man according to his deeds" (Rom. 2:5, 6). "In the place where the tree falleth, there it shall be" (Eccl. 11:3).

55. When we have then come by faith to a knowledge of all these divine attributes, should we not then also have a knowledge of the nature of God's divine majesty?

In order that we may honor, love, fear, and serve the Lord God the better, He has, besides the revelation of His acceptable will, (as already mentioned and shown) also revealed to us His divine attributes, in order that we may thereby know in what relation He stands to us, but not how He exists in His own divine being. For, as this could not be serviceable to the promotion of our salvation, it has not pleased Him to reveal anything to us about it, that we may not by presumptuous searching and seeking to know His precise nature, commit sin. And, as mere creatures, how can we comprehend our Creator? For if the works of man cannot comprehend the nature of their maker, how shall we be able to understand and comprehend the nature of the Great Creator? "For as the heavens are higher than the earth, so are My ways higher than your ways, and My thoughts than your thoughts" (Isa. 55.9) When Moses desired to see the glory of God, he received the answer, "Thou canst not see My face· for there shall no man see Me, and live" (Ex 33 20) By this understand that God cannot be seen in His divine nature, for although God's countenance is mentioned in Holy Scripture, we must not understand this in a natural sense, after the manner of men; but rather in a spiritual sense, as an effect of Him towards us God is spoken of in human terms to assist, in some measure, our weakness, and to represent and show His operations, but not His precise nature, as no image can be formed of that, as is to be seen in Isaiah 40 18, 25 "To whom then will ye liken God? or what likeness will ye compare unto Him To whom then will ye liken Me, or shall I be equal? saith the Holy One" Thus the Lord God is and remains, to us in the nature of His being, an incomprehensible God, and although we can see His operations in many things, yet "His understanding is infinite" (Ps. 147·5) And we are obliged to say with Paul: "O the depth of the riches both of the wisdom and knowledge of God! how unsearchable are His judgments, and His ways past finding out!" (Rom. 11 33) Now if God's judgments and ways are incomprehensible, how much more so is His divine being itself?

Article Fourth, of the Unity of God

56. Now there has been much said of God, and, how that He was One God. Why then is it said by so many, and also at so many places "God the Father, God the Son, and God the Holy Ghost"? Is then according to such expression, the Son God, and the Holy Ghost God, even as the Father is God? Why then are the Jews in the wrong when they say that Christians worship and profess three Gods; whereas it is otherwise acknowledged that there is but One God?

We have said and confessed that not only the Lord God is incomprehensible, but also that His judgments in regard to us are so; therefore the divine being of the Father, of the Son, and of the Holy Ghost, or the Spirit of God, as they exist in themselves, cannot be comprehended by man nor expressed in words For although it is said by some men, that there are three independent persons or beings in the Godhead, and therefore say further "God the Father, God the Son, and God the Holy Ghost," yet we do not find such expressions in Holy Scripture. We find, on the contrary, that the Son and Holy Ghost are united in the same divine being and that the Godhead is likewise attributed to them; as Christ's own words purport, "He that hath seen Me hath seen the Father" (John 14:9), and "I and the Father are one" (John 10:30).

57. But when the Lord God calls Himself to Moses, "the God of Abraham, the God of Isaac, and the God of Jacob" (Ex. 3:15), are not thereby three names mentioned?

The Lord God does indeed confess Himself to have been the God of these three persons, but not that He, on His part, consists of three persons, but that He is the God of Israel. Besides that, He declares by this statement that He is the same God that was the God of their fathers; namely, "the God of Abraham, the God of Isaac, and the God of Jacob," who sent Moses to them (Israel), and was further now also their God. But this God is not merely a God of Abraham, of I s a a c, and of Jacob, but "The God of the whole earth" (Isa. 54:5). Not "the God of the Jews only" but "of the Gentiles also" (Rom 3:29).

58. How then must these three names be understood, of which we read in Matthew 28:19: "baptizing them in the name of the Father, and of the Son, and of the Holy Ghost?"

From this it must not be understood that there are three beings, or three persons, much less that there are three Gods in heaven[1] But these names are thus differently expressed in consideration of the work of redemption and the salvation of the human race; as, the Father, the origin, the Son, the means of redemption; and the Holy Ghost, sanctification and confirmation in salvation—all of which thus happens to us from the perfection of the Great God, Creator of heaven and earth, as Paul says "Now He which stablisheth us with you in Christ, and hath anointed us, is God, who hath also sealed us, and given the earnest of the Spirit in our hearts" (II Cor. 1 21, 22) Now although there are different persons with man, such as father, mother, and son, yet must we not thus talk and judge of God after the manner of man: for we have proved that He is an incomprehensible God Hence we should rather understand under these names, "One God," as John testifies of the same, "For there are three that bear record in heaven, the Father, the Word, and the Holy Ghost· and these three are one" (I John 5:7) Of this Oneness we have also testimony in John 1 1: "In the beginning was the Word, and the Word was with God, and the Word was God " We also read of God and the Spirit in the account of creation· that "the Spirit of God moved upon the face of the waters" (Gen 1:2). And to this David refers when he says, "By the word of the Lord were the heavens made, and all the host of them by the breath of His mouth" (Ps 33:6)

59. How can it be, that these three, namely, "God the Father, God the Son, and God the Holy Ghost," are "One God," since it is so clearly written by Matthew that Jesus was baptized by John, that the Spirit of God descended like a dove, and lighted upon Him, and that a voice from heaven said: "This is my beloved Son, in whom I am well pleased," where indeed the Son was baptized, the Holy Ghost seen, and the Father's voice heard. Matt. 3:16, 17. Is it not then to be inferred that there are three Divinities in heaven?

Were we to view and consider this matter after the manner of men we would conclude and judge that there are. but this great work of God, which He has, according to His promise, accomplished supernaturally, through His great love and divine power, cannot and must not be judged and understood in a natural manner, but rather be viewed, believed, and considered as an incomprehensible work, with high admiration of God and His great, almighty, and inconceivable wisdom The person of Jesus Christ was at that time to be seen and felt in His humanity in the flesh, yet as Paul says: "God was in Christ, reconciling the world unto Himself" (II Cor. 5:19). We must also further confess with Paul: "Great is the mystery of godliness: God was manifest in the flesh" (I Tim. 3:16).

---

[1] In his desire to escape tritheism Roosen has given the impression of veering toward Antitrinitarianism. Not that he held to a philosophical rationalism which denied the deity of the Lord Jesus and the personality of the Holy Spirit; Roosen was a simple evangelical and a Biblicist. He therefore employed the language of a Biblicist rather than of a theologian in attempting to wrestle with a profound theological topic One dare not hastily accuse him of unsound doctrine on the basis of one sentence, but must compare all his statements on the Godhead Note the latter part of his answer to the fifty-ninth question, for example Roosen accepted the entire corpus of Biblical truth as God's Word but lacked the requisite theological training to enable him to express his views with theological precision Cf his excellent answer to question 62, however. J. C W.

Thus this matter remains to human reason incomprehensible: even as a father who has a son, is not the son, but the father; so also is the son not the father, but the son of the father, and as the Holy Spirit is a Spirit of God and of Christ, so He is neither the Father nor the Son, but the Holy Spirit But as we are mere natural beings, and this is supernatural and a work of God, we must view it as a godly mystery and receive it in faith Nor should we desire to search into any part of the divine nature which is incomprehensible to us; as remarked before: "O the depth of the riches, both of the wisdom and knowledge of God! how unsearchable are His judgments, and His ways past finding out!" (Rom 11·33).

60. **Have then the Jews no testimony and proof of the "Unity of God" in the Old Testament; since it seems so strange to them that Christians profess to find and worship in the divine being, "Father, Son, and Holy Ghost," through which they (the Jews), alienate themselves still more from Christianity?**

It appears that as long as they adhere so closely to Moses, and the veil remains hanging over their hearts and eyes, they cannot perceive nor understand this matter. Besides this, it does not become them to keep so distant, and, much less, to speak so blasphemously of the matter in question, inasmuch as there is so frequently mention made of the "Holy Spirit," the "Spirit of the Lord," and the "Spirit of God," in the Old Testament; as is to be seen in the beginning of the description of creation, "And the Spirit of God moved upon the face of the waters" (Gen. 1 2) And David says "The Spirit of the Lord spake by me, and His word was in my tongue" (II Sam. 23·2). And again he says, "Uphold me with Thy free spirit" (Ps 51·12). Isaiah says in lamenting over Israel "They rebelled and vexed His holy Spirit. Where is he that put His holy Spirit within him?" (Isa. 63:11). And again it is said, "I will pour out my Spirit upon thy seed" (Isa 44 3; cf. Joel 3:1).

61. **Do we then read nothing of the Son of God in the Old Testament; since it appears so strange to the Jews that we Christians honor Christ as the Son of God, whom they will not accept as the Messiah?**

As they expect a temporal Messiah, such as Moses and Elijah, and an earthly kingdom like that of David and Solomon, they remain in unbelief towards the Son of God, Jesus Christ. Otherwise they could find testimony enough of Him in the Old Testament. In the Proverbs of Solomon we find this· "Who hath ascended up into heaven, or descended? who hath gathered the wind in His fists? who hath bound the waters in a garment? who hath established all the ends of the earth? what is His name, and what is His Son's name, if thou canst tell?" (Prov 30 4) Of this Son (in the person of God) David also testifies "Thou art my Son; this day have I begotten Thee Ask of me, and I shall give Thee the heathen for Thine inheritance, and the uttermost parts of the earth for Thy possession" (Ps 2 7, 8). "Kiss the Son, lest He be angry, and ye perish from the way, when His wrath is kindled but a little Blessed are all they that put their trust in Him" (Ps 2 12). Of the Son's unity with God, Isaiah prophesies "For unto us a Child is born, unto us a Son is given· and the government shall be upon His shoulder: and His name shall be called Wonderful, Counsellor, The mighty God, The everlasting Father, The Prince of Peace" (Isa 9 6)

Article Fifth, of the Incarnation of Christ

62. **Concerning the Son of God, the Lord Jesus Christ, was He before His birth by Mary already the Son of God with the Father?**

Certainly was He before His birth by Mary, with the Father, as we have just noted in Isaiah 9.6. Of Christ Peter wrote, "Who verily was foreordained before the foundation of the world" (I Pet. 1.20). He was not only foreordained, but existed from eternity, as Micah testifies, "Whose goings forth have been from of old, from everlasting" (Micah 5.2). Therefore Christ says Himself, "O

Father, glorify Thou Me with Thine own self with the glory which I had with Thee before the world was" (John 17:5). But Paul writes of the Son yet more explicitly when he says: "Who is the image of the invisible God, the firstborn of every creature: for by Him were all things created, that are in heaven, and that are in earth, visible and invisible, whether they be thrones, or dominions, or principalities, or powers; all things were created by Him, and for Him" (Col 1·15, 16). From this His eternity is sufficiently explained.

63. Now since this is so certain and true of the Son of God that the Father testifies of Him, "This is my beloved Son," why then does Christ so frequently call Himself the "Son of man"?

This is a matter of great mystery, which surpasses all human reason. It cannot be well comprehended, how it could be, and has also come to pass, that the Great God permitted His Son, whom He had conceived from eternity, to be born man by a virgin, and yet remain His Son. Paul calls this the "mystery of godliness" (I Tim. 3.16).

64. Has then the Son of God, by His advent into this world, become that which He was not before?

It has pleased God to reconcile the human race to Himself by His Son, and thus to destroy and annihilate "sin in the flesh through sin." "For He hath made Him to be sin for us, who knew no sin, that we might be made the righteousness of God in Him" (II Cor. 5:21). And thus He became that which He was not before, for "the Word was made flesh, and dwelt among us, (and we beheld His glory, the glory as of the only begotten of the Father,) full of grace and truth" (John 1 14) He was "made of the seed of David according to the flesh; and declared to be the Son of God with power, according to the Spirit of holiness, by the resurrection from the dead" (Rom. 1·3, 4). "That . . which we have seen with our eyes, which we have looked upon, and our hands have handled, of the Word of life" (I John 1 1) was the One "who, being in the form of God, thought it not robbery to be equal with God: But made Himself of no reputation, and took upon Him the form of a servant, and was made in the likeness of men" (Phil 2.6, 7). He "was in all points tempted like as we are, yet without sin" (Heb. 4:15). Now for these reasons the Son of God also calls Himself the "Son of man"

Article Sixth, of the Fall of the Human Race

65. Why then has the Son of God come into the world?

Because the first man, Adam, who was created by God in His own image, good and perfect (Gen. 1.27), transgressed His command and thus turned away from Him, he fell under God's wrath and condemnation, and not he alone, but all who have descended from him Gen 3.1-7. And thus by one man, Adam, "sin entered into the world, and death by sin; [understand, eternal death,] and so death passed upon all men . . . Nevertheless death reigned from Adam to Moses, even over them that had not sinned after the similitude of Adam's transgression" (Rom 5 12, 14). From such death no one "can by any means redeem his brother, nor give to God a ransom for him" (Ps 49 7). "The judgment was by one to condemnation" (Rom. 5:16).

66. Has then the Son of God, Jesus Christ, come into the world to appease, take away, reconcile, and satisfy the wrath of God?

It was thus the acceptable will of God, according to His unfathomable love and mercy, that He sent His beloved and only begotten Son into the world in the flesh, again to raise and reconcile to Himself the fallen race of man. Therefore He is also called in the prophecy of Isaiah, "The Prince of Peace" (Isa. 9.6) For, although the statutes of Moses had the promise that those who kept them should "live in them" (Lev. 18 5), yet this was included under a curse. "Cursed be he that confirmeth not all the words of this law to do them" (Deut. 27:26) Now inasmuch as through the weakness of the flesh, no one could keep the law perfectly, all men were under the curse and wrath of God Gal 3.10 "For what the law could not do, in that it was weak through the flesh, God sending His own Son in the likeness of sinful flesh, and for sin, condemned sin in the flesh" (Rom. 8:3) "For as by one man's disobedience many were made sinners, so by the obedience of one shall many be made righteous" (Rom 5 19). "As sin has reigned unto death, even so might grace reign through righteousness unto eternal life by Jesus Christ our Lord" (Rom. 5 21) "As in Adam all die, even so in Christ shall all be made alive" (I Cor 15 22) Jesus "came and preached peace to you which were afar off, and to them that were nigh" (Eph 2.17, Cf Luke 2:10, Acts 10·36) "For the Son of man is come to seek and to save that which was lost" (Luke 19·10). "For God so loved the world, that He gave His only begotten Son, that whosoever believeth in Him should not perish, but have everlasting life" (John 3 16).

67. Is then the work of our salvation and redemption attributed to the Son, our Lord Jesus Christ, alone, because His name is most frequently mentioned, and He is called our Saviour?

It was thus the eternal decree of God, that He would, through His Son, accomplish the work of redemption by presenting Him as a means for the salvation of man; as is to be seen from the fact, that the angel carried the message to Mary and Joseph that they should "call His name JESUS" (Matt. 1 21, Luke 1:31) because He should "save His people from their sins " Notwithstanding, this salvation did not take place without the Father but with Him, as Paul says· "God was in Christ, reconciling the world unto Himself, not imputing their trespasses unto them" (II Cor 5 19). "But of Him are ye in Christ Jesus, who of God is made unto us wisdom, and righteousness, and sanctification, and redemption" (I Cor. 1:30). Christ came "through the tender mercy of our God, whereby the dayspring from on high hath visited us" (Luke 1 78) "But God, who is rich in mercy, for His great love wherewith He loved us, even when we were dead in sins, hath quickened us together with Christ" (Eph 2.4, 5 cf John 3 16; I John 4:9, 10) And although the work itself is accomplished through the Son, and He is therefore called the "finisher of our faith" (Heb 12 2), yet the Father must not be excluded therefrom; but we must also give Him honor, praise, and thanks for salvation, as the angels at the birth of Christ instructed us by their example to do when they said, "Glory to God in the highest" (Luke 2 14) And Paul also says: Giving "thanks unto the Father, which hath made us meet to be partakers of the inheritance of the saints in light· who hath delivered us from the power of darkness, and hath translated us into the kingdom of His dear Son in whom we have redemption through His blood, even the forgiveness of sins" (Col. 1.12-14).

68. Does then saving faith, whereby we believe that there is "One God," also require of us that we believe that Jesus Christ is the Son of God, our Saviour and Redeemer?

This must infallibly follow from saving faith in God, who is the Creator of heaven and earth, as we have before proved His (the Son's) unity with the Father; and He Himself says, "ye believe in God, believe also in Me" (John 14:1). "He that believeth on the Son hath everlasting life: and he that believeth not the Son shall not see life; but the wrath of God abideth on him" (John 3:36) "Neither is there salvation in any other. for there is none other name under heaven given among men, whereby we must be saved" (Acts 4·12) Indeed this is the foundation of the Gospel, the beginning and end of the same Again it is said: "But these are written, that ye might believe that Jesus is the Christ, the Son of God; and that believing ye might have life through His name" (John 20:31) Christ as Saviour is the message of Peter in his Pentecost sermon (Acts

2 36) to Cornelius and his house (Acts 10 36), it was Philip's to the people of Samaria and the eunuch (Acts 8·12, 37); Paul and Silas said to the jailor: "Believe on the Lord Jesus Christ, and thou shalt be saved, and thy house" (Acts 16 31).

69. Is then faith in God, and His Son Jesus Christ, sufficient for salvation?

This is indeed the chief article of true faith to salvation, when such faith is well and rigidly fixed in the heart according to Scripture, and influences the whole man "For with the heart man believeth unto righteousness, and with the mouth confession is made unto salvation" (Rom 10 10). But as the question is here more particularly asked, whether such faith alone is sufficient to salvation, we must again say that a mere oral confession that we have such faith is not sufficient to salvation, but rather a faith whereby we willingly take upon ourselves the cross of Christ, and thereby show by the fruits of our faith that we have a "faith which worketh by love" And we must also give all diligence to have our faith accompanied by the Christian virtues of knowledge, temperance, patience, godliness, brotherly kindness, and charity. II Pet 1·5-7. For if we have not these virtues with our faith, but merely make an oral confession of God and Christ, such confession can help us nothing to our salvation For "he that lacketh these things is blind and cannot see afar off" (II Pet. 1:9). Of this James also speaks· "But wilt thou know, O vain man, that faith without works is dead? Was not Abraham our father justified by works, when he had offered Isaac his son upon the altar? Seest thou how faith wrought with his works, and by works was faith made perfect? For as the body without the spirit is dead, so faith without works is dead also" (James 2 20-22, 26). For faith is not without works, that is, such works as please God, as was shown by Abraham in reality. Therefore James may well say with Peter that a "man is justified by works, and not by faith only."

Article Seventh, of Good Works

70. Now since good works along with faith are so necessary, as faith without them is good for nothing, does man merit anything with God to salvation with his good works?

Just as faith must be firm and constant if God is to be pleased therewith (Heb. 11:6), so must the Christian virtues and good works be firm and constant in love if we hope to be saved, as we have before shown from II Pet. 1.9 In Matthew 25:31-46 it is plainly to be seen that works must accompany faith to salvation, where Christ says "Come, ye blessed of my Father ." and then names each one's reward according to his works Again we find Christ saying, "They that have done good shall come forth unto the resurrection of life" (John 5 20). Cp Phil 2 12; I Cor 15 58 As however the question is asked, whether man can do anything towards God to merit his salvation, it is to be observed that he cannot, as we would thereby make God our Debtor For although salvation is promised on good works at various places in Holy Scripture, this has reference to such works as are produced by faith, love, and obedience, but it is not to be understood, that heaven may be earned thereby For it is said. "When ye shall have done all those things which are commanded you, say, We are unprofitable servants· we have done that which was our duty to do" (Luke 17.10).

71. Must we then, while we desire and strive for eternal salvation, practice no Christian virtues, and do no Christian works?

In the practice and proof of our faith our mind and striving must always be directed towards eternal life, as the needle of the compass points to the north; as Christ says: "Strive to enter in at the strait gate" (Luke 13·24). And this from the beginning unto the end of faith and life, which Paul also clearly indicates when he says· "Know ye not that they which run in a race run all, but one receiveth the prize? So run, that ye may obtain" (I Cor. 9:24; cp 15:58) "I press toward the mark for the prize of the high calling of God in Christ Jesus" (Phil. 3:14). Again Paul says, "To them who by patient continuance in well doing seek for glory and honour and immortality, eternal life" (Rom. 2:7). Thus the first and the last, the doctrine and ministry of the Gospel, is: "Work out your own salvation with fear and trembling" (Phil. 2:12). And according to the words of Christ, "He that endureth to the end shall be saved" (Matt. 10:22) So Paul also testifies, that this in his whole career was his aim, when he says "Henceforth there is laid up for me a crown of righteousness, which the Lord, the righteous judge, shall give me at that day· and not to me only, but unto all them also that love His appearing" (II Tim 4 8). Thus the course of the Christian must be in striving for eternal life. II Pet 1:11. "For we are His [God's] workmanship, created in Christ Jesus unto good works, which God hath before ordained that we should walk in them" (Eph. 2 10). To this purpose are also the words of Christ, when He says: "My sheep hear My voice . . . and I give unto them eternal life" (John 10:27, 28).

Article Eighth, of the New Covenant, or New Testament

72. Must then all believers who hope to be saved be obedient to the voice of Christ, as their Lawgiver, and follow His doctrine and example?

This we must do from the whole heart, and not merely with the mouth, as is clearly to be seen from many testimonies in Holy Scripture, as well in the Old Testament as in the New, and also from the promises and their fulfilment. As the prophet Moses says: "The Lord thy God will raise up unto thee a Prophet from the midst of thee, of thy brethren, like unto Me; unto Him ye shall hearken" (Deut. 18 15; cf. Acts 3 22). "Behold, I have given him for a witness to the people, a leader and commander to the people" (Isa. 55.4). For "God, who at sundry times and in divers manners spake in time past unto the fathers by the prophets, hath in these last days spoken unto us by His Son" (Heb. 1:1, 2). And not only by Him, but also of Him, from heaven: "This is my beloved Son, in whom I am well pleased; hear ye Him" (Matt. 17 5; cp. II Pet 1.17).

73. Does then the Old Testament not serve us any more for doctrine; since our Lord Jesus Christ, the Son of God, has come into the world, and we are commanded to hear and follow Him?

The external ordinances of the Jewish law given by Moses, in which there were all kinds of ceremonies, which the Jews were commanded to observe in their divine service, are not to be observed any more by Christians; as they were shadows and types of the sacrifice of Christ and His royal priesthood, in which the promise of God of the coming of Christ, the salvation of the human race, and what the prophets prophesied of the same, are declared. They were given as an assurance and strengthening of our faith in the Son of God, who by His coming and sacrifice has become "the end of the law" (Rom. 10:4). For through His suffering, death, and sacrifice all the ceremonies of the law came to an end, as He said at the close of His suffering, "It is finished" (John 19 30, cf. v 28). Finished was all that was promised to the fathers, typified in the ceremonies of the law, and predicted by the prophets, according to the words of Christ. Luke 18.31; 24:26, 46; I Cor. 15·3, 4.

74. Does then the moral law, taught in the Old Testament, still concern us; so that we should conform as much to it as to the doctrine of Christ and His apostles?

Yes. For all that the holy men of God have taught has been brought forth by the Holy Spirit and written for us as doctrine (II Pet. 1·21), as well as that which the apostles have written, for Christ says: "Think not that I am come to destroy the law, or the prophets: I am not come to destroy, but to fulfil" (Matt.

5.17). And all that the two tables or Ten Commandments and the doctrine of the prophets contain, remains as the chief work of the New Testament, namely, the law of the love of God, and of our neighbor; for "on these two commandments" says Christ, "hang all the law and the prophets" (Matt. 22.40). Upon this the Apostle Paul has founded his doctrine for all Christians, when he says, "Now the end of the commandment is charity out of a pure heart, and of a good conscience, and of faith unfeigned" (II Tim. 1·5).

Article Ninth, of the Christian Church or Communion

75. Now since the ceremonial divine service distinguished heathenism from Judaism, which latter, in its time, comprised the people of God, the Temple of Jerusalem being their house of worship, and consequently their center of communion, in what then does the church of God now consist, so that they who belong thereto may be considered as, and called, the people and children of God?

Of this the Lord Himself has spoken through Jeremiah, as also through Ezekiel: "I will make a covenant of peace with them; it shall be an everlasting covenant with them: and I will place them, and multiply them, and will set My sanctuary in the midst of them for evermore" (Ezek. 37:26). "But this shall be the covenant that I will make with the house of Israel, After those days, saith the Lord, I will put My law in their inward parts, and write it in their hearts, and will be their God, and they shall be My people" (Jer. 31:33). But now this new covenant is the Gospel of God the Father, which has been proclaimed through His only beloved Son, as also through His disciples, for "God, who at sundry times and in divers manners spake in time past unto the fathers by the prophets, hath in these last days spoken unto us by His Son" (Heb. 1.1). "For God so loved the world, [i e., the whole human race,] that He gave His only begotten Son, that whosoever believeth in Him should not perish, but have everlasting life" (John 3:16). So that it may now be said, "The time is fulfilled, and the kingdom of God is at hand: repent ye, and believe the Gospel" (Mark 1.15) As was prophesied before through Isaiah, "I will also give Thee for a light to the Gentiles, that Thou mayest be my salvation unto the end of the earth" (Isa 49:6). Thus the Son of God "became the author of eternal salvation unto all them that obey Him" (Heb. 5:9). Through such faith, then, believers became God's people and children of God in the communion and church of Christ. Gal. 3 26; Rom 8 16. And this Son of God is set by the Father as the Head over the church, according to the words of Paul. Eph. 1:22; Col. 1:18, 19; Isa. 55:4.

76. Will then the Lord Jesus, as the Head of the evangelical church or communion, govern, protect, superintend, and lead the same alone: as the head does the other members of the body; or as the man is the head over his wife and children?

Since the Son of God has been chosen, ordained, and confirmed thereto by the Father (Matt. 28:18), He has not only shown Himself as the Head and Ruler of His members, but also went before them as a Leader with the pattern of His life; gave them commandments and interdictions, besides the guidance of His Spirit in holy truth, for their preservation to eternal life, as He says Himself, "My sheep hear My voice, and I know them, and they follow Me: and I give unto them eternal life" (John 10:27, 28). And: "Take My yoke upon you, and learn of Me; for I am meek and lowly in heart: and ye shall find rest unto your souls. For My yoke is easy, and My burden is light" (Matt. 11.29, 30). Further, "Teaching them to observe all things whatsoever I have commanded you" (Matt. 28 20).

Article Tenth, of the Deacons and Ministers of the Christian Church or Communion

77. Has then the Son of God, the Lord Jesus, also appointed persons in His church, and over His communion, as superintendents, deacons, and teachers?

Yes He has appointed several overseers to serve His church and communion in His bodily absence, to teach His members the doctrine, commandments, and ordinances left by Him, as also to preach the Gospel, to which He Himself appointed several in the days of His incarnation, whom He called apostles (Matt. 10 1-3; Luke 6 13-15), and sent them forth to proclaim the Gospel, as He did also at His ascension, with a declaration of His power to do the same, when He says: "All power is given unto Me in heaven and in earth. Go ye therefore, and teach all nations . . ." (Matt. 28 18, 19; cp. Mark 16:15). Thus has God the Father, together with His Son, for the edification and improvement of the church, according to the testimony of St Paul, appointed "some apostles; and some, prophets; and some, evangelists, and some, pastors and teachers; . . . for the edifying of the body of Christ" (Eph. 4.11, 12; cp. I Cor. 12:28). Which body is the church of Christ.

78. Is this still thus performed by the Father, and Christ the Son, without the means or co-operation of man?

Just as the Lord God, together with His Spirit and Word, has always effected the salvation of man through the external co-operation of man, and in I Kings 19 16, Elias is commanded to anoint Elisha in his stead as a prophet, so it still pleases God to do the same under the Gospel dispensation, as is to be seen from Christ's own words when He says: "The harvest truly is plenteous, but the labourers are few; pray ye therefore the Lord of the harvest, that He will send forth labourers into His harvest" (Matt. 9·37, 38; cp Luke 10 2) Thus the chief work of obtaining men for God's harvest or field of labor, is ordained by the Lord, and received from Him through prayer, but besides this the members of the church are to look for such men as fear God, are lovers of the church and of divine truth, and are thus good examples in doctrine, as Luke testifies of Christ (Acts 1:1), where he alludes to his having written all that Christ did and taught Thus we see that the first church and apostles did as above remarked, when they wanted to ordain an apostle in Judas' place; that is, they looked to fitness, prayed God, and said: "Thou, Lord, which knowest the hearts of all men, shew whether of these two Thou hast chosen, that he may take part in this ministry" (Acts 1:24) And this Peter observed faithfully, being commanded before all others to feed the flock of Christ And Paul, the "chosen vessel" of the Lord, observed the same thing, when he writes to Timothy, "And the things that thou hast heard of me among many witnesses, the same commit thou to faithful men, who shall be able to teach others also" (II Tim. 2 2); "Holding the mystery of the faith in a pure conscience" (I Tim. 3:9). And together with a blameless life, such men must also have a good report, not only of those within the church, but also "of them which are without," so that their office be not blasphemed (I Tim 3.7; cf. 4.12). Such men must then continue in their ministry, and minister according to "the ability which God giveth" (I Pet. 4:11). They must not neglect the gift that is in them, which was given them by prophecy, "with the laying on of the hands of the presbytery" (I Tim. 4:14). They do not feed the flock of Christ with the design of temporal gain, neither for the fleece nor the milk— "not for filthy lucre, but of a ready mind; neither as being lords over God's heritage, but being ensamples to the flock" (I Pet. 5:2, 3)

79. Must then the teachers not be maintained by the church; that is, receive pay for their service: Or must they labor to maintain themselves, doing as the Apostle Paul did, who labored day and night, that he might not be chargeable to any? Acts 18:3; 20:34; I Cor. 4:12; II Thess. 3:8.

In the choosing of evangelical teachers and those who devote themselves to the office of such, all temporal designs must cease On the contrary, the welfare and good government of the church, and the honor of God, must be kept in view He who is thus chosen must, on his part, accept and act in the ministry out of love to the utmost welfare of the church, thus devoting himself to the service of God and the church according to the example of Paul. Gal. 1:16 If he has, however, opportunity to maintain himself and those entrusted to his care, he is to follow the example of Paul, as he testifies of himself, "It is more blessed to give than to receive" (Acts 20 35). As otherwise, if one resorts to the ministry for the enjoyment of temporal gain, it has more the appearance that he is seeking improper gain than that of the fruit of love and affection which is otherwise required. I Pet. 5·2, 3. For the striving for temporal gain renders a minister unworthy before God, and soon unfit for his ministry among men

80. Must then such ministers receive nothing at all from the church for their service, for the maintenance of themselves and those entrusted to them, but must rather maintain themselves?

If with such the design of temporal gain is not the motive of their ministry, but that they devote themselves thereto out of love, and serve with the gift and "ability which God giveth," in such case the church is bound in love, on her part, to provide for their necessities: For, if a minister serves the church out of love and cordial affection, the church is, according to the words of Christ and the doctrine of Paul, under obligation, and out of mutual love, in duty bound, to provide for him according to his necessities; for thus teaches the latter in these words: "And we beseech you, brethren, to know them which labour among you, and are over you in the Lord, and admonish you; and to esteem them very highly in love for their work's sake. And be at peace among yourselves" (I Thess. 5 12, 13). "Let him that is taught in the word communicate unto him that teacheth in all good things" (Gal 6:6). And of himself he says: "If we have sown unto you spiritual things, is it a great thing if we shall reap your carnal things?" (I Cor. 9 11).

81. Thus, then, may a minister receive pay for his service if he stands in need of it, since Christ says, "The labourer is worthy of his hire" (Luke 10:7)?

If pay is demanded by the minister for his service, there is no more room for love, but it is to be feared that by such an one the flock is fed for the sake of the fleece and milk; as the Lord God complains of such, "Woe be to the shepherds of Israel that do feed themselves! should not the shepherd feed the flocks? Ye eat the fat, and ye clothe you with the wool, ye kill them that are fed: but ye feed not the flock?" (Ezek. 34:2, 3). Against this militate the words of Christ, "Freely ye have received, freely give" (Matt. 10·8). But if a minister, in his superintendence of the church, performs his duty faithfully before the Lord, then the church also has its duty to perform towards the minister, and indeed each member for himself. But when Christ says: "The labourer is worthy of his hire," this has reference to the duty and obligation of the church and those who receive his service, and that they shall do this to their minister as a reward for what he has done for them. As Paul also compares it, "Thou shalt not muzzle the ox that treadeth out the corn" (I Cor. 9:7; cp. I Tim 5.18). And to this also Paul has reference when he speaks of the duty of members, "That they which preach the Gospel should live of the Gospel" (I Cor. 9.14).

82. But how can it be reconciled, or how does it agree when Christ says: "The labourer is worthy of his hire," and Paul says: "The Lord hath ordained that they which preach the Gospel should live of the Gospel;" and yet Christ says, "Freely ye have received, freely give." Do not these things militate against one another?

They do not militate against one another, and can well be reconciled, if it only be considered under what sense and intention each of them was spoken, and that on all sides love should be exercised and have the precedence. For one treats of the teacher and his duty, the other of the hearers and their duty. Now when these matters are on all sides judged of rightly they can easily be reconciled. But if the teacher will continually insist upon the duty or obligation of his hearers, and wants to have observed towards him what is recorded in Matt. 10:10; I Cor. 9:14, but on the other hand forgets his duty, which he is to perform out of love and not for the sake of gain, and again when the hearers insist upon the teacher performing his duty towards them but forget their own—in such case the work of love will be at a stand, become fruitless and eventually be extinguished. But where people act and continue honestly in love they do not seek their own advantage but that of others. They seek what is for the promotion of their neighbor. I Cor. 10 24; 13.5. And when the words, Matt. 10 8, Ezek. 34:2, 3; I Pet. 5:2, 3 are properly understood and considered, it will be clearly seen that they concern the teacher and not the hearers But concerning the words, I Thess. 5:12, 13; Gal 6:6, I Cor. 9 11, which concern the hearers, it is to be remarked that when they are observed without reluctance, it goes well in the church and love may abide. Whatever else may then appear at variance may be reconciled.

83. What kind of a service in the church is that where members are called assistants and governors?

This is a service where members dispatch all cases concerning the welfare of the church that do not concern the ministerial service, and who have a particular oversight over the poor, over widows and orphans, and over aged, frail, and infirm persons so that no one suffer want. Such persons consequently receive the given alms into safekeeping and distribute them among the needy, as we read that Peter says: "It is not reason that we should leave the Word of God, and serve tables. Wherefore, brethren, look ye out among you seven men of honest report, full of the Holy Ghost and wisdom, whom we may appoint over this business" (Acts 6·2, 3). From which service honorable aged women are also not to be excluded. I Tim 5 9, 10, Tit. 2:3, but are to perform such service in their sphere, and particularly among their own sex.

Article Eleventh, of the Entrance into the Church or Communion

84. Can we become members of the communion or Christian church by affirming that we believe the Gospel, and that there is a God who sent Jesus Christ, or must yet more be done if we will become members of the church or communion?

Faith in the Gospel, which testifies of God and His Son Jesus Christ, is the beginning or first stage of entrance into the church of Christ But in order to become a member of the same, a sound conversion and an entire change of life must take place. For it is said, "Repent ye, and believe the Gospel" (Mark 1 15). As was manifested in many, who, when Peter and other apostles preached the Gospel to them at the day of Pentecost, whereby their hearts were touched, so that they said, "Men and brethren, what shall we do?" received the answer: "Repent, . . ." (Acts 2 37, 38) As also the words of Christ show, when He says "Thus it is written, and thus it behoved Christ to suffer, and to rise from the dead the third day and that repentance and remission of sins should be preached in His name" (Luke 24 46, 47). Which is also testified by Paul when he says, "The times of this ignorance God winked at; but now commandeth all men every where to repent" (Acts 17:30).

85. What kind of work is repentance and what use is there in it that one does repent?

True, evangelical repentance, a repentance that is valid before God, is no small or insignificant matter, but a great one, inasmuch as the pardon of sins is promised thereon It consists in two points: (1) In true knowledge of God and His divine attributes: (2) In a knowledge of our own dangerous condition For without a true knowledge of God and His holy will and a knowledge of our inability to fulfil the same there is no pardon of sin to be expected. On the contrary, if anyone will obtain the favor of God he must see his sinful condition, and now he has, like the prodigal son, abused his heavenly Father's goods and mercy, and turned them "into lasciviousness" (Jude 4). Through this two-fold knowledge he will, with David, have respect unto the Lord's ways. Ps 119 15. Besides, he will behold "the goodness and severity of God" (Rom. 11:22). And now the goodness of God leadeth him to repentance. Rom. 2:4. Thus repenting, he says with a deep sigh in his heart, "O wretched man that I am! who shall deliver me from the body of this death?" (Rom. 7 24). Under the burden of his sins, he does with David, "go mourning all the day long" (Ps. 38.6). In such a condition, man has come to a knowledge of himself, and is far advanced in repentance and sorrow for his sins

86. Is it then no true and full repentance when we repent of and mourn over our sins?

To have a knowledge of our sins, and to repent of them before men—to say that we are sorry for them—is not yet a true, yea scarcely a half repentance. True repentance, a repentance that will be valid before God, must be shown and attested by a contrite heart and heartfelt sorrow before God, so that we cry out before Him. "I acknowledge my transgressions: and my sin is ever before me. Against Thee, Thee only, have I sinned and done this evil in Thy sight" (Ps. 51:3, 4) A truly penitent one will say with the prodigal son "Father, I have sinned against heaven, and before Thee, and am no more worthy to be called Thy son; make me as one of Thy hired servants" (Luke 15.18, 19).

87. Is it also no full and true repentance if we repent of our sins, mourn over them, and pray God for pardon?

Although this is the chief part of repentance, still it is no full repentance unless it is connected with a holy resolution to forsake sin and amend our lives. For this is the purport of the ground and foundation of the entrance into the Christian church, laid by Christ. "Repent. for the kingdom of heaven is at hand" (Matt. 4:17). Of which amendment of life, Solomon also speaks very properly when he says of sins, "Whoso confesseth and forsaketh them shall have mercy" (Prov. 28 13). Sins must not only be confessed and forsaken, but also put wholly away from one, as God speaks through Isaiah "Wash you, make you clean; put away the evil of your doings from before Mine eyes; cease to do evil; learn to do well, seek judgment" (Isa. 1 16, 17) And James says: "Draw nigh to God, and He will draw nigh to you. Cleanse your hands, ye sinners, and purify your hearts, ye double minded. Be afflicted, and mourn, and weep let your laughter be turned to mourning, and your joy to heaviness" (James 4 8, 9) On such the Lord will look in mercy, as He speaks through Isaiah, I will look "even to him that is poor and of a contrite spirit, and trembleth at My word" (Isa. 66 2). "Wherefore come out from among them, [i e., out from among the ungodly] and be ye separate, saith the Lord, and touch not the unclean thing, and I will receive you, and will be a Father unto you, and ye shall be My sons and daughters, saith the Lord Almighty" (II Cor. 6 17, 18). Thus going on from stage to stage is a repentance that is valid before God, as we have thereby the promise that though our "sins be as scarlet, they shall be as white as snow; though they be red like crimson, they shall be as wool" (Isa 1:18)

88. When, then, a person has come to the faith, and also to true repentance and amendment of life through the ministry and the reading of the Word of God; what more remains for him to do so that he may become a member of the church, and have a mind at rest for himself?

When a person is in possession of true and saving faith, so that he believes that there is a God, and also "that He is a rewarder of them that diligently seek Him" (Heb. 11:6),—with such a person faith does not stand still but goes on from stage to stage, from virtue to virtue, and from commandment to commandment, such person showing a filial obedience in everything that may be serviceable to his soul's salvation; so that the words fully apply to him: "God be thanked, that ye were the servants of sin, but ye have obeyed from the heart that form of doctrine which was delivered you" (Rom 6:17). This proof of obedience is then a willingness, to take upon ourselves the yoke of Christ, as He calls all penitent hearts unto Him: "Come unto Me, all ye that labour and are heavy laden, and I will give you rest. Take My yoke upon you, and learn of Me; for I am meek and lowly in heart: and ye shall find rest unto your souls" (Matt 11 28, 29). And this is the free, open "fountain . . . for sin and for uncleanness" (Zech. 13:1), to which the apostles directed all afflicted and anxious souls of men; as did Philip, the eunuch (Acts 8.35); Peter, Cornelius and his house (Acts 10.36), and Paul, the jailer (Acts 16:31).

Article Twelfth, of External Water Baptism on Faith

89. What then is required of man in the Gospel, to show his obedience when he takes upon himself the yoke of Christ?

The first proof of his obedience is that he submits to the commandment of Christ and becomes baptized on his confession of faith; as is to be seen: "Teach all nations, baptizing them in the name of the Father, and of the Son, and of the Holy Ghost" (Matt 28 19); as was done with many at the day of Pentecost at Jerusalem, after hearing the sermon of Peter. All who gladly received the words of the apostles were baptized. Acts 2.41. So the people of Samaria when they believed the preaching of Philip, who preached to them "concerning the kingdom of God, and the name of Jesus Christ, they were baptized, both men and women" (Acts 8 12). Further, the eunuch, (Acts 8 38), Cornelius and his house, (Acts 10:48); the jailer, (Acts 16 33). Paul himself was baptized after he was taught and instructed by Ananias (Acts 9 18). So that baptism is a work that properly belongs to faith and true repentance.

90. In what respect then is Christian baptism serviceable to believing and penitent persons? Are they also benefited thereby?

Christian external water baptism implies that it is a commandment of God, given by the Son of God, and that it is conducive to the benefit of man in various respects, if it is received with a sincere heart, and the obligation which it imposes is properly observed.

1. It signifies the burying of the old man of sin, according to the words of Paul when he says: "Know ye not, that so many of us as were baptized into Jesus Christ were baptized into His death? Therefore we are buried with Him by baptism into death: that like as Christ was raised up from the dead by the glory of the Father, even so we also should walk in newness of life" (Rom. 6.3, 4).

2. It signifies the pardon, washing off, and absolution of sin; for thus said Peter to the contrite hearts at the day of Pentecost: "Be baptized every one of you in the name of Jesus Christ for the remission of sins, and ye shall receive the gift of the Holy Ghost" (Acts 2.38). And Ananias said to Paul: "Brother Saul, . . . why tarriest thou? arise, and be baptized, and wash away thy sins, calling on the name of the Lord" (Acts 22 13, 16). Through which is represented the purification which takes place through the blood of Christ; as is to be seen from the words of Christ· Matt. 26 28; Col. 1:14; I John 1 7; Rev. 1:5.

3 The fulfilling of "all righteousness," according to the declaration of Christ (Matt. 3.15).

4. "The answer [covenant] of a good conscience toward God" (I Pet. 3·21)

91. Is it also stated in the Gospel, to whom baptism is to be administered, or are some excluded therefrom?

This question may be answered in a twofold manner; namely, that baptism must be viewed in a general and also in a particular manner The law of Moses was given for the children of Israel alone, and not for the Gentiles, as David testifies: "He sheweth His word unto Jacob, his statutes and judgments unto Israel He hath not dealt so with any nation" (Ps 147 19, 20). But the law of the Gospel is given for all men, without distinction of Jew or heathen Matt 28 19; Mark 16 15. Circumcision was also only commanded to be performed on the male sex, and not on the female Gen. 17.10. On the contrary, baptism requires no distinction, not even between men and women, as is to be seen in the case of the people of Samaria Acts 8 12, 16:15. This also was the case of those who were baptized at the day of Pentecost, and that of the heathen centurion, Cornelius Acts 10.47, 48.

92. Is then baptism of so general a nature that it should be administered to all men, even as it is said of the Gospel that it should be preached to every creature? Mark 16:15.

In the administration of baptism, as in the functions of the ministry, no distinction is made, but all those who are of a capable understanding to give ear to the words of the ministry, who can be taught, and who can also receive the doctrine of the Gospel in faith and thereby become fit subjects for baptism, after embracing the same by repentance and amendment of life, all such may be and have been baptized This is shown above from Acts 8 12; 10·47, 48; 16.15 For all the persons here alluded to, after the Gospel was preached to them and they were exhorted to faith by repentance and amendment of life and received the Gospel, were baptized And although children belong to the human race, yet we cannot see, either from the command of Christ, from His doctrine, nor from the practice of the apostles that baptism becomes them, or that they were baptized And why not? Because they have no ears to hear, nor hearts to understand Matt 11:15.

93. May then by virtue of the command of Christ, as also according to the doctrine and practice of the apostles, no infants or small children be baptized?

We cannot see that the command of Christian baptism extends to small children, and we also do not find in the whole New Testament that the apostles in their ministry spoke to children, much less that they baptized such Further, we cannot see that small children are or can be possessed of that which is represented by and required in baptism. For very young children are not capable of receiving the doctrine of the Gospel, nor have they committed any sins of which they can repent, or of which they can amend their lives Much less can they receive any matter of faith or believe in Christ Jesus, as Paul plainly speaks of the acceptance of faith: "How shall they believe in Him of whom they have not heard?" and then he proceeds to confine faith to hearing, and hearing to the Word of God (Rom 10 14, 17) So also Moses testifies of children that they have "no knowledge between good and evil" (Deut 1 39). Yea, the Lord Himself testifies of them that they "cannot discern between their right hand and their left hand" (Jonah 4.11). And we also daily see of children, that if they are in the greatest danger of fire and water, they by no means know how to save themselves from them, thus showing that they live in complete innocence and without any knowledge of things about them

94. Now since evangelical Christian baptism should only be administered on faith, repentance, and amendment of life, why then do some baptize infants, although these have not the said qualifications?

They do this on account of original sin which, according to their declaration, has come on all men through the fall of Adam: and this they endeavor to prove from the words of Paul, Rom. 5:12-14. Paul, however, adds that through the death of Christ they were reconciled, the charge of original sin being taken away, and that it does not consequently rest any more on children. Rom 5 18, 19 Others who baptize infants defend the practice from the will and discretion of the parents, as also from the practice of the Roman Catholic Church, thus baptizing their children on the faith of the church, and making them, as they think, members of the same.

Again, others hold baptism as a sign of the covenant, through which children become united with the church as their parents are. And as circumcision was a sign of the Old Covenant, so baptism was ordained and instituted as a like sign for the New Covenant.

Others again want to prove from Heb. 11.6 that children have faith if they are born of Christian parents, it being impossible without faith to please God. Some conclude from the words of Christ: "Suffer little children, and forbid them not, to come unto me: for of such is the kingdom of heaven" (Matt 19.14), that if the kingdom of heaven belongs to children they must have faith, or else they could not please God; which they also infer from Matt. 18 6 where Christ says, "But whoso shall offend one of these little ones which believe in me, it were better for him that a millstone were hanged about his neck, and that he were drowned in the depth of the sea."

95. How is it possible that there are so many different opinions among those who baptize infants, since they are agreed in the matter itself, there being so much misunderstanding as to the ground on which they administer baptism? Is it not proper that we should have, in a matter o fso much importance, a clear and express command, and a firm ground?

As far as we are concerned we will not judge those who believe in infant baptism on account of their opinions, but will leave them to answer to God themselves for the practice of such baptism. But we for our part cannot in the least agree with any of them, for we hold ourselves bound in this matter to follow the express command and order of Christ, as also the doctrine and order of the apostles, by whom the command is established, first to teach, and then to baptize those who have believed. We see that the apostles everywhere followed this command, but do not find that they baptized children. Therefore we believe this chief command, not from inference or probable evidence, but from the infallible Word of the holy Gospel, so that we can say to the candidate for baptism with Philip: "If thou believest with all thine heart, thou mayest" (Acts 8:37). And here the words of Christ are in place: "Teach all nations, baptizing them" (Matt. 28.19). "He that believeth and is baptized shall be saved" (Mark 16.16). Thus we see that doctrine and faith go before baptism.

96. Is it then only men and women that are to be baptized, as is testified and shown of the people of Samaria? Acts 8:12.

It must not be merely men and women, for the command concerns all nations, it being said: "Preach the Gospel to every creature" (Mark 16 15); that is, to all mankind. The law indeed concerned chiefly men, particularly the Ceremonial Law. But the Gospel concerns all mankind who have arrived at the age of discretion, and possess a knowledge of good and evil, whether they are married or unmarried, and who have ears to hear and hearts to understand the conditions of it, according to Matt. 11:29. It concerns those who voluntarily take upon themselves the yoke of Christ to follow Him, and who, from the hearing of and faith in the Gospel, say with the eunuch, "What doth hinder me to be baptized?" (Acts 8:36). It includes those who thus feel themselves impelled to yield to the requisitions of the Gospel, as did the people at the day of Pentecost. For those who gladly received the words of Peter were baptized.

97. Is there then a certain age appointed at which people are to be baptized, as the Lord God had appointed the eighth day for circumcision, or are we to

follow the example of Christ who was baptized as is thought, in His thirtieth year?

In respect of the administration and reception of Christian baptism, we do not find any certain age appointed at which a person is to receive it, as in the case of circumcision Nor do we read that Christ was baptized at the age of thirty years, but indeed that He was still considered as a son of Joseph when He was about that age. Luke 3:23. Thus we see that the baptism of the Gospel is not confined to any certain age, but rather that it depends on the emotion of the human mind. That is, a person should receive it when he finds himself convinced and impelled by the power of the living Word of God to yield obedience to God and Christ, at the same time amending his life, and believing the Gospel. Mark 1.15. Now when a person has come to this state, then is the proper time for him to be baptized "for the remission of sins" (Acts 2 38) as Peter exhorts and as Paul remarks that Ananias directed him to do. Acts 22:16

98. Are men's sins pardoned and washed off through baptism?

The sins which men do are not washed off by external baptism, as this is liberally expressed by Ananias, else it would be necessary to practice this continually, as was done under the law with the sin offering. For if any one sinned against the law or became impure, he had to sacrifice, purify himself, and become reconciled to God. But for this purpose baptism is not instituted, to apply it at any time for the purification of sin. Heb. 9·22, 23. So Peter also says in respect of baptism that it is "not the putting away of the filth of the flesh, but the answer of a good conscience toward God" (I Pet. 3:21). For after we have received baptism unto repentance and amendment of life, on faith in Jesus Christ, the same secures unto us the pardon of sins committed. This takes place through the precious blood of Christ, the free and open "fountain . . . for sin and uncleanness," of which Zechariah prophesied (Zech 13 1), and whereby he signifies the death of Christ, "In whom we have redemption through His blood, even the forgiveness of sins" (Col. 1:14). So that it is not water in baptism that has the power and efficacy to take away sin, and cleanse men from it. "But if we walk in the light, as He is in the light, we have fellowship one with another, and the blood of Jesus Christ His Son cleanseth us from all sin" (I John 1:7).

Article Thirteenth, of the Fruits and Works of Faith

99. Now if we have received Christian baptism on faith, knowledge of sin, and pardon of the same, is this sufficient to salvation, or must yet something more be done in order to be saved?

Yes. For baptism binds the person who believes in Jesus Christ and is baptized to different things, as well in temporal as in spiritual matters, which matters are comprehended in the Gospel, that is, to observe and give proof of the doctrine of the Gospel For after the Lord Jesus had commanded His disciples to preach the Gospel to all nations, "baptizing them in the name of the Father, and of the Son, and of the Holy Ghost" He also added: "Teaching them to observe all things whatsoever I have commanded you" (Matt. 28:19, 20). To this Paul also refers when he says: "Know ye not, that so many of us as were baptized into Jesus Christ were baptized into His death? Therefore we are buried with Him by baptism into death: that like as Christ was raised up from the dead by the glory of the Father, even so we also should walk in newness of life" (Rom 6:3, 4). So Paul also exhorts, "work out your own salvation with fear and trembling" (Phil. 2 12).

100. Now since baptism, on faith in Jesus Christ, is not sufficient to salvation, but there must be, as I perceive, yet something more done, in what does this consist, or what may it be?

Yes, certainly there must be yet something more done to obtain salvation, namely, that we bring forth fruits of faith as a good tree in the vineyard that does not cumber the ground Luke 13 7. We are to be found as fruitful grafts—grafted into the spiritual olive tree Jesus Christ, as Paul teaches, Rom. 11 24 For such Christ Himself calls fruitful branches in Him—who is the "true vine" (John 15:5). And of all such it is required that they walk worthy of the vocation wherewith they are called. Eph. 4:1. We are to be as good trees that bring forth fruits worthy of conversion, who give as much diligence as possible to excel in good works. Tit 3.1, 8. "For we are His workmanship, created in Christ Jesus unto good works, which God hath before ordained that we should walk in them," says Paul (Eph. 2 10, cp Tit 2.14). Consequently there must be, with such, a total conversion and change of life. For as they yield their members servants to uncleanness and to iniquity unto iniquity, even so now they must [after their baptism] yield their members servants to righteousness and holiness Rom. 6 19. To which the words of Christ also refer, when He says, "Let your light so shine before men, that they may see your good works, and glorify your Father which is in heaven" (Matt. 5.16).

101. What is intimated to the candidate for baptism at the reception of the same when he is "baptized in the name of the Father, and of the Son, and of the Holy Ghost"?

A great deal, and this comprises the chief articles through which salvation has been effected for him, and without which no salvation could have been obtained.

1. That God the Father is the origin from which the means of salvation are prepared and bestowed upon him "For God so loved the world, that He gave His only begotten Son, that whosoever believeth in Him should not perish, but have everlasting life" (John 3 16). To which Paul also refers when he says: "Giving thanks unto the Father, which hath made us meet to be partakers of the inheritance of the saints in light: . and hath translated us into the kingdom of His dear Son" (Col. 1:12, 13). "But God, who is rich in mercy, for His great love wherewith He loved us, even when we were dead in sins, hath quickened us together with Christ" (Eph. 2·4, 5).

2. That he is baptized on his faith in the name of the Father, and has received the adoption of the sons of God, as Paul says: "For ye are all the children of God by faith in Christ Jesus" (Gal. 3:26) He then has free access to the Father, and may address Him in his prayers "Our Father which art in heaven" (Matt 6.9). To this Paul adds. If we are "children, then heirs, heirs of God, and joint-heirs with Christ" (Rom. 8 17).

102. What does the name of Son show the candidate for baptism in the reception of the same?

1. That the Son of the living God is the means of his salvation "Neither is there salvation in any other· for there is none other name under heaven given among men, whereby we must be saved" (Acts 4:12) "In whom we have redemption through His blood, even the forgiveness of sins" (Col 1 14) And not only so; but he is also through the Son redeemed from the power of hell and death (Heb 2 14) so that he can say. "O death, where is thy sting? O grave, where is thy victory? The sting of death is sin, and the strength of sin is the law. But thanks be to God, which giveth us the victory through our Lord Jesus Christ" (I Cor. 15·55-57).

2 That Christ is his Mediator and Advocate with the Father "For there is one God, and one mediator between God and men, the man Christ Jesus" (I Tim. 2 5) On the strength of this John comforts the faithful members of Christ when he says. "My little children, these things write I unto you, that ye sin not. And if any man sin, we have an advocate with the Father, Jesus Christ the righteous" (I John 2·1).

103. What is effected for the candidate for baptism, thereby, that he is baptized in the name of the Holy Ghost?

1. It shows unto him, that the Holy Ghost was a co-worker in the divine being, along with the Father and the Son, in the accomplishment of his salvation.

2. That He shall further abide with him as his Comforter. John 14:16, 17. "The Spirit [Himself] beareth witness with our spirit, that we are the children of God" (Rom. 8 16); having thus, if he walks like a faithful child, the spirit of adoption, whereby he cries, "Abba, Father" (Rom. 8:15)

3. It is especially serviceable to the strengthening of all such in their pilgrimage, that they will, according to the promise of Christ, be guided by the Holy Spirit "into all truth" (John 16:13).

104. Should it claim the particular attention and consideration of such candidates for baptism that they are "baptized in the name of the Father, and of the Son, and of the Holy Ghost"?

It necessarily claims the consideration of such, that through the holy appellation and reception of such baptism they have become the adopted of God, as they should also consider themselves to be, as Paul says· "Ye are not your own. For ye are bought with a price: therefore glorify God in your body, and in your spirit, which are God's" (I Cor. 6 19, 20). And again he says· "I beseech you therefore brethren, by the mercies of God, that ye present your bodies a living sacrifice, holy, acceptable unto God, which is your reasonable service" (Rom. 12 1). Thus we show "what manner of spirit" we are of. Luke 9:55.

Article Fourteenth, of the Lord's Supper, or Breaking of Bread

105. Is there any thing important and particular in the Gospel, for persons baptized to perform, as a chief commandment and precept of Christ?

The Lord Jesus has commanded all the members of His church or communion to observe His (the Lord's) Supper, which He has instituted with bread and wine, and also observed Himself For in the last night when He was betrayed and ate the last passover with His disciples, "He took bread, and gave thanks, and brake it, and gave unto them, saying, This is My body which is given for you: this do in remembrance of Me Likewise also the cup after supper, saying, This cup is the new testament in My blood, which is shed for you" (Luke 22 19, 20). "For this is My blood of the new testament, which is shed for many for the remission of sins" (Matt 26 28). And the holy and highly enlightened Apostle Paul, sent out by the Lord Jesus to preach the Gospel of God, (Rom 1 1), after testifying how he received the command for observing the Lord's Supper, adds "For as often as ye eat this bread, and drink this cup, ye do shew the Lord's death till He come" (I Cor. 11:26).

106. Was then the Lord's Supper also observed to His remembrance by the church after His death?

Yes. For it is clear and evident that the same was taught by the apostles in the primitive church and observed by the believers of that time, as we read: "And they continued stedfastly in the apostles' doctrine and fellowship, and in breaking of bread and in prayers .... And breaking bread from house to house, did eat their meat with gladness and singleness of heart" (Acts 2.42, 46). So we also read that the believers at Troas met on a Sabbath "to break bread" when Paul passed that way, and that he then served them with the same Acts 20 7, 11. But as it was observed in a disorderly manner by the Corinthians, Paul reproved them on that account, and told them that they did not observe it as instituted by Christ, but to their own prejudice. He therefore represented to them the proper manner of observing this ordinance, as he had received it of the Lord, as is amply to be seen. I Cor 11:18-29.

107. Does it then stand so well with believers that if they are baptized on their faith, and observe the Lord's Supper or the breaking of bread externally, that they can console themselves with the hope of eternal life?

Just as external baptism alone brings no salvation, unless we do that on our part which is required of us in the Gospel, so can the external rite or observance of the communion not save the person baptized, if he does not endeavor also to fulfil his Christian calling, as is required of the faithful children of God. Therefore the Apostle Paul, when representing to the believers at Corinth the observance of the ordinance, enjoins that each one before partaking of the same shall examine his life and conversation, as to how he stands with God and his neighbor in respect of the same. He says: "But let a man examine himself, and so let him eat of that bread, and drink of that cup. For he that eateth and drinketh unworthily, eateth and drinketh damnation to himself, not discerning the Lord's body" (I Cor 11.28, 29).

108. Were it not better to abstain from partaking of the Lord's Supper, so as not to partake of it to one's own damnation, since people are so frail and fallible and frequently commit sin before they are aware of it?

Not to partake of the communion, or to neglect the same, from such a view or from such thoughts, would be done more from contempt for the command of Christ than from the fear of God, and might easily be an occasion for continuing in sin. But if we seriously take into consideration the command of Christ, and thereby find ourselves bound to the observance of the communion, it will incite us the more powerfully to give strict heed to our life and conversation—to avoid sin, to bring our faults the more earnestly before the Lord, and to pray for the pardon of our sins Thus the observance of the Lord's Supper will be serviceable to our comfort and pardon through the merits of Christ, since Christ says in His word: "This cup is the new testament in My blood, which is shed for you" (Luke 22 20; cp Matt. 26·28). But to continue knowingly and wilfully in sin, and to abstain from partaking to get clear of God's just punishment, is rather more a proof of wickedness than of the fear of God For he who from contempt neglected to keep the passover amongst the Israelites, did not go unpunished Num. 9.13. Much less will he go unpunished who despises the command of Christ And although those were not to keep the passover who were, according to the law, unclean, yet was the condition annexed that they had to purify themselves and keep the passover on "the fourteenth day of the second month" And he who did not do this was to be "cut off from among his people" (Num. 9.11, 13). Thus the command of Christ is established "This do in remembrance of Me" (Luke 22:19). So also Paul teaches, "But let a man examine himself, and so let him eat of that bread, and drink of that cup" (I Cor. 11:28). This teaches that we are not to stand still in this work but are to continue in it. If we then find ourselves, by examination, not pure before God, but guilty of something, we must first become reconciled to God and our neighbor, and then "eat of that bread, and drink of that cup"

109. Are then the bread and wine of the communion the real body and blood of Jesus Christ, since they are so called of Christ, and it is so strictly declared by Paul, that "he that eateth and drinketh unworthily, eateth and drinketh damnation to himself"?

The Lord Jesus in instituting His Supper, indeed speaks of them, bread and wine, as such, namely This is My body; this is My blood Matt 26 26-28; Mark 14·22-24 This declaration however, that the external bread and wine of the communion are the real body and blood of Christ, must not be literally understood, but is to be taken in a spiritual and mysterious sense, as is to be seen from the conversation of Christ with the Jews about the eating of His flesh and the drinking of His blood. John 6·54, 55 As this was however literally understood by the Jews and many of His disciples, He said; "The flesh profiteth nothing; the words that I speak unto you, they are spirit, and they are life" (John 6:63). So we are also to understand the words of Christ about the institution of the holy communion in a spiritual sense, and therefore He concludes the matter with the words: "This do in remembrance of Me" (Luke 22 19). The same language is also twice used by Paul in reference to such bread and wine, as follows: "This do in remembrance of Me" (I Cor. 11 24; cp. v. 25). And since the apostles, whenever they speak of the communion, call it the "breaking of bread" (Acts 2·24, 46; 20.7, 11; I Cor. 10.16; 11 23-26), it cannot be understood by us as the real body and blood of Christ, but must be understood in a spiritual sense, as a holy sign of the body and blood of Christ. So Paul also calls and represents it. I Cor. 10:16

110. Now if the said bread is merely common bread, such bread as we use for food, how then can we eat it unworthily to our own damnation?

Although the passover of the Jews consisted merely of the flesh of lambs, such as was eaten by them otherwise, yet no one that was uncircumcised—no heathen nor Jew that was according to the law unclean—was permitted to eat thereof. Such were not permitted to eat thereof: (1) Because it was an institution of the law; (2) Because it consisted of meat set apart for the worship of God; (3) Because it was to be kept as a memorial of their (the Jews') deliverance from Egypt; when the "destroyer" passed over their houses and spared their first-born, and (4) Because it brought to their minds the knowledge and remembrance of the divine favors shown to their ancestors, and that it was a command given by God, as already remarked. Now then, since the passover was expressly set apart for these purposes, it was a matter of God, and sacred in His sight, and therefore it was also to be kept sacred by the Israelites, and partaken of in purity. Thus we are also to understand the matter of the breaking of bread in the communion, that it is to be observed: (1) On account of its being commanded by Christ, who instituted it in memory of His sufferings and death, and enjoined it as a holy ordinance, and that it is therefore also to be considered by us as holy; (2) Because it—the breaking of bread—represents and signifies to us, for the proper, separate observance of the same, such dear and precious things, of the sacrifice of Christ, the breaking of His body, the shedding of His blood on the cross for our reconciliation with God, the pardon of our sins and our preservation to eternal life. Wherefore it is proper that we should observe and regard it as holy. Paul recognizes this when he says: "The cup of blessing which we bless, is it not the communion of the blood of Christ? The bread which we break, is it not the communion of the body of Christ" (I Cor. 10.16)?

111. Are there yet more such comparisons and expressions in Holy Scripture, where to external things the name of divine things is given, and whereby it is shown that the words of Christ about the bread and wine of His supper were spoken in significance of His body and blood?

Holy Scripture is full of expressions which signify internal, divine, spiritual, and heavenly things, which things are denominated by the names of external things, which represent and show to us divine, spiritual, and heavenly things. Thus Christ calls Himself the door of His sheep, and says: "The good shepherd giveth his life for the sheep" (John 10:11); the "true vine," and believers "the branches" (John 15:5); "the way" (John 14 6); His Father the "husbandman," and Peter a "rock." And Joseph said to Pharaoh, in explaining his dream, that the seven "good kine" and the seven "good ears," were "seven years of plenty," and the seven "ill favored kine" and "seven empty ears," were seven years of famine. Gen. 41:26-29. Likewise did he say of the dreams of the chief butler and chief baker that the "three branches" and the "three baskets" were three days. Gen. 40·12-18 So they also saw and experienced themselves what their dreams signified. Further, David calls the water which the "three mighty men" fetched at the risk of their lives, at the gate of Bethlehem, and from among their enemies, the "blood of the men," and "poured it out unto the Lord." II Sam 23:16, 17. Paul speaks of the two wives of Abraham, and their two sons, Isaac and Ishmael: "Which things [he says] are an allegory," namely, that they signify the "two covenants" (Gal 4:24). Thus he also speaks of the rock which Moses smote in the wilderness and from which water issued, that this "rock" was Christ. I Cor. 10:4. Now these things are called that which they signify, and such expressions there are in great abundance in Scripture

112. Must then the communion be only observed in memory of the death and sufferings of Christ?

The Lord God not only commanded the children of Israel to eat the passover and to celebrate the feast of the passover in memory of their deliverance from Egypt, but also to renew the memory of the faithful fulfilment of the promise given to their fathers; thereby reminding them of the favors of God, as the Lord remonstrated with them through Micah, when they had in a great measure ceased to regard these matters, when he says, "That ye may know the righteousness of the Lord" (Micah 6:5). Thus must also the observance of the Lord's Supper not serve us merely as a common memorial of the death and sufferings of Christ, but should remind us particularly of God's great love and favors shown to us, inasmuch as He has bestowed unto us such a precious Passover, even Christ, the beloved Son of God, who has been sacrificed for us (I Cor. 5 7); thereby showing that we are reconciled to Him, and have obtained peace with God through Jesus Christ (Rom. 5.1). Further it should remind us of what has been effected for us through the advent of Christ, as well as through His doctrine, example, suffering, and death, in order that we may thereby remember His great love through which we are so dearly bought, as Paul says: "Ye are not your own For ye are bought with a price: therefore glorify God in your body, and in your spirit, which are God's" (I Cor. 6.19, 20).

113. Does the observance and usage of the Lord's Supper serve as a memorial and knowledge of the great favors of God, conferred upon us through Christ?

It serves all pious and godly persons in many respects, as a consolation, as a strengthening and encouragement in their pilgrimage, as also as an assurance that:

1. The Lord's Supper is left to them as a testament; as also that the suffering and the death of Christ redound to the pardon of their sins and the restoration of eternal life

2. That just as they partake of bread and wine in the holy communion, so they shall also partake of Christ and His merits, as Christ says in a parable: "I am the living bread which came down from heaven: if any man eat of this bread, he shall live forever: and the bread that I will give is My flesh, which I will give for the life of the world . . . . For My flesh is meat indeed, and My blood is drink indeed He that eateth My flesh, and drinketh My blood, dwelleth in Me, and I in him" (John 6:51, 55, 56). Therefore Christ sets the cup of His supper before believers as a testament left by Him, when He says: "This cup is the new testament in My blood, which is shed for you" (Luke 22 20) In Him they also have a faithful Assistant, who watches over them like a shepherd over his flock. Psalm 23:1. Matt. 28:20.

Thirdly and lastly, it represents to all believers the unity of the spirit, which they have with one another through the unity of faith and the hope of salvation conferred upon them by Christ wherein they are through this ordinance all one, provided that they show the unity of the Spirit, as Paul says: "For we being many are one bread, and one body: for we are all partakers of that one bread" (I Cor. 10:17).

114. Is there also a set time when and how often the Lord's Supper is to be observed by the church, as was the case with the passover among the Israelites?

God had appointed the children of Israel a certain time when they were to observe the passover; namely, according to their year, on the fourteenth day of the first month. Exodus 12 6 But as it regards the Lord's Supper, we find no fixed time when and how often it is to be observed by the church, there being no such time appointed in the primitive church; which is evident from Acts 2:42-47, where it is said: "And they continued stedfastly in the apostles' doctrine and fellowship, and in breaking of bread, and in prayers . . . and breaking bread from house to house, did eat their meat with gladness and singleness of heart." And at Troas it was, in consequence of an accidental visitation of Paul, observed on a Sabbath evening Acts 20.7-11. However, it is well to be observed that as often as we partake of the communion, we "shew the Lord's death till He come" (I Cor. 11:26).

Article Fifteenth, of the Commandment of Love

115. Has the Lord Jesus, besides baptism and the Lord's Supper, yet also given other high commandments to His church, which were not given under the Old Testament dispensation?

The Lord has indeed given some such commandments, none that abrogate the chief commandments of the law of Moses, but such indeed as make said law more perfect and binding. For Christ says: "I am not come to destroy, but to fulfil" (Matt. 5:17). But particularly is this to be observed in reference to the commandment of love, which is the chief commandment, the whole substance of the law of Moses; namely: "Thou shalt love the Lord thy God with all thine heart, and with all thy soul, and with all thy might" (Deut. 6·5). Further, "Thou shalt love thy neighbour as thyself" (Lev. 19:18). "On these two commandments hang all the law and the prophets" (Matt. 22:40). This means that we should well stand the test of these commandments, and walk in perfect love, and that in the exercise of such love all that is contained in the law and the prophets is fulfilled as Paul testifies: "The end of the commandment is charity out of a pure heart, and of a good conscience, and of faith unfeigned" (I Tim. 1·5).

116. Where and how is the commandment of love made and cited more perfectly by Christ than it was in the law of Moses?

Under the law of Moses, the love of their neighbor was not understood to extend farther than to their brethren, the Israelites, who alone were considered as neighbors. Under the Gospel, however, "brotherly kindness and charity" (II Pet. 1 7) are required For Christ says: "If ye love them which love you, what reward have ye? do not even the publicans the same?" (Matt. 5:46) And when a certain lawyer asked Christ, who, according to the law, was his neighbor, He told him the story of the Samaritan (Luke 10·29), thereby declaring to him that he was to exercise love towards all those who stood in need of his help. Thus He teaches that not only he who was his brother according to the covenant of circumcision, was his neighbor, but that we should show our labors of love, without distinction, to all those to whom we can be of service. At the same time He also enjoined brotherly love as strictly as it was ever commanded in the law, and said to His disciples: "A new commandment I give unto you, That ye love one another . . . . By this shall all men know that ye are My disciples, if ye have love one to another" (John 13:34, 36). "He that loveth not knoweth not God; for God is love" (I John 4:8). Therefore Peter also so strictly and earnestly enjoins love, when he says: "Above all things have fervent charity among yourselves: for charity shall cover the multitude of sins" (I Pet. 4:8). We are to exercise not only "brotherly kindness," but also "charity" or, love towards all mankind (II Pet. 1:7), loving also our enemies. Matt. 5:44.

Article Sixteenth, on Revenge

117. Is there then in this doctrine of showing love towards all men without distinction, nothing contrary to the law, since the Jews had to fight against their enemies through the hand of the Lord? How then must a Christian act in this matter, when he is to show love towards all men?

It pleased God at that time to exterminate the seven different proscribed nations, who were His enemies, through the Jews, with whom the latter were not permitted to enter into any treaty of peace, nor their children into marriage relations. Ex. 34.12, 16. Otherwise they had to show love towards all strangers in their country. Ex 23 9 But now that "God was in Christ, reconciling the world unto Himself" (II Cor. 5:19), our benevolence must be shown to all men, without distinction II Pet 1 7 This is expressly taught by Christ "Ye have heard that it hath been said, An eye for an eye, and a tooth for a tooth: But I say unto you, That ye resist not evil: but whosoever shall smite thee on thy right cheek, turn to him the other also . . . Ye have heard that it hath been said, thou shalt love thy neighbour, and hate thine enemy. But I say unto you, Love your enemies, bless them that curse you, do good to them that hate you, and pray for them which despitefully use you, and persecute you . . . . For if ye love them which love you, what reward have ye? do not even the publicans the same? And if ye salute your brethren only, what do ye more than others? do not even the publicans so?" (Matt. 5:38-47). In a similar manner the Apostle Paul exhorts believers when he says: "Dearly beloved, avenge not yourselves, but rather give place unto wrath: for it is written, Vengeance is mine; I will repay, saith the Lord. Therefore if thine enemy hunger, feed him; if he thirst give him drink: for in so doing thou shalt heap coals of fire on his head" (Rom 12.19, 20). Thus must orthodox Christians through welldoing silence the ignorance of unwise and foolish men.

118. Has true love—the love required in the Gospel—also certain signs, whereby it may be known?

Certainly has that love which extends to all mankind also certain signs. For wherever the true love of God is founded in the hearts of men, men are also kindled in love towards their fellow creatures "He that saith he is in the light, and hateth his brother, is in darkness even until now" (I John 2.9). "Charity suffereth long, and is kind; charity envieth not; charity vaunteth not itself, is not puffed up, doth not behave itself unseemly, seeketh not her own, is not easily provoked, thinketh no evil; rejoiceth not in iniquity, but rejoiceth in the truth" (I Cor. 13:4-6) "Love worketh no ill to his neighbour: therefore love is the fulfilling of the law" (Rom. 13.10). Thus a true Christian is, through love, free from all desire of revenge.

Article Seventeenth, on the Swearing of Oaths

119. Are there yet more such matters, to which Christ alluded and which are practiced by worldly governments, which are forbidden in the law of Christ?

It is also a plain commandment of Christ that in testimony about disputes about temporal matters we should not swear an oath, which is otherwise customary under worldly government. This was no commandment of the Mosaic law, but there was a commandment that the children of Israel were not to swear falsely. Lev. 19 12. The swearing of oaths was, however, customary among men from the time of Abraham, as is to be seen in the case of Abraham himself, who took an oath from his servant. Gen 24:2, 3. Isaac bound himself by an oath to king Abimelech in a treaty of peace Gen. 26·31. So also Jacob and Laban confirmed their "covenant" by an oath Gen. 31:53. Now since the swearing of oaths is no commandment of God and matters of truth can be as strongly attested without an oath as with it, Christ directs His people, whose calling it is to be "speaking the truth in love" (Eph 4 15), to pursue the shortest and safest way of truth He says: "Ye have heard that it hath been said by them of old time, Thou shalt not forswear thyself, but shalt perform unto the Lord thine oaths. But I say unto you, Swear not at all; neither by heaven, for it is God's throne: nor by the earth; for it is His footstool; neither by Jerusalem; for it is the city of the great King. Neither shalt thou swear by thy head, because thou canst not make one hair white or black. But let your communication be, Yea, yea; Nay, nay· for whatsoever is more than these cometh of evil" (Matt 5 33-37) From this it is to be seen that the Lord Jesus does not merely abolish and forbid that which was adopted by man without commandment, but that He at the same time forbids that which the law mentions about swearing falsely, and also directs how we can testify to the truth without swearing

Article Eighteenth, on Matrimony

120. Are there yet more things changed, or made perfect, by the Lord Jesus, which are also mentioned in the law?

Concerning the state of matrimony, Christ made amends for the abuses and decline which had crept into it in consequence of being suffered under the law of Moses, and also reproved them Of which God also complains in this matter contrary to His will. Mal. 2:14, 15. Further, Christ also again brought the state of matrimony to its primitive order For when He was asked by the Pharisees whether it was "lawful for a man to put away his wife for every cause?" he answered, "Have ye not read, that He which made them at the beginning made them male and female, and said, For this cause shall a man leave father and mother, and shall cleave to his wife and they twain shall be one flesh? Wherefore they are no more twain, but one flesh What therefore God hath joined together, let not man put asunder" (Matt. 19:4-6) And when the Jews again asked: "Why did Moses then command to give a writing of divorcement, and to put her away?" Jesus answered: "Moses because of the hardness of your hearts suffered you to put away your wives· but from the beginning it was not so. And I say unto you, Whosoever shall put away his wife, except it be for fornication, and shall marry another, committeth adultery: and whoso marrieth her which is put away doth commit adultery" (Matt 19.7-9) From this it is clearly to be seen, that Christ teaches all Christians, that a man is bound to his wife by the bond of matrimony as long as she lives, and that the wife is also bound to her husband by the same tie as long as she lives. "But if her husband be dead, she is at liberty to be married to whom she will; only in the Lord" (I Cor. 7:39).

121. Are then all marriages made by the Lord, as the words of Christ purport?

As God is an omniscient God, and His actions are incomprehensible to man, we cannot come to a settled conclusion about this matter But if we take into consideration the providence of God, we must confess that there are also persons united by God in matrimony who enter into this state for their mutual punishment, or who must be a punishment to others thereby. This is seen in the case of Samson, whose marriage became an occasion of punishment to the Philistines Judges 14:1, 2 So we also see how married people frequently live to the punishment of each other. But where the true fear of God exists with people, there we may be assured that He is the author of marriage, for "great is His mercy toward them that fear Him" (Ps 103·11). And of this Abraham was assured when he sent for a wife for his son Isaac. Not knowing who she would be, he said to his servant, who was in such matters considerate and cautious· "The Lord ... shall send His angel before thee, and thou shalt take a wife unto my son" (Gen. 24:7).

Now when the servant met her, he turned to God in prayer, and when Laban understood the message he said, "The thing proceedeth from the Lord: we cannot speak unto thee bad or good" (Gen. 24 50).

122. Are there also means whereby we may come to such a state of marriage, and whereby we may be assured that the Lord God has appointed a consort for man?

There are indeed means whereby we may be assured that we have come to the matrimonial state by the direction of God, if we only fear the Lord (Ps 103 11), as was said to King Asa. "The Lord is with you, while ye be with Him" (II Chron 15:2). We have an example in the patriarchs Abraham, Isaac, and Jacob, when we observe how they feared God and how by means of prayer they obtained the consorts appointed for them by the Lord. For "the eyes of the Lord are upon the righteous, and His ears are open to their cry" (Ps. 34:15) So we also see that Jacob prayed God to be with him on his journey, when for the purpose of obtaining a consort he moved from his father's house to Mesopotamia. Gen. 28:20. "The effectual fervent prayer of a righteous man availeth much" (James 5 16). And the Apostle John says: "This is the confidence that we have in Him, that, if we ask any thing according to His will, He heareth us" (1 John 5:14).

123. Is not every one at liberty to enter into a state of matrimony with whom he pleases?

The faithful Christian is not at liberty to do so. But the wholesome doctrine of the Gospel, when properly observed by him, will direct him how to act in this matter. But that it is not pleasing to God that men should enter into the matrimonial state according to the dictates of their carnal minds is to be seen from the marriages before the flood. For it is said: "The sons of God saw the daughters of men that they were fair, and they took them wives of all which they chose" (Gen. 6 2). So were also the children of Israel—who were otherwise called the people of God—expressly forbidden to intermarry with the sons and daughters of the land of Canaan, whom the Lord had proscribed So we are also not permitted to marry those who are too nearly related to us by consanguinity Lev. 18·6-18. Beyond these exceptions, however, we are at liberty to marry whom we please, only so that, according to the admonition of Paul, it be done "in the Lord" (I Cor. 7.31). That is, those who intend entering into the state of matrimony, should do so in prayer and in the fear of God. Under these conditions, then, they are at liberty to marry as they please· the rich to the poor, the old to the young, widows to the single, if such persons are free in their conscience from others, and are of the same religious faith, and attend the same worship.

124. May then not persons, men and women, join themselves together of their own accord, without this being done by a minister of religion?

All intimate connection between men and women without the bond of matrimony is called fornication, about which we have a command in the law of Moses, "There shall be no whore of the daughters of Israel, nor a sodomite of the sons of Israel" (Deut. 23·17) Therefore Paul also says: "To avoid fornication, let every man have his own wife, and let every woman have her own husband" (I Cor. 7:2). Also: "Marriage is honourable in all, and the bed undefiled: but whoremongers and adulterers God will judge" (Heb 13.4).

Article Nineteenth, of Ecclesiastical Punishment, or Excommunication

125. Now if any member of the church peradventure transgresses any of these commandments of Christ, or acts contrary to them, is there also some punishment ordained by the church for such transgression?

If such transgression takes place wilfully, out of contempt for the commandment, the person so transgressing is disobedient to the Gospel. Rom. 2:8. Particularly is this true if his course of life is such that he thereby gives others occasion to speak evil of the same and the doctrine of the Gospel is thereby blasphemed. But the conduct of such person is to be examined into from different points of view: whether it consists of faults, errors, or intentional and voluntary sins and transgressions, with or without repentance; as also with the difference, whether the offence exists between him and God, or between him and his brother or neighbor. Now if such offence is only the consequence of an error, or an overhasty action, whereby the erring person overstepped the bonds of his calling, such matter may be made good again by a brotherly admonition, exhortation, and instruction, and repentance on the part of the offender, according to the doctrine of Paul: "If a man be overtaken in a fault, ye which are spiritual, restore such an one in the spirit of meekness, considering thyself, lest thou also be tempted" (Gal. 6:1) "Him that is weak in the faith, receive ye, but not to doubtful disputations" (Rom. 14.1). And when this is done in love, it may be serviceable to much good, and thus it behooves us to do according to the doctrine of Christ, when one brother sins against another, for Christ says: "If thy brother shall trespass against thee, go and tell him his fault between thee and him alone if he shall hear thee, thou hast gained thy brother. But if he will not hear thee, then take with thee, one or two more, that in the mouth of two or three witnesses every word may be established. And if he shall neglect to hear them, tell it unto the church" (Matt. 18.15-17).

126. Must we then proceed and act differently with those who sin against God?

In such cases we must proceed with caution and distinguish well whether the sins committed are such against which damnation is pronounced in Scripture, or whether they are such as may be atoned for through repentance, or whether the offended proves himself obstinate, and continues in his wicked course of life. Of such Paul says, "But after thy hardness and impenitent heart treasurest up unto thyself wrath against the day of wrath and revelation of the righteous judgment of God" (Rom 2 5). Now in case of such transgression of the commandment of Christ, in consequence of which the church is evil spoken of by those who are "without," the sentence of the church must, according to the instructions of Christ, be pronounced against such offender. And if there is no heartfelt repentance and sorrow for sin, no desire to avoid evil, observable in such person, he must be cut off from the church as a dead and unfit member, and swept out as a leaven, being considered, according to the instruction of Christ, as "an heathen man and a publican" (Matt 18.17). And so also Paul writes "Know ye not that a little leaven leaveneth the whole lump? Purge out therefore the old leaven, that ye may be a new lump" (I Cor. 5:6, 7) "For what have I to do to judge them also that are without? do not ye judge them that are within? But them that are without God judgeth. Therefore put away from among yourselves that wicked person" (I Cor. 5.12, 13). "Them that sin rebuke before all, that others also may fear. I charge thee before God, and the Lord Jesus Christ, and the elect angels, that thou observe these things without preferring one before another, doing nothing by partiality" (I Tim 5.20, 21)

Article Twentieth, of Excommunication or Exclusion from the Church

127. Now if such persons as before alluded to, are punished by the church for their wicked and unchristian course of life is this done merely for the terror of others?

It is done, not merely as a terror to others and as an example of the punishment of sin, but also as a warning to the offender, in order to bring him, according to the commandment of Christ and His apostles, to repentance and amendment of life. So it is also to serve as a declaration that the church will not suffer itself to be blasphemed, on his account, by others, or by those "without." Therefore such person is to be so far shunned that he has nothing more to do in the church and its communion. He is not to be recognized by the brotherly kiss or salutation, or no more so than one who never was connected with the church, until the time of his conversion, his amendment of life and conversation.

128. How are we to conduct ourselves towards such, so long as they are without the pale of the church?

If they still adhere to the church, hear the Word of God, are no blasphemers and abusers—in such cases we are diligently to exhort them again to become reconciled to God and the church, and, in as far as we see that they are in earnest, we are to reach them the helping hand to their restoration. Nevertheless, this must be done with great caution and foresight, so that the offender does not fall in too great sorrow and that we do not act against God's will in such case. But when the person thus excluded from the church still continues in vice, sin, and shame, and there is no hope for his amendment, we must refer such case to the just judgment of God, but for all that perform God's commandment towards him; that is, show and exercise Christian love towards him as towards our neighbor. Matt. 5:48; 19.19; 22 39; Mark 12·31; Gal 5:14; 6.10.

Article Twenty-First, of the Reception Again of the Penitent

129. Now if such a person as above alluded to has, through proper reproof and exhortation, come to conversion and amendment of life, how is he then to be dealt with?

In such case the church is bound to show cordial love and sympathy for him, and, out of joy at his return, to encourage in him the hope that if he continue in his good intention he will again be received as a member of the church of Christ and become united to the same, as is clearly shown in the parable of the lost son, when Christ says. "Likewise, I say unto you, there is joy in the presence of the angels of God over one sinner that repenteth" (Luke 15 10). So it behooves us, according to this, again to receive such an one with joy, as Paul writes to the Corinthians "Sufficient to such a man is this punishment, which was inflicted of many So that contrariwise ye ought rather to forgive him, and comfort him" (II Cor. 2·6, 7)

130. Has then civil government no power to inflict punishment in the Christian church, or is such government not recognized in the doctrine of the Gospel as a legitimate authority?

The office of such government consists in the administration of temporal affairs, and is not abrogated by the Gospel, and although such government does not appear to be instituted by Christ in the evangelical church (Luke 22:25, 26), yet believers are taught and commanded in the Gospel to be "subject unto the higher powers," for Christ says: "Render therefore unto Caesar the things which are Caesar's; and unto God the things that are God's" (Matt. 22:21). But in whatever concerns spiritual and divine things, "we ought to obey God rather than men" (Acts 5:29). For Christ Himself is appointed as the Head of the church, and He prescribes rules, privileges, and laws for the same, which are, according to the word of God, to be administered spiritually, as shown before from Matt. 18·15-17, and as Christ further declares, "Whatsoever thou shalt bind on earth shall be bound in heaven: and whatsoever thou shalt loose on earth shall be loosed in heaven" (Matt. 16.19).

131. Is there also testimony in Holy Scripture of such great and heinous sins of which it may be understood that they are bound in heaven and are damnable, if people die therein?

Such testimony we have in abundance, how that God is displeased with a carnal and sinful course of life, as Paul mentions at different places—as for instance in Rom 1:29-32; 8:6, 7, at which latter place he says· "To be carnally minded is death . . . enmity against God" And again he says: "Neither fornicators, nor idolators, nor adulterers, nor effeminate, nor abusers of themselves with mankind, nor thieves, nor covetous, nor drunkards, nor revilers, nor extortioners, shall inherit the kingdom of God" (I Cor. 6.9, 10). So it is further said of others of a similar character: "That they which do such things shall not inherit the kingdom of God," by which understand, such as continue in such a course of life, as Paul further testifies when he says: "If ye live after the flesh, ye shall die. but if ye through the Spirit do mortify the deeds of the body, ye shall live" (Rom 8:13)

Article Twenty-Second, of the Office of Civil Government

132. Are there not also many sins amongst the afore-mentioned which are punished by the civil law, whereby the delinquent may also be condemned to death? How then is the church to act in such case?

There are two different kinds of laws; namely, a spiritual law, and a worldly law. The spiritual law is the Scripture, written as the Word of God, and which is to be used in the church in all cases as a guide or rule, to distinguish between good and evil He that is spiritual, compares spiritual things with spiritual. "For the word of God is quick, and powerful, and sharper than any twoedged sword, piercing even to the dividing asunder of soul and spirit, and of the joints and marrow, and is a discerner of the thoughts and intents of the heart" (Heb. 4 12). If therefore any matter in the church is adjudged according to the Word of God, the persons appointed to judge the same do not adjudge such matter according to their own understanding, but the Word of God speaks the sentence, which convinces the heart of the sinner that he is guilty before God, and that he deserves such punishment. "For true and righteous are His judgments" (Rev. 19·2). But the sentence of the church, which is passed upon the sinner according to the Word of God, is not intended for his destruction but for his amendment—for the "destruction of the flesh [that is, the destruction of the lusts of the flesh], that the spirit may be saved" (I Cor. 5 5) that such persons may again be converted and saved, as the Word of God speaks of such sinners. Isaiah 1:16-18; Ezekiel 18 21-23; Luke 15:32. And from the sin from which the sinner is loosed through his reception again into the church, he shall also be loosed in heaven Matt. 16:19.

133. By what authority then do civil judges and civil government judge criminals, if this is not done according to the sense of the Gospel?

The civil laws, according to which criminals are judged and many of them condemned to death, are not founded on the doctrine of the Gospel, but they are such laws as were in part given by God to the children of Israel under the Old Testament dispensation. Otherwise, they are such as were given by rulers high in authority or by wise men for the welfare and in behalf of their country's subjects, which laws were consequently ratified by kings and emperors and other high authorities, for the peace and tranquility of their countries and cities, as also for the punishment of the bad and protection of the pious. Wherefore Peter also exhorts all faithful Christians in the following language: "Submit yourselves to every ordinance of man for the Lord's sake: whether it be to the king, as supreme; or unto governors, as unto them that are sent by Him for the punishment of evildoers, and for the praise of them that do well" (I Pet. 2:13, 14). And when the Apostle Paul stood bound before the judgment seat, in consequence of the envy of the Jews, although he was free from every crime he appealed unto Caesar, as the head of the highest worldly authority at that time. Acts 25:11.

134. Have then civil governments the power to make laws whereby judges may judge men and even condemn them to death?

"There is no power but of God: the powers that be are ordained of God

Whosoever therefore resisteth the power, resisteth the ordinance of God: and they that resist shall receive to themselves damnation" (Rom. 13·1, 2). Daniel said, "He removeth kings, and setteth up kings" (Dan. 2:21). So did also the Lord Jesus Christ Himself, submit to the paying of tribute money, and commanded to "render . . unto Caesar the things which are Caesar's" (Matt. 22:21) "Wherefore ye must needs be subject, not only for wrath, but also for conscience sake. For for this cause pay ye tribute also· for they are God's ministers, attending continually upon this very thing" (Rom. 13:5, 6). So that we are in duty bound, for the Lord's sake, not merely to be "subject unto the higher powers," but also, as Paul teaches, to make "supplications, prayers, intercessions, and giving of thanks," not only for men in general but also "for kings, and for all that are in authority, that we may lead a quiet and peaceable life in all godliness and honesty" (I Tim 2:1, 2). "For he is the minister of God to thee for good. But if thou do that which is evil, be afraid, for he beareth not the sword in vain: for he is the minister of God, a revenger to execute wrath upon him that doeth evil. . . Render therefore to all their dues· tribute to whom tribute is due; custom to whom custom; fear to whom fear; honour to whom honour" (Rom. 13·4, 7).

135. Must we then submit and be obedient to civil government in all things? If so, how then can we at the same time follow the law of Christ and the government, since they frequently militate against one another?

Since civil governments derive their power from God it is evident that they also depend on God Therefore we must regard the commandments of God more than those of worldly governments Consequently, whenever the commandments of worldly authority militate against those of God, the latter must, according to the example of the apostles, have the preference. For when they were forbidden to preach any more in the name of Jesus, they answered: "Whether it be right in the sight of God to hearken unto you more than unto God, judge ye" (Acts 4.19). Therefore it also behooves us to obey God above all things, without which we cannot, agreeably to our faith and according to the example of Paul, have a good conscience before God. For Paul says he exercised himself "to have always a conscience void of offence toward God, and toward men" (Acts 24:16). Thus, whatever we are in duty bound to do towards civil government, according to the Word of God that we should willingly do, but not that which is contrary to the Word of God and militates against it.

136. But if government would insist upon having its commands observed and executed, or else attach punishment to nonperformance, how would we be able to escape or resist the same?

All that we could do against such proceedings would have to be done in all meekness and discretion. We would have to entreat government in such case not to burden our hearts and consciences, stating that it was not from any evil design that we refused yielding obedience to its commands but from fear of acting against the commandments of God, which we were not permitted to do. But should our prayer not be regarded, then we should have rather to suffer everything that God would permit to be done unto us than to yield obedience in violation of our conscience and act contrary to the commandments of God In such case we would have to consider well the words of Peter, when he says: "For this is thankworthy, if a man for conscience toward God endure grief, suffering wrongfully" (I Pet 2 19) But if our sufferings should be too grievous to be borne, or if we should not be tolerated on account of not yielding the demanded obedience, then Christ directs us as to the ways and means we are to adopt and how we are to act in such case; namely, "When they persecute you in this city, flee ye into another" (Matt. 10:23).

137. Is the state of the Christian of such a nature that he is to bear everything that a worldly government and unreasonable men may do unto him? And,

if so, is not then his calling a hard one, and how do the words of Christ agree therewith, when He says, "My yoke is easy, and My burden is light" (Matt. 11:30)?

Such thoughts and imaginations arise from the weakness of the flesh and from human nature, and as long as these have the upper hand in a person it is very hard for him to suffer all things which may come in his way. But where the love of God reigns in the hearts of men through the power of saving faith there the Lord is their strength and vital power, so that they fear no misfortune that may befall them on account of the testimony of His Word. Ps. 27:1. For their hearts are firmly fixed in the Lord, so that they may well say with David: "Whom have I in heaven but Thee? and there is none upon earth that I desire beside Thee. My flesh and my heart faileth but God is the strength of my heart, and my portion forever" (Ps. 73:25, 26). "Many are the afflictions of the righteous: but the Lord delivereth him out of them all (Ps. 34.19) For this reason also the life of a Christian is called a warfare, in which he must spend his days as "an hireling" (Job 7:1). Wherefore Paul also exhorts to "fight the good fight of faith" (I Tim. 6.12), to be "rejoicing in hope; patient in tribulation; continuing instant in prayer" (Rom. 12:12). For where evil is endured and wrong suffered for conscience' sake, there the pious soul is "strong in the Lord, and in the power of His might" (Eph. 6 10) and can thus by meeting his adversary by well doing "put to silence the ignorance of foolish men" (I Pet. 2.15) For "when a man's ways please the Lord, he maketh even his enemies to be at peace with him" (Prov. 16:7).

138. Now if striving and suffering are the duty of Christians, on what then does their hope rest, and on what is it founded?

That striving thus is the calling of orthodox Christians has already been fully mentioned, in which their Lord and Chief has gone before them, for He says: "The servant is not greater than his lord If they have persecuted Me, they will also persecute you" (John 15 20). "Ye shall be hated of all nations for My name's sake" (Matt. 24 9). "Yea, the time cometh, that whosoever killeth you will think that he doeth God service" (John 16 2). Therefore He also says: "If any man will come after Me, let him deny himself, and take up his cross daily, and follow Me" (Luke 9:23) For "we must through much tribulation enter into the kingdom of God" (Acts 14:22). Now since the highly enlightened Apostle Paul, as a faithful follower of his Lord in this warfare and as a pattern of all the faithful has testified this in the foregoing quotation, namely, that we must thus enter into the kingdom of God, this gives good encouragement—is even a great comfort in this life, so that we may well say, "I reckon that the sufferings of this present time are not worthy to be compared with the glory which shall be revealed in us" (Rom. 8:18). To us, who look not at the things which are seen but at the things which are not seen, "our light affliction, which is but for a moment, worketh for us a far more exceeding and eternal weight of glory" (II Cor. 4:17, 18). "Because Christ also suffered for us, leaving us an example, that ye should follow His steps" (I Pet. 2:21). For the ground on which our hope rests is the Word of the Lord, which, as Paul says, was "written for our learning, that we through patience and comfort of the Scriptures might have hope" (Rom. 15:4). And this was also the comfort and protection of the prophet Jeremiah in all his sufferings, for he says, "Thy word was unto me the joy and rejoicing of mine heart" (Jer. 15:16). David expresses himself in a similar manner (Ps. 119:92), and Paul says that we know that "tribulation worketh patience; and patience, experience; and experience, hope: and hope maketh not ashamed" (Rom. 5.3-5). Now although the pious are tried through many sufferings yet they can say: "Whether we live, we live unto the Lord; and whether we die, we die unto the Lord: whether we live therefore, or die, we are the Lord's" (Rom. 14.8).

Article Twenty-Third, of the Resurrection of the Dead

139. Shall then pious and orthodox Christians, who thus strive "through faith," never die, while nevertheless the contrary is seen and certified, it being "appointed unto men once to die" (Heb. 9:27)?

In Holy Scripture there are two different lives, and two different deaths spoken of. We must therefore distinguish in what manner the righteous does not die, since it is said, that "it is appointed unto men once to die" (Heb. 9:27), as it is also manifest that all men, the pious as well as the wicked, are subject to natural death, and have to die, as Solomon says: "And how dieth the wise man as the fool" (Eccl. 2:16). For although Adam lived 930 years, Methuselah 969, Noah 959, Abraham 175, and many pious people lived to a great age; yet was the end of them all: "And he died." "For as in Adam all die, even so in Christ shall all be made alive" (I Cor. 15:22).

140. Is there then yet also another death, except the natural death, and another life, except the natural life?

Undoubtedly there is yet a death other than the natural death; and also a life other than the natural life. For natural death must be preceded by a spiritual death (a death unto sin) if we are to come to that state in which we shall never die. In spiritual death (death unto sin) we remain naturally alive, but come to a state in which we die in the Lord so that we live eternally and never die. That is, if we die unto our worldly lusts, thereby we crucify and mortify our carnal affections and lusts, which "war against the soul," doing as Paul says, "Reckon ye also yourselves to be dead indeed unto sin, but alive unto God through Jesus Christ our Lord" (Rom. 6:11). And "For ye are dead, and your life is hid with Christ in God . . . . Mortify therefore your members which are upon the earth" (Col 3:3, 5). They that are Christ's have crucified the flesh with the affections and lusts" (Gal. 5:24) Such can then say: "For to me to live is Christ, and to die is gain" (Phil. 1:21). Thus men can die unto sin and live unto God. And if they die a natural death, according to the decree of God, as far as their bodies are concerned they go the way of all the earth, but as it concerns their souls, they go from this temporal and toilsome life to an eternal and happy rest. For "their works do follow them" (Rev. 14:13). "He [the righteous] shall enter into peace: they shall rest in their beds, each one walking in his uprightness" (Isa 57:2). Thus we see that we must not understand under natural death, eternal death. That there is however also another life after this natural life, is proved from the words of Christ, when He says: "He that believeth in Me, though he were dead, yet shall he live" (John 11:22).

141. Shall then only the pious, who first die a spiritual death (a death unto sin) and then also a natural death, live again, while the wicked remain in death?

Not only the pious, after having laid off this temporal life, or died a natural death, shall again be raised and made alive, but also the ungodly. For since all the descendants of Adam have fallen under the power of death, through one man's, Adam's sin, although they have not "sinned after the similitude of Adam's transgression" (Rom. 5:12, 14), so also through one man, Christ, comes the resurrection of the dead: "For as in Adam all die, even so in Christ shall all be made alive" (I Cor. 15:22). Of this also Daniel testifies in the following words: "And many of them that sleep in the dust of the earth shall awake, some to everlasting life, and some to shame and everlasting contempt" (Dan. 12:2). "Awake and sing, ye that dwell in dust" (Isa. 26:19). And Christ Himself says: "Marvel not at this: for the hour is coming, in the which all that are in their graves shall hear His [Christ's] voice, and shall come forth; they that have done good, unto the resurrection of life; and they that have done evil, unto the resurrection of damnation" (John 5:28, 29). So Christ also says to Martha. "I am the resurrection and the life" (John 11:25). "In this was manifested the love of God toward us, because that God sent His only begotten Son into the world, that we might live through Him" (I John 4.9).

142. How can this come to pass, that the dead, who are mouldered in the earth, can again arise and live?

The precise nature of how this will come to pass is not necessary for us to know, much less to search into it. That it will, however, come to pass through the power and might of God is abundantly revealed to us, as David testifies when he says: "Thou turnest man to destruction; and sayest, Return, ye children of men" (Ps. 90:3). And Job says, "I know that my Redeemer liveth, and that He shall stand at the latter day upon the earth" (Job 19 25). From this it is evident that the resurrection of the dead can and will take place through the omnipotence of God, although this may appear to our understanding strange, and even impossible. But what is impossible with man is possible with God. For just as the Lord God created everything out of nothing, so He is also able to reanimate and again to put together the decayed body of man, and that with a single word, as is to be seen in the case of Lazarus John 11 43, 44 This the Psalmist also affirms, when he says: "Return, ye children of men" (Ps. 90:3, cp. Ezek. 37:10). So also Paul speaks of this matter as follows, "For if we believe that Jesus died and rose again, even so them also which sleep in Jesus will God bring with Him" (I Thess 4 14). Besides this, however, the Apostle Paul does in some measure relieve our wonder by comparing the resurrection of the dead with the seed in the ground, as is to be seen in I Cor. 15:35-38. So he also treats somewhat of the nature of the resurrection: "It is sown in corruption, it is raised in incorruption; it is sown in dishonour, it is raised in glory: it is sown in weakness, it is raised in power: it is sown a natural body, it is raised a spiritual body" (I Cor. 15:42-44)

Article Twenty-Fourth, of the Last Judgment and Eternal Life; also of Eternal Death

143. Now since mankind have a like ingress into the world, and a like egress out of it, will it then also be so with the resurrection of the dead?

No. For although the resurrection shall take place in like manner, yet will the consequence be unlike; as a great difference will be made in regard to the lives which men have led in this world. For, while one will be banished from the presence of the Lord and excluded from heaven, the other will be received into the favor of God; that is, into heavenly and eternal glory. Matt. 25.40, 41. Further, the day here alluded to, the day of judgment, will come to pass as Malachi prophesies. "The day cometh, that shall burn as an oven; and all the proud, yea, and all that do wickedly, shall be stubble: and the day that cometh shall burn them up, saith the Lord of hosts, that it shall leave them neither root nor branch. But unto you that fear My name shall the Sun of righteousness arise with healing in His wings" (Mal 4.1, 2). So Daniel also says: "And many of them that sleep in the dust of the earth shall awake, some to everlasting life, and some to shame and everlasting contempt" (Dan. 12.2). And all this is confirmed by Christ Himself. John 5:29, Matt. 25 32, 33.

144. Is the time also known when this shall come to pass, or when the day of judgment shall come?

The precise time or hour of this day is not revealed or made known to us in Holy Scripture, but the certainty and nature of it is. For when the disciples asked the Lord Jesus: "When shall these things be? and what shall be the sign of Thy coming, and the end of the world?" He put them in mind of various preceding signs of war and of darkness in the sun, moon, and stars, and also of many other tribulations, but said, "The end is not yet." Now since no one knows any thing of the day and hour of this day, not even the angels in heaven, but the "Father only," (Matt. 24·36) who has put in His own power the event of this day, how then should sinful and frail man imagine through his presumption to have found out, by peculiar wisdom, the time of this awful event, and thereby, like Martha, trouble himself with many things, and forget the one thing needful? Therefore Christ commands us to "watch and be ready," like those servants who wait on their master, not knowing when he would come. Mark 13.35. So Paul also testifies, saying: "But of the times and the seasons, brethren, ye have no need that I write unto you. For yourselves know perfectly that the day of the Lord so cometh as a thief in the night" (I Thess. 5·1, 2). And Christ Himself says, "Except those days should be shortened, there should no flesh be saved but for the elect's sake those days shall be shortened" (Matt 24 22).

How, or in what manner the Day of the Lord will come, is predicted in Matt 24, as it was also previously by the prophets Joel, for instance, says "The day of the Lord cometh, for it is nigh at hand, a day of darkness and of gloominess, a day of clouds and of thick darkness ... for the day of the Lord is great and very terrible" (Joel 2 1, 2, 11) On which day, as Peter says, "The heavens shall pass away with a great noise, and the elements shall melt with fervent heat, the earth also and the works that are therein shall be burned up. Seeing then that all these things shall be dissolved, what manner of persons ought ye to be in all holy conversation and godliness" (II Pet 3 10, 11)

145. Shall it then, on that day, be revealed how men lived during their lifetime, and what they did, and shall they at the same time be judged thereby?

It appears clearly that every one will receive his reward according to his works. Now since all men are, through the Gospel, called, exhorted, and urged to repentance and amendment of life, but many live in a state of disobedience thereto, therefore God "hath appointed a day, in the which He will judge the world in righteousness by that man whom He hath ordained, whereof He hath given assurance unto all men, in that He hath raised Him from the dead" (Acts 17:31). "For we must all appear before the judgment seat of Christ; that every one may receive the things done in his body, according to that he hath done whether it be good or bad" (II Cor. 5.10). Therefore Christ also exhorts "Take ye heed, watch and pray: for ye know not when the time is" (Mark 13 33). "For as a snare shall it come on all them that dwell on the face of the whole earth Watch ye therefore, and pray always, that ye may be accounted worthy to escape all these things that shall come to pass, and to stand before the Son of man" (Luke 21 35, 36) For which reason Paul also writes to the Romans as follows: ". . . not knowing that the goodness of God leadeth thee to repentance? But after thy hardness and impenitent heart treasurest up unto thyself wrath against the day of wrath and revelation of the righteous judgment of God; who will render to every man according to his deeds: to them who by patient continuance in well doing seek for glory and honour and immortality, eternal life: But unto them that are contentious, and do not obey the truth, but obey unrighteousness, indignation and wrath, tribulation and anguish, upon every soul of man that doeth evil" (Rom 2.4-9).

146. How or in what manner, shall then the judgment be held, and sentence pronounced?

This is circumstantially described by Matthew, who received the same from the mouth of the Lord Jesus, in the following words "When the Son of man shall come in His glory, and all the holy angels with Him, then shall He sit upon the throne of His glory: and before Him shall be gathered all nations; and He shall separate them one from another, as a shepherd divideth his sheep from the goats· and He shall set the sheep on His right hand, but the goats on the left Then shall the King say unto them on His right hand, Come, ye blessed of my Father, inherit the kingdom prepared for you from the foundation of the world. . . . Then shall He say also unto them on the left hand, "Depart from Me, ye cursed, into everlasting fire, prepared for the devil and his angels" (Matt. 25:31-41).

147. What will then properly be the great difference in the condition of the said parties, when each of them shall have gone to the place to which he will be doomed?

There has already been much said about the circumstance that those who are disobedient to the truth, the Gospel, shall be doomed to Hell, to dwell with the devil and his angels, where there is prepared for them disgrace and wrath, tribulation and anguish "everlasting destruction from the presence of the Lord, and from the glory of His power" (II Thess 1 9) They "shall cast them into a furnace of fire: there shall be wailing and gnashing of teeth" (Matt. 13:42), where the "smoke of their torment ascendeth for ever and ever" (Rev. 14:11). This is to be seen in the representation of the rich man. Luke 16 25. Such "shall have their part in the lake which burneth with fire and brimstone" (Rev. 21.8), "where their worm dieth not, and the fire is not quenched" (Mark 9 44), but where they "shall be tormented day and night for ever and ever" (Rev. 20.10). This is indeed a dreadful end of the ungodly, who were during their lifetime disobedient to the Gospel.

148. What shall, on the contrary, be the ultimate condition of the pious when they shall have come to the place allotted them after the judgment?

For them there will be perpetual glory, great rejoicing, and sweet joy and rest. They shall be in the presence of the Great God and the Lord Jesus Christ, as also in the company of Abraham, Isaac, and Jacob and of all the holy men of God, and surrounded by a great host of angels, thus being in everlasting joy at the "right hand of God," where "there are pleasures for evermore" (Ps. 16:11). They will find themselves in a state of happiness, of which the Apostle Paul says, "Eye hath not seen, nor ear heard, neither have entered into the heart of man, the things which God hath prepared for them that love Him" (I Cor. 2.9). "They shall hunger no more, neither thirst any more: neither shall the sun light on them, nor any heat. For the Lamb which is in the midst of the throne shall feed them, and shall lead them unto living fountains of waters: and God shall wipe away all tears from their eyes" (Rev. 7.16, 17). Thus are the pious to be with the Lord to all eternity, as the spirit of revelation says· "Behold the tabernacle of God is with men, and He will dwell with them, and they shall be His people, and God Himself shall be with them, and be their God" (Rev. 21:3). In this state, then, there will be unspeakable joy and glory, and perfect happiness without end, a happiness to express which all tongues on earth would have to be silent and dumb while the saints in heaven, the elect of God, sing with heart, soul, and spirit, the heavenly hosanna, saying: "Blessing, and glory, and wisdom, and thanksgiving, and honour, and power, and might, be unto our God for ever and ever. Amen" (Rev. 7:12).

Bibliography

Bender, H. S.: *Conrad Grebel, c. 1498-1526 The Founder of the Swiss Brethren.* The Mennonite Historical Society, Goshen, Indiana, 1950.
Bender, H. S.: "The Anabaptist Vision," *The Mennonite Quarterly Review,* Goshen, Indiana, XVIII, 2 (April 1944), 67-88.
Bender, H. S.: "The Mennonite Conception of the Church and Its Relation to Present Day Needs," *The Mennonite Quarterly Review,* Goshen, Indiana, XIX, 2 (April 1945), 90-100.
Bender, H. S., and Horsch, John: *Menno Simons' Life and Writings,* Scottdale, Pennsylvania, 1936.
Bender, H. S.: *Mennonite Origins in Europe,* M.C.C, Akron, Pennsylvania, 1942, 34-41
Blanke, Fritz. "Beobachtungen zum ältesten Tauferbekenntnis," *Archiv Fur Reformationsgeschichte,* Jahrgang 38, Heft 2/3, Leipzig, 242-249.
Brunk, Geo. R.: *Ready Scripture Reasons,* Mennonite Publishing House, Scottdale, Pennsylvania, 1926
Burckhardt, Paul: *Die Basler Taufer Ein Beitrag zur Schweizerischen Reformationsgeschichte,* Basel, 1898, 103-125.
Burkhart, I. E.· "Menno Simons on the Incarnation," *The Mennonite Quarterly Review,* IV, 2 (April 1930), 113-139, IV, 3 (July 1930), 178-207; 2 (April 1932), 122, 123.

Complete Works of Menno Simons [1496-1561], The, Elkhart, Indiana, 1871.
Correll, Ernst H.: *Das schweizerische Taufermennonitentum Ein soziologischer Bericht,* Mohr, Tübingen, 1925, 24-54.

Fretz, J. Winfield: "Mutual Aid Among Mennonites," *The Mennonite Quarterly Review,* Goshen, Indiana, I, XIII, 1 (January 1939), 28-58; II, XIII, 3 (July 1939), 187-209.
Friedmann, Robert: "The Anabaptist Genius and Its Influence on Mennonites Today," *Proceedings of the first Conference on Mennonite Cultural Problems,* Held at Winona Lake, Indiana, August 7 and 8, 1942, 20-25.
Friedmann, Robert· "Anabaptism and Pietism," *The Mennonite Quarterly Review,* Goshen, Indiana, I, XIV, 2 (April 1940), 90-128; II, XIV, 3 (July 1940), 149-169.
Friedmann, Robert: *Mennonite Piety Through the Centuries,* The Mennonite Historical Society, Goshen College, Goshen, Indiana, 1949.
Friedmann, Robert: "Spiritual Changes in European Mennonitism, 1650-1750," *The Mennonite Quarterly Review,* XV, 1 (January 1941), 33-45.
Friedmann, Robert: "The Encounter of Anabaptists and Mennonites with Anti-Trinitarianism," *The Mennonite Quarterly Review,* Goshen, Indiana, XXII, 3 (July 1948), 139-162
Friesen, J. J.: *An Outline of Mennonite History,* Newton, Kansas, 1944, 32-37.
Funk, Henry: *Restitution or An Explanation of Several Principal Points of the Law* Originally Published in Philadelphia, A D, 1763 . . . , (Elkhart, Indiana, 1915)

Gingerich, Melvin· *Service for Peace, a History of Mennonite Civilian Public Service* The Mennonite Central Committee, Akron, Pennsylvania, 1949

Händiges, Emil· *Die Lehre der Mennoniten in Geschichte und Gegenwart Nach den Quellen dargestellt* . . , Eppstein und Ludwigshafen am Rhein, (c. 1921,) 5-78
Hansen, George: *Ein Fundamententbuch der Christlichen Lehre,* Mennonitische Verlagsanstalt, Elkhart, Indiana, 1893
Hege, Christian and Neff, Christian *Mennonitisches Lexikon,* Weierhof (Pfalz) und Frankfurt am Main, Bd I 1913-24, Bd II, 1937 Note especially the following articles· *Bann, Bergpredigt, Bibel, Chiliasmus, Exegese, Eid, Gemeinde, Gemeindeverfassung, Gemeindezucht, Inspiration, Krieg, etc*
Hershberger, Guy F.· *War, Peace, and Nonresistance,* Scottdale, Pennsylvania, 1944.
Horsch, John: "The Early Mennonite View on Christian Stewardship," *Christian Monitor,* Scottdale, Pennsylvania, May 1931, 145.

Horsch, John: "The Faith of the Swiss Brethren," *The Mennonite Quarterly Review*, I, IV,4 (October 1930), 242-266, II, V,1 (January 1931), 7-27; III, V,2 (April 1931), 128-147; IV, V,4 (October 1931), 245-259

Horsch, John: *Infant Baptism, Its Origin Among Protestants and The Arguments Advanced For and Against It*, Scottdale, Pennsylvania, 1917

Horsch, John: *Menno Simons, His Life, Labors, and Teachings*, Scottdale, Pennsylvania, 1916, 223-299.

Horsch, John: *Mennonites in Europe*, Scottdale, Pennsylvania, 1942, 293-380.

Horsch, John: *The Principle of Nonresistance as Held By the Mennonite Church . .* , [First Edition,] 1927; Second Edition, Revised and Enlarged, Scottdale, Pennsylvania, 1939.

Horsch, John. *Die biblische Lehre von der Wehrlosigkeit*, Scottdale, Pennsylvania, 1920

Horsch, John "The Relation of the Old Testament Scriptures to the New Testament," *Christian Monitor*, Scottdale, Pennsylvania, November 1938, 329.

Horsch, John: "The Teaching of the Early Mennonite Fathers on Predestination," *Christian Monitor*, Scottdale, Pennsylvania, July 1938, 198f.

Horsch, John "Washing the Saints' Feet," *Gospel Herald*, Scottdale, Pennsylvania, April 27, 1939, 83.

Kauffman, Daniel, Editor: *Bible Doctrine* . . . , Scottdale, Pennsylvania, 1914.

Kauffman, Daniel, Editor: *Doctrines of the Bible* . . . , Scottdale, Pennsylvania, 1928.

Krahn, Cornelius. *Menno Simons (1496-1561), Ein Beitrag zur Geschichte und Theologie der Taufgesinnten*, Heinrich Schneider, Karlstrasse 28, Karlsruhe i. B., 1936, 103-179.

Lind, Millard: *Answer to War*, Mennonite Publishing House, Scottdale, Pennsylvania, 1952

Littell, Franklin H. *The Anabaptist View of the Church*, The American Society of Church History, Philadelphia, Pennsylvania, 1952.

Mennonite Central Committee, Handbook of Information on the, M.C C., Akron, Pennsylvania, July 1943, "Our Heritage of Faith," 23f.

Philip, Dietrich [1504-68] *Enchiridion or Hand Book of the Christian Doctrine and Religion* . . . , Elkhart, Indiana, 1910.

Rideman, Peter: *Rechenschaft unserer Religion, Lehr und glaubens, von den Brüdern, so man die Hutterischen nennt, ausgangen 1565* Aufs Neue herausgegeben und gedruckt im Verlag der Hutterischen Bruder in U.S A., Canada und England. Cotswold-Bruderhof, Ashton Keynes, Wilts., England, 1938. English Edition, 1950

Rutenber, Culbert G : *The Dagger and the Cross*, Fellowship Publications [New York 32, N.Y., 1950].

Simons, Menno, *The Complete Works of*, Elkhart, Indiana, 1871.

Sippell, Theodore: "The Confession of the Swiss Brethren in Hesse, 1578," *The Mennonite Quarterly Review*, XXIII, 1 (January, 1949), 22-34.

Smith, C. Henry: *The Story of the Mennonites*, Mennonite Book Concern, Berne, Indiana, 1945.

Smucker, Donovan E · "The Theological Triumph of the Early Anabaptist Mennonites," *The Mennonite Quarterly Review*, Goshen, Indiana, XIX, 1 (January 1945), 5-26.

Stauffer, Ethelbert. "The Anabaptist Theology of Martyrdom," *The Mennonite Quarterly Review*, Goshen, Indiana, XIX, 3 (July 1945), 179-214.

Töws, Aron A.: *Mennonitische Martyrer der junsten Vergangenheit und der Gegenwart* [Abbotsford, British Columbia, 1949].

Twisk, Peter J. [1565-1636]: *The Peaceful Kingdom of Christ or An Exposition of the 20th Chapter of the Book of Revelations*, Elkhart, Indiana, 1913.

van Braght, Thieleman J.· *The Bloody Theater or Martyrs' Mirror*, (1660), English Edition, Mennonite Publishing House, Scottdale, Pennsylvania, 1950.

von Muralt, Leonhard· *Glaube und Lehre der Schweizerischen Wiedertäufer in der Reformationszeit*, Zürich, 1938, 27-47.

Wenger, J. C · *Separated unto God*, Mennonite Publishing House, Scottdale, Pennsylvania, 1952.

BIBLIOGRAPHY 163

Wenger, J C.: "The Relation of the Christian to the Old Testament Scriptures," *Christian Monitor*, Scottdale, Pennsylvania, September 1939, 266f
Wenger, J. C.· "The Theology of Pilgram Marpeck," *The Mennonite Quarterly Review*, Goshen, Indiana, XII, 4 (October 1938), 205-256.
Wenger, J. C. "Pilgram Marpeck, Tyrolese Engineer and Anabaptist Elder," *Church History*, IX, 1 (March 1940), 24-36, especially 33-35.
Wenger, J. C : "The Schleitheim Confession of Faith," *The Mennonite Quarterly Review*, XIX, 4 (October 1945), 243-253.
Wenger, J. C.: "Concerning the Satisfaction of Christ. An Anabaptist Tract on True Christianity," *The Mennonite Quarterly Review*, XX, 4 (October 1946), 243-254
Wenger, J C.· "Two Kinds of Obedience A Swiss Brethren Tract on Christian Freedom." *The Mennonite Quarterly Review*, XXI, 1, (January 1947), 18-22
Wenger, J. C.: "Concerning Divorce. A Swiss Brethren Tract . . . ," *The Mennonite Quarterly Review*, XXI, 2 (April 1947), 114-119.
Wenger, J. C.: "Martin Weninger's Vindication of Anabaptism," *The Mennonite Quarterly Review*, XXII, 3 (July 1948), 180-187.
Wenger, J. C.: "Three Swiss Brethren Tracts," *The Mennonite Quarterly Review*, XXI, 4 (October, 1947), 275-284.
Wenger, J. C.: "Two Early Anabaptist Tracts," *The Mennonite Quarterly Review*, XXII, 1 (January, 1948), 34-42
Wenger, J. C.: *Glimpses of Mennonite History and Doctrine*, Herald Press, Scottdale, Pennsylvania, 1949.
Wenger, J. C.: "The Church as a Brotherhood," *Gospel Herald*, Scottdale, Pennsylvania, XLII, 37 (September 13, 1949), 897f.
Wenger, J. C.: "Ought We Abandon Close Communion?" *Gospel Herald*, Scottdale, Pennsylvania, XLII, 9 (March 1, 1949), 193f.

Yoder, Edward. *Our Mennonite Heritage*, M C.C, Akron, Pennsylvania, 1942
Yoder, Edward "What Is Mennonitism?" *Proceedings of the second Annual Conference on Mennonite Cultural Problems*, Held at Goshen, Indiana, July 22 and 23, 1943, 106-112.

www.ingramcontent.com/pod-product-compliance
Lightning Source LLC
Chambersburg PA
CBHW050815160426
43192CB00010B/1775